M&A Disputes

The Wiley Finance series contains books written specifically for finance and investment professionals as well as sophisticated individual investors and their financial advisors. Book topics range from portfolio management to e-commerce, risk management, financial engineering, valuation and financial instrument analysis, as well as much more. For a list of available titles, visit our Web site at www.WileyFinance.com.

Founded in 1807, John Wiley & Sons is the oldest independent publishing company in the United States. With offices in North America, Europe, Australia, and Asia, Wiley is globally committed to developing and marketing print and electronic products and services for our customers' professional and personal knowledge and understanding.

M&A Disputes

A Professional Guide to Accounting Arbitrations

A. VINCENT BIEMANS
GERALD M. HANSEN

WILEY

Published by John Wiley & Sons, Inc., Hoboken, New Jersey.

Published simultaneously in Canada.

Library of Congress Cataloging-in-Publication Data:

Names: Biemans, A. Vincent, 1977- author. | Hansen, Gerald M., 1967- author.
Title: M & A disputes : a professional guide to accounting arbitrations / A. Vincent Biemans, Gerald M. Hansen.
Other titles: Mergers and acquisitions disputes
Description: Hoboken, New Jersey : John Wiley & Sons, 2017. | Series: Wiley finance series | Includes index. |
Identifiers: LCCN 2017009404 (print) | LCCN 2017014047 (ebook) | ISBN 9781119331933 (pdf) | ISBN 9781119331940 (epub) | ISBN 9781119331919 (cloth)
Subjects: LCSH: Consolidation and merger of corporations–Accounting. | Arbitration (Administrative law)
Classification: LCC HG4028.M4 (ebook) | LCC HG4028.M4 .B54 2017 (print) | DDC 657/.96—dc23
LC record available at https:// lccn.loc.gov/2017009404

Cover Design: Wiley
Cover Images: © maxuser/Shutterstock

Printed in the United States of America

10 9 8 7 6 5 4 3 2 1

The authors would like to thank their wives, Lenora and Rachel, for their love and support and, importantly, their willingness to listen to excited work stories that have GAAP as the protagonist.

Contents

Preface

Why This Book

M&A transactions continue to be an important part of the corporate and investment landscape. Many of the purchase agreements governing those transactions contain post-closing purchase price adjustment mechanisms. As a result, after-the-fact adjustments to the purchase price are commonplace.

In many instances, those adjustments remain limited to a series of uncontroversial accounting true-ups. Purchase price adjustment mechanisms can, however, have a significant impact on the deal value to one or both parties. Sellers and buyers can be easily caught off guard by a sizeable proposed adjustment, problems with the company's accounting, or some perceived unreasonable position by the counterparty. In some instances, the impact on the ultimate purchase price paid by buyers and received by sellers can make or break transactions.

In the event of a dispute regarding a post-closing purchase price adjustment, the purchase agreement commonly provides for the matter to be brought before an independent accountant for resolution. The parties rely on their attorneys and accountants to advise them on the successful resolution of those disputes before the accounting arbitrator. The resolution process, however, can be opaque for those unfamiliar with it and the area is under-published. Moreover, there are distinguishing characteristics and unique considerations when comparing the field of M&A accounting arbitrations and the broader legal and accounting professions.

This book seeks to provide guidance to current and potential practitioners, whether in-house or at a professional services firm, in resolving—and perhaps preventing—M&A disputes.

It aims to provide the reader with an in-depth walkthrough of the M&A dispute resolution process and practical guidance on achieving the best results for their clients from the diligence phase through final resolution. It also seeks to provide would-be arbitrators with the handhelds needed to arrive at an informed and appropriate award. In addition to a discussion of the post-closing purchase price dispute resolution process, this book also discusses steps the transaction parties can take to potentially mitigate the scope and severity of any post-closing purchase price dispute.

The Organization of the Book

We have organized the book into five separate, but interrelated, parts.

The first part—The M&A Dispute Framework—provides an introduction to purchase price adjustment mechanisms, an overview of the post-closing purchase price adjustment process, and the dispute resolution process before the accounting arbitrator. It also provides a more specific introduction to net working capital adjustment mechanisms. We selected net working capital adjustment mechanisms as the primary basis for discussion throughout most of this book for its prevalence in practice as well as the analogous applicability of many of the identified issues to other adjustment mechanisms. Notably, post-closing adjustment mechanisms and the related dispute resolution process can be—and often are to some extent—customized as they are contractual in nature. Notwithstanding, the (net working capital) adjustment mechanisms and resolution procedures generally have more in common than they are different.

The second part—Core Concepts and Issues—discusses a variety of recurring elements across purchase price adjustments and disputes, including the nature of GAAP, the common requirement of consistency with historical accounting practices, the determination of target net working capital, transaction-specific adjustments, selected audit topics, and subsequent events.

The third part—The Accounting Arbitration—provides a discussion of the dispute resolution process from the selection and retention of the accounting arbitrator through the arbitration award. Included are various considerations for the parties in preparing their submissions to the arbitrator as well as considerations for the arbitrator in reaching a determination on the items in dispute.

The fourth part—The Disputed Items—provides a detailed discussion of the drivers of many disputed items and several common categories of disputed items such as inventory, accounts receivable, and contingent liabilities. We discuss the genesis of such disputed items, important considerations when evaluating them, and how to present them to an accounting arbitrator. Although we cover some relevant accounting guidance, the emphasis is not on discussing all the ins-and-outs of GAAP. This book is not intended to be a technical accounting manual.

The final part—Other Topics—closes out the book with a discussion of several important topics, including the impact of contractual choices in the purchase agreement, the interaction between indemnification provisions and net working capital adjustment mechanisms, other purchase price adjustment mechanisms, and finally a brief discussion of international considerations.

Acknowledgments

We want to express our appreciation to our clients, their retained professionals, and our current and former colleagues, including, but certainly not limited to: Cees Hardeman, Dale Kitchens, Catherine Madrid, Hans van Sonderen, Rebecca Szelc, and Greg Wolski. We have learned a great deal from all of them throughout the years about both M&A transactions and disputes as well as a variety of other topics. We look forward to continuing to do so.

We want to thank Stuart McCrary for introducing us to Bill Falloon at Wiley. In addition, we want to thank Bill and everybody else at Wiley who worked on this book, including Shelley Flannery, Judy Howarth, Julie Kerr, and Caroline Maria Vincent.

Finally, we want to thank Amanda Nauert for her review of the manuscript and her improvements to the final product. We also greatly appreciate Teddy Tankersley's willingness to acts as a sounding board on a variety of topics.

About the Authors

A. Vincent Biemans is a Managing Director of Berkeley Research Group, LLC ("BRG"). He assists U.S. and European buyers and sellers with their M&A disputes both as a (party-retained) advisor and as a (jointly retained) neutral accounting arbitrator. In addition to advising on M&A disputes, he also has significant experience developing complex damages and valuation assessments. He has been involved with engagements across a wide variety of industries and with economic interest covering a broad size spectrum (from less than $1 million to more than $10 billion).

Prior to joining BRG, Mr. Biemans served at several professional services firms, including a public multinational consultancy; a litigation, valuation, and financial advisory boutique; and a law firm. He started his career in an advisory practice in The Netherlands, where he advised clients ranging from startup ventures to publicly traded multinationals. He moved to the United States in early 2007.

Mr. Biemans is a Certified Public Accountant (CPA). He also holds the Chartered Financial Analyst (CFA), Accredited in Business Valuation (ABV), Certified Fraud Examiner (CFE), and Chartered Global Management Accountant (CGMA) designations. He holds advanced degrees in accountancy (post-graduate), economics (M.Sc.), and fiscal law (LL.M.). He is a member of various professional organizations.

Gerald (Jerry) Hansen is also a Managing Director of BRG. He is a CPA and forensic accountant with extensive experience across a variety of accounting, audit, and financial forensics services including M&A disputes (as an arbitrator and an expert), audit services, expert services, forensic due diligence, and fraud investigations. He has served at a Big 4 public accounting firm, a multinational consultancy, as well as global corporations in a career spanning over 25 years. Mr. Hansen previously served as the Southwest Region leader of Ernst & Young's Transaction Forensics practice, a specialty practice that focused on disputes, investigations, and forensic due diligence services that stem from contemplated and completed merger and acquisition transactions. He also has in-house experience in software revenue recognition, mortgage banking, and insurance claims.

Mr. Hansen has provided dispute-, forensic-, and audit-related services to clients in a wide range of industries including real estate, technology, energy, transportation, manufacturing, software, food services, publishing, automotive, healthcare, retail, staffing services, advertising, and financial services. He is a contributing author to *The Litigation Services Handbook* as well as the AICPA book *The Guide to Investigating Business Fraud*, in addition to other articles and presentations. He holds a BBA in Finance from Southern Methodist University and an MS in Accounting from the University of Virginia.

PART One

The M&A Dispute Framework

CHAPTER 1

Introduction to M&A Disputes

The purchase and sale of a business is typically an extensive process involving the identification of potential counterparties, due diligence, negotiation of a price and the purchase agreement, and finally the closing of the transaction. The closing represents the culmination of months of hard work often involving the assistance of a variety of advisors, including investment bankers, transaction counsel, and accountants.

The closing, however, does not necessarily mean that the transaction is fully completed and the purchase price is set. Many contracts governing the acquisition of a company or a business contain one or more mechanisms that allow for post-closing adjustments to the purchase price based on a predetermined metric such as net working capital; earnings before interest, taxes, depreciation, and amortization (EBITDA); or some other metric. Such mechanisms and any resulting proposed purchase price adjustments may be resolved amicably between the parties. On the other hand, the adjustment process may lead to post-closing disputes between the parties regarding the appropriate amount of the purchase price adjustment.

THE TRANSACTION LIFECYCLE

Purchase price adjustments are generally implemented after the closing of the transaction. The underlying mechanisms, however, are agreed upon prior to the closing. Moreover, the actual post-closing adjustments may well find their genesis in pre-closing events. Shown here is a sample representation of the lifecycle of a typical merger and acquisition transaction.

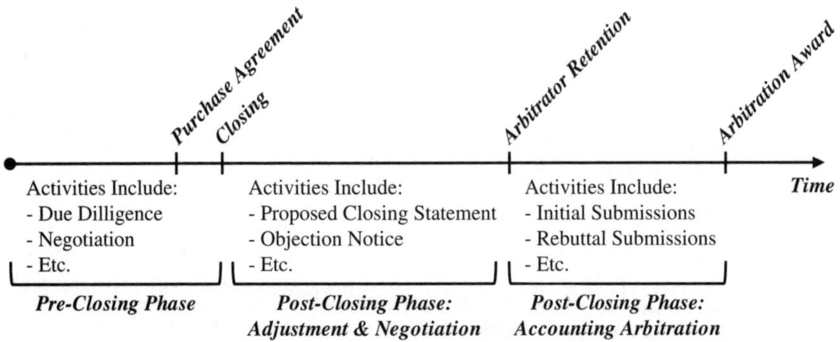

Sample Transaction Lifecycle with NWC Adjustment

M&A transactions can take a variety of forms and can follow varying timelines. Notwithstanding, the transaction lifecycle can generally be broken down into two major time periods—pre-closing and post-closing—with a variety of activities occurring in each period. For example, if the seller initiates the sales process, it may perform a variety of activities early on in the process to identify potential buyers and to get the company ready for sale. Once the field of potential buyers has narrowed, the parties can engage in further information exchanges, the buyer can perform its due diligence, and the parties can negotiate the purchase agreement.

The purchase agreement can incorporate both a negotiated purchase price amount (e.g., $1 billion) as well as a variety of adjustments that need to be made to arrive at the amount that is to ultimately be paid by the buyer. By means of example, the purchase price may be set on a debt free/cash free basis, that is, the agreed upon purchase price of $1 billion assumes the company has no debt and no cash. To arrive at the amount ultimately owed by the buyer, the company's debt and cash at closing have to be, respectively, deducted from and added to the negotiated purchase price amount (of $1 billion).

Transactions routinely provide for purchase price adjustments to be implemented post-closing. For example, many purchase agreements contain a net working capital adjustment mechanism in order to have the final purchase price—i.e., after any post-closing adjustments—reflect the actual amount of net working capital that was transferred with the business as of the closing date. Such adjustments are made post-closing because, among other things, it is typically not possible to correctly quantify the net working capital on the closing date itself because of the time necessary to perform a typical "closing of the books."

In such situations, the purchase agreement can provide for a preliminary closing statement based on which the preliminary purchase price is calculated and paid at closing. Subsequent to closing, the buyer is commonly contractually required to submit a proposed closing statement with updated net working capital amounts and any resulting purchase price adjustment. The seller may disagree with the buyer's calculations and send a—contractually provided for—objection notice. In the case of disagreement regarding any proposed adjustments, the purchase agreement commonly provides for negotiations between the parties, which are typically aided by the exchange of information between them.

In the event the parties cannot resolve the implementation of the purchase price adjustment between them, the purchase agreement may provide for the disputed items to be submitted to an accounting arbitrator for resolution. The dispute phase will typically at least involve the parties tendering initial and rebuttal submissions (with supporting documentation) to the accounting arbitrator for consideration and resolution of the dispute.

The focus of this book is on disputes arising after the closing of an M&A transaction and their resolution through accounting arbitration. Of course, the parties' pre-closing activities can have an impact on the post-closing purchase price adjustment process. For example, the level of sell-side and buy-side due diligence performed prior to closing can result in the preemptive identification and resolution of potential problem areas and, generally, increase the parties' knowledge of the accounting of the company being sold/acquired. Moreover, the negotiation of the purchase agreement and the precise language of its provisions can have a significant impact on the implementation of any purchase price adjustment mechanisms and the ultimate purchase price paid and received.

CATEGORIES OF PURCHASE PRICE ADJUSTMENT PROVISIONS

Contractual post-closing purchase price adjustment mechanisms are found in purchase agreements that are structured as stock purchases as well as in those that are structured as asset purchases. Post-closing purchase price adjustments can range from immaterial in the context of the transaction to large amounts that significantly impact the economics for the buyer and seller. There are three broad categories of potential contractual post-closing adjustments to the purchase price:

1. Adjustments to the purchase price based on the financial position or performance of the target company as of or through the closing date
2. Adjustments to the purchase price based on the financial performance of the target company subsequent to the closing date
3. Adjustments to the purchase price based on the allocation of financial responsibility through representations, warranties, and indemnifications in the purchase agreement

Each of those categories of post-closing adjustments can lead to disputes between the parties to the transaction. In addition to contractual purchase price adjustment disputes, there are also disputes related to the transaction and/or the purchase price that are based directly on the legal framework governing the transaction as opposed to the underlying contract. An example of a possible legal challenge that can lead to an adjustment to a share purchase price is a Delaware appraisal action. Another example of a legal challenge related to alleged under- or overpayment can be an action based on allegations of transaction fraud. Parties can also end up in dispute regarding a transaction that was never consummated based on, for example, allegations that one of the parties wrongfully failed to close. As this book focuses on accounting arbitrations, which generally find their basis in being preemptively agreed upon as a form of alternative dispute resolution, non-contractual purchase price adjustment disputes are outside the scope of this book (although we discuss transaction fraud briefly in Chapter 22).

As it relates to contractual purchase price adjustments, agreements governing larger transactions generally contain at least a choice of law and forum selection clause. Many agreements, however, go much further and contain arbitration and/or expert determination clauses complete with prescribed procedures and an agreed-upon timeline for dispute resolution. The agreed-upon choices for alternative dispute resolution and the associated procedures can differ dependent on the nature of the potential dispute. In other words, one purchase agreement can contain multiple avenues for dispute resolution. For example, an agreement can simultaneously contain (i) an overall clause that prescribes New York law as the governing law and the federal court for the Southern District of New York as the venue of choice, (ii) an arbitration clause that arranges for an American Arbitration Association appointed arbitrator to decide any indemnification-related disputes, and (iii) a clause that provides for an independent accountant to resolve any post-closing net working capital disputes.

In general, the perceived benefits of alternative dispute resolution include the relative efficiency of the process, as it is often both faster and cheaper than traditional litigation, as well as the ability to tailor procedures and discovery. The limitations on discovery tend to be especially attractive to foreign transaction parties, for which the U.S. discovery process is often significantly more extensive than the obligations that are imposed by their home jurisdictions. In addition, especially in the event of a would-be venue that is smaller and less used to foreign litigants, some foreign parties may fear that they would be at a disadvantage due to local biases. Of course, alternative dispute resolution also has downsides, including a commonly perceived tendency of arbitrators to arrive at split or compromise decisions as well as significant limitations on the ability to appeal an arbitration ruling. In the case of purchase price adjustment clauses, the efficiency benefits of alternative dispute resolution can be further increased by having, what are essentially, accounting disputes analyzed and decided by accountants.

The first category of purchase price adjustment disputes—adjustments based on the target company's financial position or performance as of or through the closing date—is as close as it gets to contract-based pure accounting disputes. The underlying adjustment mechanisms include those based on the amounts of net working capital, debt (or net debt), and/or cash and cash equivalents that are transferred with the company at closing. The adjustment mechanisms can also incorporate performance measures such as EBITDA, earnings before interest and taxes (EBIT), or a variety of custom measures that cover a defined period prior to closing. For example, the contractual purchase price adjustment formula can incorporate the company's Adjusted EBITDA for the 12 months leading up to closing into the calculation of the ultimate purchase price. Not surprisingly, purchase agreements routinely arrange for purchase price disputes related to category 1 adjustment mechanisms to be brought before an independent accountant. Coates (2012)—in his analysis of a sample of M&A agreements for the period from 2007 through 2008—found that "83% of contracts containing price-adjustment clauses also contained clauses mandating arbitration of disputes arising out of those price-adjustment clauses."[1]

Importantly, disputes related to category 1 adjustment mechanisms center on the quantification of an adjustment, if any. Generally, there is not the two-step of actionable wrongful conduct and damages that is common in general civil litigation. Indeed, the need for some form of adjustment is generally not indicative of wrongful behavior. The existence of a dispute does not belie this; the parties may simply disagree on the appropriate accounting and need assistance in quantifying (part of) the adjustment.

Category 2 adjustments—adjustments based on post-closing performance—are commonly referred to as earn-out provisions and allow the seller of a company to retain some interest in the upside of the company's financial performance while protecting the buyer against paying upfront for expected performance that may never materialize. In a sense, disputes in the second category are often not about adjusting an estimated purchase price, but about quantifying what should be the ultimate purchase price based on post-closing performance. Those disputes can encompass accounting issues and/or various legal and non-accounting factual allegations about wrongful conduct. The accounting issues are frequently resolved by accounting arbitrators. The non-accounting aspects of such disputes are typically brought before attorney arbitrators or judges, but can still involve accountants to provide consulting services and/or educate the trier of fact on the relevant accounting issues as a retained expert.

Disputes in the third category—adjustments based on representations, warranties, and indemnifications—are typically legal in nature. Moreover, although the related payments may be considered adjustments to the purchase price from an accounting perspective, the purchase agreements typically treat those items as payments between the parties and not explicitly as purchase price adjustments, unless for accounting or tax purposes. In our experience, it is highly uncommon for disputes in the third category to be brought before an independent accountant.

Notwithstanding, the findings of the independent accountant in relation to a dispute in the first category can indirectly impact the outcome of disputes in the second and third categories. By means of example, the accounting arbitrator can rule on the amount that should be included on the balance sheet as of the closing date for a partially performed contract, which would fall under the first category. That starting balance and the associated accounting can then have an impact on the amount of revenue that should be recognized in the year subsequent to closing. As a result, the accountant's ruling related to balance sheet work-in-progress accounting can impact the amount of the earn-out owed to the seller for performance subsequent to closing. Similarly, by means of another example, the independent accountant could rule on the appropriate amount to be included on the balance sheet as a tax accrual. If the purchase agreement also contains a clause that arranges for indemnification of prior period taxes in excess of the applicable tax accrual, the ruling of the independent accountant in the context of a category 1 adjustment could very well impact a purchase price adjustment in relation to category 3.

As this book relates to accounting arbitrations as opposed to civil litigation, it focuses primarily on the conception, negotiation, and adjudication of the first category of post-closing purchase price adjustments. The most prevalent adjustment mechanism in this category is for the amount of net working capital that exists on the target company's balance sheet as of the closing date. Post-closing net working capital adjustments also form the bulk of post-closing disputes that are brought before an accounting arbitrator.

Given their prevalence in practice as well as the analogous applicability of many of the identified issues to other adjustment mechanisms, the majority of this book will focus on net working capital–based adjustment mechanisms and disputes. Notwithstanding, we mention other purchase price adjustment mechanisms and disputes throughout this book where appropriate. We also specifically discuss certain other adjustment mechanisms, including EBITDA-based adjustments and earn-outs in Chapter 22.

ACCOUNTING ARBITRATIONS VERSUS EXPERT DETERMINATIONS

Post-closing purchase price adjustment disputes before an independent accountant can take the formal form of an accounting arbitration or of an expert determination. There are a variety of legal consequences that may be associated with the selection of one over the other regarding, for example, the accountant's legal powers and the enforceability of the conclusion.

The parties may (or may not) preemptively select one formal approach over the other in the purchase agreement. The dispute resolution process before the independent accountant and the issues at play, however, are typically the same whether the parties opt for expert determination or arbitration.

Since for purposes of this book the terms are essentially interchangeable, we will refer to both *arbitrations* and *expert determinations* as accounting arbitrations or arbitrations throughout this book. Similarly, we will refer to the independent accountant as the accounting arbitrator or arbitrator whether he or she was retained to issue an arbitration award or to render an expert determination. The same is not uncommon in various articles and other publications on the topic of M&A disputes.

OVERVIEW OF THE BOOK

In this book, we will cover the various aspects of the accounting arbitration process as well as selected common arguments and issues. We will use the net working capital adjustment mechanism as the basis for most of our discussion.

First, we provide an overview of the dispute phase to briefly introduce the post-closing dispute resolution process

(Chapter 2) as well as an overview of post-closing net working capital adjustments (Chapter 3). Those two chapters will provide the reader with foundational information to place the subsequent chapters in context.

We then address some of the core concepts and issues at the foundation of many post-closing purchase price adjustments and disputes, including the nature of GAAP (Chapter 4), the concept of *past practices in accordance with GAAP* (Chapter 5), and several other important and commonly recurring items (Chapters 6–9).

After this, we discuss the post-closing purchase price dispute process in more detail. We start off with opportunities for mitigation that are available to the parties prior to the dispute being brought before the accounting arbitrator (Chapter 10). We then discuss the entire dispute process from retention of the accounting arbitrator through the award (Chapters 11–14).

After discussing the process, we discuss common sources of adjustments, including some specific financial statement accounts (Chapters 15–19). We include technical accounting guidance as well as advice on the documentation and presentation of arguments to the accounting arbitrator.

Finally, we cover other relevant topics, including a discussion of purchase agreements and their relevant provisions (Chapter 20), the interaction of net working capital adjustments and indemnification provisions (Chapter 21), other adjustment mechanisms (Chapter 22), and selected international considerations (Chapter 23).

Overall, this book is meant to provide in-depth professional guidance for practitioners. It cannot, however, exhaustively cover each possible variation. There are few absolute truths in a field for which the framework is predominantly set by contractual arrangements between sellers and buyers in combination with accounting guidance. In order to keep the book readable, we have attempted to avoid inserting "typically" or "generally" into every statement even when exceptions can exist. We urge the reader to carefully evaluate the facts, circumstances, and legal context of the individual cases with which he or she comes into contact. As we cover the various topics, we have attempted to illustrate important concepts with examples. Those examples are simplified to illustrate specific concepts, are fictitious, and are not meant to capture the full nuance of real-world matters.

NOTE

1. *See* John C. Coates IV, "Managing Disputes through Contract: Evidence from M&A," *Harvard Business Law Review*, Vol. 2, 2012, p. 333.

CHAPTER 2

The Post-Closing Adjustment and Dispute Process

The previous chapter introduced the transaction lifecycle and briefly discussed how the activities in the pre-closing phase can impact a purchase price adjustment dispute in the post-closing phase. We now highlight the different elements of the post-closing purchase price adjustment process in more detail to provide a framework for the rest of the book. Although we introduce the dispute resolution process in this chapter, we cover it much more extensively later in the book.

FROM CLOSING TO DISPUTE

The transaction has closed and the parties are in the honeymoon period. Nothing spoils this pleasant period like an accounting arbitration. How do the parties get from a mutually agreeable closing to a formal dispute? The answer—a disagreement regarding the need for, or the appropriate amount of, an adjustment to the purchase price.

The parties are due their respective bargained-for items as documented in the purchase agreement. In many transactions, there is a purchase price adjustment mechanism that allows for upward or downward adjustments to the purchase price based on a specific metric. If the parties cannot agree on the purchase price adjustment, the purchase agreement commonly provides for an accounting arbitration process.

Following are the typical steps the parties go through from the closing of a transaction to the commencement of an accounting arbitration:

1. After the closing of the transaction, the buyer obtains control of the company and gains direct access to the company's books and records. The purchase agreement typically provides for a defined period of time for the buyer (e.g., 30 days) to prepare a proposed closing statement that contains, among other things, a proposed final amount of net working capital as of the closing date and any resulting adjustment to the purchase price.
2. After the buyer submits its proposed closing statement to the seller, the seller typically has a predetermined period of time (also, e.g., 30 days) to analyze the proposed closing statement and to assess whether the seller agrees or disagrees with one or more of the buyer's proposed adjustments. If the seller agrees with all of the proposed adjustments, the purchase price is updated and the transaction is finalized. If, after review and the exchange of information between the parties, the seller rejects all or part of the buyer's proposed adjustments, the seller submits a written response detailing any objections (commonly referred to as an "objection notice").
3. If an objection notice is submitted, the parties enter a contractually agreed-upon negotiation phase. In this phase a further exchange of information and negotiation takes place to attempt to resolve or narrow the adjustments that the seller objected to prior to entering the dispute phase.
4. Any remaining unresolved adjustments are then submitted to an accounting arbitrator for resolution in accordance with the relevant purchase agreement.

In the remainder of this chapter, we first discuss the common steps reflected in the previous summary in more detail. We then provide and discuss the common steps that are part of the dispute process.

The Proposed Closing Statement and Proposed Purchase Price Adjustment

For a transaction with a purchase price adjustment provision, the first step in the post-closing process is the buyer's assessment of its acquisition and the preparation of a "proposed closing statement" or "closing balance sheet." Most purchase agreements provide an agreed-upon time period, often 30 to 90 days, for the buyer to prepare the proposed closing statement.

The proposed closing statement contains the adjusted net working capital as well as the impact of any adjustments on the purchase price. Specifically, the adjusted net working capital amount is compared to the (preliminary) amount of net working capital used as of the closing date. Any surplus or deficiency is used to calculate the proposed purchase price adjustment. By means of example, if the purchase price paid at closing was $100 million based on a preliminary net working capital amount of $20 million and the buyer's post-closing calculation of net working capital shows $15 million, the buyer would propose a $5 million purchase price reduction.

The above is a simplistic summary of what can be a complicated process. Purchase agreements can vary in their definition of net working capital, its components, and the standard for quantifying it. By means of example, the purchase price can be calculated on a cash free/debt free basis. For some transactions, that can mean that the cash is retained by the seller and the company's debt is paid off at closing. For other transactions, that can mean that the purchase price is negotiated without giving consideration to cash and debt. As of the closing date, the cash that transfers with the company will have to be added to the purchase price and the debt, potentially including a variety of debt-like items, will have to be deducted. In such instances, the purchase agreement will have to carve-out cash and cash equivalents from the net working capital definition and set the boundaries between net working capital and debt, which could otherwise overlap. Purchase agreements can also provide for a host of other exclusions, additions, or limitations, which may or may not be GAAP compliant. Such transaction-specific items can include a wide variety of items such as, for example, an agreed upon cap on warranty accruals or the contractual exclusion of certain inventory items from the net working capital calculation.

Finally, there are also purchase agreements that provide for the seller to prepare the proposed closing statement. This is much less common because for most transactions the seller already prepares the net working capital or other metric that is used to derive the purchase price paid at closing. Moreover, after the closing, the buyer has control of the company and, in many instances, direct access to its books and records.

Accepting or Objecting to Post-Closing Purchase Price Adjustments

Upon receiving the buyer-prepared proposed closing statement, including any proposed purchase price adjustment, the seller commonly has a contractually agreed-upon opportunity to review and either accept or object to the buyer's calculations. Purchase agreements commonly provide for (i) a specified time for review by the seller, (ii) a requirement for the seller to prepare an objection notice that specifically addresses any adjustment that the seller disagrees with and identifies the grounds for its disagreement, and (iii) any items to which the seller has not objected to be deemed accepted and final.

The proposed closing statement is typically the buyer's only opportunity to propose adjustments to the purchase price based on a net working capital adjustment mechanism and the objection notice is typically the seller's only opportunity to dispute such proposed adjustments.

Under normal circumstances, the objection notice should not contain a blanket objection to all adjustments proposed by the buyer. The individual objections are generally required to have a basis in the purchase agreement. On some occasions, the parties are still in the process of exchanging information as the objection notice becomes due. In such instances, the parties can agree to extend the deadline for the seller's objection notice or the seller can object *pro forma* to the items for which it has not yet received sufficient information to come to a fully informed conclusion. Extending the deadline may result in a cleaner process, but the latter approach has the benefit of taking a series of uncontested items off the table.

The Negotiation Period

In the event the seller submits an objection notice, many purchase agreements provide for a period of negotiation (e.g., 30 days) between the parties to resolve the objections prior to a formal dispute resolution process.

During this negotiation period, the parties will share and discuss information regarding their positions on the adjustments proposed by the buyer. Frequently, the seller will request additional supporting documentation from the buyer to more fully understand the basis for the buyer's proposed adjustments. It is not unusual for several of the proposed adjustments to be resolved between the parties during this negotiation period.

Example: Misplaced and Found Inventory

- After the closing, the buyer counts the inventory, finds items missing, and adjusts the inventory balance to incorporate the results of the count in its proposed closing statement. The proposed closing statement, thus, reflects a variety of missing items and a downward adjustment of the purchase price.
- The seller objects to the adjustment as it believes there was no inventory missing as of the closing date.
- Subsequent to the objection notice, the seller is able to help the buyer find the missing items, which the company keeps in a special supply closet in one of its offices.

The negotiation process is not only an opportunity for the parties to exchange information. It also allows the parties to critically assess their positions and the positions of their counterparty. As various items are often discrete, as opposed to interdependent, it is common for multiple items to be resolved as the parties trim and exchange their respective "weak" positions. We discuss the negotiation process and the "resolution matrix" that can assist a party in analyzing its position across various items in Chapter 10.

Unresolved Disputed Items Submitted to an Accounting Arbitrator

If the parties are unsuccessful in reaching an agreement on all of the seller's objections to the buyer's proposed closing statement, the unresolved items, now the "disputed items," are submitted to an accounting arbitrator for a final and binding determination. The accounting arbitration process is often specifically provided for in purchase agreements for which such a process is relevant (i.e., transactions with post-closing purchase price adjustment provisions related to an accounting metric such as net working capital).

The types of disputed items that typically end up being submitted to an accounting arbitrator for resolution—as opposed to being resolved through negotiation—are often proposed adjustments that are significant in dollar amount, involve real or perceived departures from the company's historical accounting practices, require significant judgment under GAAP, and/or involve real or perceived departures from provisions of the purchase agreement such as transaction-specific non-GAAP adjustments. For example, the buyer proposes to reduce accounts receivable by $1 million based on its assessment that certain older receivables should be written off in accordance with GAAP. The seller perceives the change as based on the buyer's preference for a strict accounts receivable aging methodology to determine the allowance for doubtful accounts. The seller disputes the proposed adjustment as violating the purchase agreement provision requiring the use of the seller's historical accounting policies.

The disputed items that end up being tendered to the accounting arbitrator for resolution are documented, discussed, and supported in the various submissions to the accounting arbitrator. After considering the information provided by the parties, the accounting arbitrator renders a determination on each of the disputed items, formally resolving the dispute.

THE DISPUTE RESOLUTION PROCESS

Purchase agreements commonly provide a framework for calculating net working capital as well as procedures to finalize the amount and resolve any related disputes. Purchase agreements, however, do not necessarily specify each element of the accounting arbitration process. Either way, a typical dispute resolution process includes the following steps:

1. Retention of the accounting arbitrator
2. Parties' initial submissions
3. Parties' rebuttal submissions
4. Arbitrator interrogatories and document requests
5. Hearing (optional and relatively uncommon)
6. Arbitration award

This section provides a brief overview of those major elements of the dispute resolution process (i.e., the activities from the engagement of the arbitrator through resolution). We discuss the mechanics of the arbitration process, including the selection of the accounting arbitrator and the various submissions to the accounting arbitrator, in more detail in later chapters.

Retention of the Accounting Arbitrator

The first step in the formal dispute resolution phase is the retention of the independent accountant. In order to retain the accounting arbitrator, the parties first have to agree on his or her selection. Purchase agreements vary in the extent of guidance they provide on the selection of the accounting arbitrator, ranging from very little guidance to highly specific instructions. For example, some purchase agreements simply state that the parties will jointly select and retain an accounting arbitrator while other purchase agreements include a list of individuals in order of preference. More is discussed on this topic in Chapter 11.

After selecting an accounting arbitrator, the parties have to agree with each other and the accountant on the terms of the engagement. That can involve substantial effort and multiple drafts of the accountant's engagement letter as that letter typically defines the dispute, lays out the procedures to be followed, and establishes the boundaries of the arbitrator's authority. As a result of the selection process and the detail commonly included in the engagement letter, the retention of the independent accountant can take much longer than the parties anticipated when the purchase agreement was drafted.

Example: Arbitrator Retention Process and Delays

- Day 1: The parties agree to submit the disputed items to the independent accountant for resolution in accordance with the purchase agreement.
- Day 3: The parties approach the accountant named in the agreement to serve as the arbitrator.
- Day 9: The accountant declines the engagement due to a conflict of interest.
- Day 11: The parties identify another accountant at a similar firm and approach that accountant to serve as the arbitrator.
- Day 15: The second potential arbitrator makes a disclosure to the parties resulting from his firm's conflict check, but

states that he or she believes it does not threaten his or her independence. The second potential arbitrator believes the disclosed item does not need to stand in the way of his or her retention.

- Day 18: The parties have a conference call with the second potential arbitrator.
- Day 21: The parties agree to proceed with the retention of the second potential arbitrator.
- Day 24: The second potential arbitrator provides a draft engagement letter to the parties.
- Day 28: Both parties provide comments to the draft engagement letter.
- Day 30: The second potential arbitrator circulates a revised draft engagement letter to the parties that incorporates the proposed changes.
- Day 32: The parties approve the engagement letter.
- Day 33: The engagement letter is finalized and executed.

The Proceedings before the Accounting Arbitrator

Purchase agreements vary in the level of detail provided regarding the accounting arbitration proceedings. Purchase agreements can range from providing only general guidelines regarding the submissions to the arbitrator to including a detailed process.

It is not uncommon for the detailed arbitration process to be first set forth in the independent accountant's engagement letter or agreed to immediately after his or her retention. The process is generally more involved than a simple exchange of information and positions. By means of example, the following schedule, or some variation thereof, is commonly used for accounting arbitrations:

1. The parties simultaneously provide their initial submissions to the accounting arbitrator.
2. The parties simultaneously provide their rebuttal submissions to the accounting arbitrator.

3. The accounting arbitrator sends his document requests and/or interrogatories to the parties.
4. The parties submit responses to the accounting arbitrator's document requests and interrogatories.
5. An (optional) in-person hearing may be held in some matters.
6. The accounting arbitrator issues the award.

The time between each step in the process varies from matter to matter depending on the scope of the items in dispute, scheduling conflicts of the parties and the accounting arbitrator, and other factors. The initial submissions, rebuttal submissions, and the parties' responses to the arbitrator's document requests and interrogatories are also provided to the opposing party. In practice, the arbitrator often cross-forwards the parties' submissions upon having received the submissions from both sides.

The initial and rebuttal submissions should generally be accompanied by all supporting documentation necessary for the accounting arbitrator to review and assess the respective parties' position on each item in dispute. At a minimum, the parties typically include the purchase agreement, the preliminary closing statement, the buyer's proposed closing statement, and the seller's objections thereto as well as a selection of correspondence and supporting documentation already exchanged between the parties with their initial submissions. In addition, the parties can submit additional factual and financial supporting documentation, including, for example, various spreadsheets, company documents reflecting business or accounting practices, and historical financial statements. In addition to the typical supporting documentation, the parties can also include affidavits from individuals that are knowledgeable regarding the company's accounting or other relevant topics. The parties can also include expert reports or expert affidavits with their submissions, such as an expert report that discusses the industry in which the company operates to provide context for the argued accounting treatment.

After the initial submissions, the parties typically have an opportunity to provide rebuttal submissions. In most cases, the sole purpose of rebuttal submissions is to provide each party an opportunity to provide rebuttal arguments and accompanying supporting documentation in response to the positions of the other party as presented in their respective initial submissions. Rebuttal submissions are generally not intended to facilitate the raising of new issues. It is not uncommon for parties to abandon (concede) some of their positions in their rebuttal submissions based on the support provided with the opposing party's initial submission.

After receiving the initial and rebuttal submissions, the independent accountant will, if necessary, issue document requests and interrogatories that include questions for the parties. In some proceedings there can be multiple rounds of arbitrator document requests and/or interrogatories based on the nature and complexity of the disputed items and the information already provided by the parties.

In addition to written submissions and the accompanying supporting documentation, there can be a hearing before the accounting arbitrator. If the parties elect to have a hearing, it is typically a one-day event consisting of presentations from both sides and an opportunity for the arbitrator to ask questions in person.

The Arbitration Award

After analysis of the information provided by the parties and in accordance with the terms of the applicable purchase agreement, the independent accountant provides the parties with a determination for each of the disputed items in the agreed-upon level of detail (the "award"). In practice, the award can range from a one-page schedule to a fully reasoned award report that incorporates a detailed discussion of the independent accountant's considerations in support of his or her conclusion. In addition to decisions on the individual disputed items, the award can also include a calculation of the impact on the purchase price and an allocation of the fees and expenses of the independent accountant between the parties. The parties can preemptively provide for the type of award in the purchase agreement or, as commonly occurs, they can decide on it later in the process, for example, at the time of the retention of the accounting arbitrator.

A key aspect for an appropriate resolution of a post-closing purchase price dispute is for the parties, their advisors, and the accounting arbitrator to understand the specific mechanics and requirements for preparing the final closing statement including the net working capital (or other purchase price adjustment trigger).

Purchase agreements vary and often contain transaction-specific provisions that may include, for example, non-GAAP measures for specific items. The arbitrator and the parties should be careful to closely observe the provisions of the purchase agreement that governs the transaction at hand in presenting and reaching a determination regarding the disputed items.

CHAPTER 3

Post-Closing Net Working Capital Adjustments

At a basic level, a company's net working capital is the difference between its total current assets and its total current liabilities. In summary, current assets are cash and other assets that are reasonably expected to be realized in cash, sold, or consumed during the normal operating cycle of the business.[1] Current assets include items such as accounts receivable, inventory, and prepaid expenses. Similarly, current liabilities include short-term liabilities such as accounts payable, accrued liabilities, and the current portion of long-term debt. In essence, net working capital is the short-term capital available to be used by the business in its day-to-day operations.

For purposes of many valuation analyses, the analyst considers whether the company has sufficient working capital to operate its business. If the company has a shortfall of or excess working capital, an adjustment needs to be made to the value of the company. Such adjustments can have a dollar-for-dollar impact on the valuation.

Example: Comparative Valuation Impact

- Company A and B are identical. Company A has sufficient working capital to operate its business (no excess or shortfall). Company B has the same amount of working capital and in addition has a bank account with $1 million in surplus cash (i.e., excess working capital).

- The value of Company B is $1 million higher than Company A as the buyer could buy Company B, extract $1 million, and end up with the same company as if the buyer had purchased Company A.
- *Note*: The example is simplified and ignores possible complications such as adverse tax effects. Moreover, excess cash is—in practice—not necessarily transferred with the company but may be extracted by the seller prior to closing.

NET WORKING CAPITAL ESTIMATION AND ADJUSTMENT

On the date the transaction is closed, neither the seller nor the buyer can necessarily precisely determine the amount of net working capital that is transferred with the business. Even if the closing date were at the end of a quarter or fiscal year, which is typically not the case, not enough time would be available to go through the regular end-of-period closing of the books.

As the company uses its working capital to operate its business (e.g., during the months prior to the closing date), the composition and amount of the company's net working capital is subject to continuous change. Indeed, every sale, purchase, and payment as well as the simple passage of time can result in changes to the composition and/or amount of the company's net working capital. Moreover, the company's accounting for many transactions and various elements of net working capital are normally not in real-time. Rather, the company's accounting naturally lags behind the underlying events, only recording certain events at the end of the day, week, month, or reporting period. While some events can be recorded in the company's books in (near) real-time, other accounting items can generally not be finalized until the company closes its books for the relevant period.

Transaction parties vary in their approach to selecting the preliminary amount of net working capital that is utilized to determine the purchase price to be paid at closing. On the one hand, some purchase agreements simply contain an agreed-upon amount that was determined some time prior to closing. At the other extreme, some agreements have an elaborate pre-closing estimation procedure that involves a proposed amount of net working capital to be used at closing, objections thereto, and even pre-closing dispute resolution procedures. Most agreements, however, fall somewhere in between these two extremes. The transaction is often closed using a purchase price amount based on the estimated net working capital at closing, a target amount of net working capital, or an otherwise agreed-upon amount. We discuss the determination of the target net working capital in Chapter 6.

After the closing, the amount of net working capital that was transferred with the company can generally be determined more precisely as opposed to being estimated without the benefit of typical closing of the books procedures. Notwithstanding any dispute related to the determination of the net working capital, once the net working capital is determined post-closing, the purchase price can be adjusted and a payment made between the parties, if any, to close out the transaction. There are three common elements to this net working capital true-up process (barring a dispute):

1. The target net working capital, which is part of the agreed-upon purchase price for the transaction. In other words, if the final net working capital is the same as the target net working capital, the final purchase price equals the originally agreed upon purchase price amount.
2. The estimated or preliminary amount of net working capital as of the closing date. The amount to be paid as of the closing date is calculated based on this preliminary amount, which can be different than the target net working capital and may result in a preliminary purchase price adjustment at closing.
3. The post-closing calculation of the final net working capital as of the closing date, which is determined after the fact and based upon which the final purchase price is determined.

The adjustment of the purchase price is commonly dollar-for-dollar. In other words, a one-dollar difference between the preliminary amount based upon which the transaction closed and the final net working capital amount that is determined after the fact, results in a one-dollar purchase price adjustment (relative to the amount paid at closing). The following is an example of this process.

Example: Adjustment Arithmetic

- The seller and the buyer agree to transact a company for a purchase price of $100 million, including a target amount of net working capital of $10 million.
- Prior to closing, the seller and the buyer agree on an estimated amount of net working capital for purposes of closing the transaction in an amount of $8 million.
- On the closing date, the buyer pays seller $98 million, which is calculated: $100 million (purchase price) – $10 million (target net working capital) + $8 million (estimated net working capital).
- After closing, the actual net working capital turns out to be $11 million. The purchase price is adjusted to $101 million, which is calculated: $100 million (purchase price) – $10 million (target net working capital) + $11 million (actual net working capital).
- The buyer makes an additional payment of $3 million, which is calculated: $101 million (final purchase price) – $98 million (paid at closing).

The above implementation of a dollar-for-dollar impact starting with the first dollar does not always apply. For example, some purchase agreements contain a minimum threshold below which no purchase price adjustment takes place. The applicable purchase agreement includes the relevant provisions that may specify a minimum threshold or other custom mechanics applicable to the agreed upon post-closing net working capital–based purchase price adjustment.

AN APPROACH TO DEFINING AND QUANTIFYING NET WORKING CAPITAL

To determine the final amount of net working capital that was transferred with the business as of the closing date, the parties need to have defined net working capital and selected an approach to quantifying it. Three general contractual approaches are to determine the amount of net working capital (i) in accordance with U.S. GAAP, (ii) in accordance with the company's historical accounting practices, or (iii) in accordance with the company's historical accounting practices consistent with GAAP, GAAP as applied consistently with the company's historical accounting practices, or a similarly worded arrangement. We use the shorthand "*past practices in accordance with GAAP*" for the third approach throughout this book. We also generally use "GAAP" as shorthand for U.S. GAAP.

All three methodologies (and a variety of other methodologies) can be encountered in practice. In our experience, *past practices in accordance with GAAP* is a very common general approach. Utilizing *past practices in accordance with GAAP* as the methodology for determining the amount of net working capital generally has important advantages over the other two methodologies. Although, the formula can be customized with, for example, carve-outs and prescribed measurement methodologies for specific items, it does not require the parties to negotiate the quantification of the individual components of net working capital. Moreover, the company already tracks and quantifies its current assets and liabilities as part of its regular accounting, which typically should be in accordance with GAAP. In addition, the target net working capital—to which the closing date net working capital is compared—is commonly determined based on the company's historical accounting practices. In other words, utilizing *past practices in accordance with GAAP* provides for a comprehensive and objective framework that is—or at least should be—already in use by the company.

In many situations, the formula would falter without both of its book-ends (i.e., past practices and GAAP). Excluding the context of the company's historical accounting practices and simply prescribing *in accordance with GAAP* as the methodology for the proposed closing statement often insufficiently narrows possible outcomes. GAAP by itself is not narrowly prescriptive on many accounting topics. Rather, it provides companies with many acceptable accounting choices across various assets and liabilities to allow the company to tailor its accounting to its specific facts and circumstances. Including the company's *past practices* incorporates the accounting choices as the company has historically made them and thus narrows the possible outcomes. It also increases comparability with historical financial information, including the basis on which the target net working capital was derived.

Eliminating GAAP from the equation and having the closing statement prepared *in accordance with past practices* should in many instances greatly concern the buyer. The seller may have historically implemented non-GAAP compliant accounting practices that would then—pursuant to the purchase agreement—be used to determine part of the purchase price. Without the contractual requirement that those past practices comply with GAAP, the buyer may be exposed to an unexpected and disadvantageous purchase price adjustment without a contractual basis to challenge the additional payment. The buyer is typically not in a position to verify that net working capital is accounted for in accordance with GAAP until after the transaction has closed.

Although, there is a place for other formulas—and again they are used in practice—utilizing the formula of *past practices in accordance with GAAP* can be a comprehensive and appropriate basis for calculating net working capital. Notwithstanding, that formula certainly does not eliminate all potential issues. There are a variety of issues and ambiguities that can occur and lead to disputes between the parties when utilizing *past practices in accordance with GAAP*. We discuss the concept of *past practices in accordance with GAAP* and some of its potential limitations more extensively in Part 2 of this book.

THE DEMARCATION AND QUANTIFICATION OF NET WORKING CAPITAL

Net working capital is comprised of a set of balance sheet accounts, namely current assets minus current liabilities. In considering each potential component of net working capital, there are three questions to be answered:

1. Should a particular item be included on the balance sheet or not? In accounting terms, this question relates to "recognition."
2. If it is to be included on the balance sheet, should a particular item be considered a current or a non-current asset or liability? In accounting terms, this question relates to "classification."
3. If an item is to be included as a current asset or current liability on the balance sheet, the remaining question is: for what amount? In accounting terms, this question relates to "measurement."

In addition, there is often a fourth question that needs to be asked in the context of a purchase price adjustment:

4. Are there any (partial) contractual exceptions or customizations to the determination of net working capital that deviate from *past practices in accordance with GAAP*? The purchase agreement can provide for a variety of customizations and contractual limitations. For example, the purchase agreement can provide for items to be included with or excluded from net working capital that would otherwise be treated differently under GAAP.

As illustrated here, the answers to those four questions set the boundaries for the quantification of the net working capital components for transactions involving net working capital purchase price adjustment provisions.

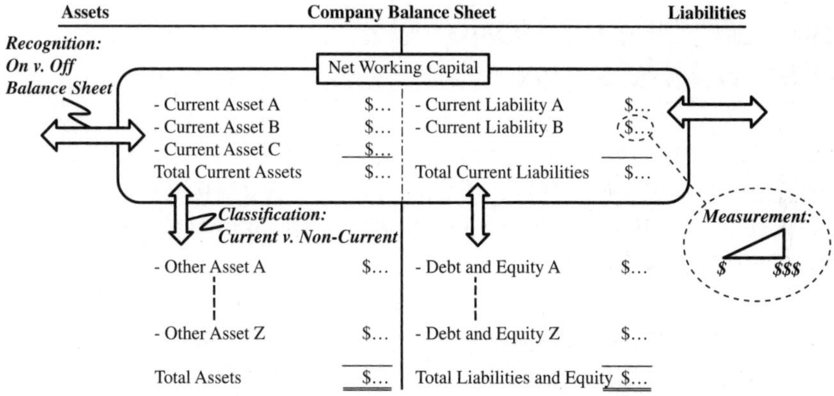

Demarcation and Quantification of Net Working Capital

Each of the overarching concepts of recognition, measurement, and classification can lead to disputes between the parties. Ahead, we provide a brief discussion of each of those three concepts and examples of potential disputes. In practice, the parties can disagree on one or more of those questions for one or more items in net working capital for a variety of reasons, including those related to GAAP guidance, the interpretation of the company's historical accounting practices, specific contractual provisions, and the facts and circumstances surrounding the company and the transaction. We discuss common and some uncommon disputed items in more detail in Chapters 15–19.

Recognition

A company's balance sheet reflects the financial position of the company and includes its assets and liabilities. It should not include any other assets or liabilities. On its face that seems reasonably straightforward and in most instances it is. There are, however, several complications.

Common disputes between sellers and buyers related to the recognition of the assets and liabilities of the company include those surrounding the existence of assets as of the closing date, the recognition of contingent liabilities, and a variety of accruals that can result from the timing of the closing.

Disputes that relate to the question whether all current assets included on the balance sheet were present/existed at closing are very common. By means of example, the buyer may count the inventory post-closing, find some of the inventory is missing, and conclude that it must not have existed as an asset of the company as of the closing date. The seller may disagree and conclude that the buyer's count is unreliable or that any inventory shrinkage must have occurred after the closing date.

The question whether contingent liabilities should be recognized on the balance sheet can require substantial judgment. Under GAAP a contingent liability is recognized if it is probable that the liability has been incurred and the amount of the loss can be reasonably estimated.[2] Sellers and buyers can disagree on one or both of those two requirements. By means of example, the company may be subject to an ongoing sales tax audit at the time of closing. The seller may oppose a buyer-proposed adjustment to recognize a tax liability. The seller could argue that the audit may result in a tax liability, but that the chance of that happening does not rise to the level of "probable" under GAAP.

Under accrual accounting, transactions and events are generally recorded in the period in which they occur as opposed to, for example, the moment that cash is received or expended. This is part of the application of the "matching principle" in accrual accounting. There are a variety of balance sheet accruals that come into play to facilitate the recording of the financial impact of events and transactions in the correct period. Ensuring that transactions near the end of an accounting period are recorded in the correct period is commonly referred to as related to *cutoff* in accounting parlance. Because the timing of the closing typically differs from the end of the company's regular reporting period, additional accruals and *cutoff* issues may become relevant in an M&A transaction that are not normally applicable to the company. By means of example, the company may pay its rent for each month on the last day of the month. There would be no rent accrual needed for purposes of the financial statements as of the end of a month, quarter, or year. In the event of a closing on January 15, however, the buyer may argue that the company should recognize half a month's rent as a pre-closing expense. That could result in the accrual of a liability (that is part of and lowers net working capital) for that half a month of unpaid rent in order to comply with GAAP. The seller may argue that the company does not historically make such bookings intra-month and booking them at month-end is an appropriate simplification under GAAP.

Finally, it is noteworthy that the GAAP notion of "assets of the company" does not necessarily fully align with legal ownership of the assets. Similarly, recognition of liabilities under GAAP does not necessarily align with the existence of legal obligations. As a result, it is—for example—possible for more than one company to have the same asset on their balance sheet or for no company to be allowed to include an asset. That being said, this distinction is not normally a driver of disputes—rather the appropriate GAAP treatment is—and accordingly we do not discuss this in more detail.

Measurement

The measurement of the amount at which an asset or liability should be included on a company's balance sheet ranges from accounting-based arithmetic to the application of judgment and estimation. The items that require significant qualitative judgment, estimation, and the careful consideration of relevant facts and circumstances to implement in accordance with

GAAP tend to lend themselves to differing views and potential disputes between the parties.

By means of illustration, inventory valuation disputes are very common. Those disputes often center on the assessment of the value or utility of the inventory as of the closing date as compared to the recorded historical costs. Considering the historical costs is part of the measurement process and commonly requires only mechanical processing and arithmetic. The disputes often center on the items for which subsequent measurement may indicate excess, obsolete, or otherwise impaired inventory (at least according to one of the parties). The identification of those items and the impact on the measurement of the inventory and any related inventory allowances requires judgment and estimation. The correct appropriate application of judgment and estimation are topics on which the parties may very well disagree.

We discuss the complications associated with using accounting estimates in general with the nature of GAAP in Chapter 4. We also discuss the common issues and disputed items associated with several accounting estimates throughout the disputed items part of this book.

Classification

A company's net working capital is the difference between its total current assets and total current liabilities. Current assets are assets that are reasonably expected to be realized, sold, or consumed during the normal operating cycle of the business.[3] For companies that have multiple operating cycles per year, GAAP prescribes a one-year time period for the segregation of current assets.[4] In parallel to current assets, the defining factor for current liabilities is that their liquidation is reasonably expected to require the use of current assets (or the creation of other current liabilities).[5]

Disputes related to the distinction between current and non-current assets typically center around the length of the time period that should be used to segregate them. A buyer may seek to use a one-year period to segregate current and non-current assets, while the seller may argue that a longer operating cycle is justified based on the operations of the business. Importantly, the one-year minimum is very much ingrained as the *de facto* distinction within the accounting community and buyers can be caught off guard when confronted with the broader GAAP guidance. Notably, the one-year period is so ingrained—without the same being true for the rest of the GAAP context—that it is not uncommon for even professionally supported parties to be caught off-guard by the notion of the operating cycle requiring a longer segregation criterion than one year.

Example: Current Does Not Necessarily Mean One Year

- A company sells its services in the form of two-year service contracts on specialized equipment. The company manufactures certain installable parts that it needs to perform its services in-house.
- At the onset of each two-year service contract the company commences fabrication of specialized parts for the entire period of the contract. Dependent on workload, the parts are completed over a period ranging from 1 to 18 months.
- After closing, the buyer seeks to exclude from current assets all parts that are not reasonably expected to be needed within one year and an accompanying adjustment to the purchase price in an amount of $4 million. The seller argues that its operating cycle is longer than one year and none of its inventory should be reclassified.

Disputes regarding the classification of liabilities can include those related to the segregation of the current portion of a long-term liability or accrual as a current liability. Historically, the company may not have made that split for each relevant item—and it may have been less significant for purposes of preparing the financial statements—or the company may not have recognized the relevant accrual altogether.

Example: Recognition and Classification of a Lease Concession

- A company leases its office building and expenses the quarterly lease payments as it incurs them. The company is in the third year of its ten-year lease commitment. When it entered into the lease, the company received a one-year lease concession.
- After closing, the buyer argues that the company should have straight-lined the rent (annual rent expense = 9 years * annual rent payment/10 years). The buyer seeks to recognize an associated deferred rent accrual and deduct it from net working capital.
- The seller admits that it should have recognized the accrual, but responds that only the current portion of the deferred rent should be deducted from net working capital, which would eliminate most of the net working capital impact.
- *Note*: Dependent on the purchase agreement this issue may be (partially or exclusively) captured in the adjustment for debt and debt-like items.

Transaction-Specific Items

Using *past practices in accordance with GAAP* may be generally attractive for the parties to a transaction. Notwithstanding, it may not be specific enough or a perfect fit for all items based on the context of the transaction, the facts and circumstances surrounding the company, or other needs of the parties. There may be one or more items that require a predefined custom treatment for purposes of determining the closing net working capital. In order to accommodate those special items, the parties may choose to partially deviate from an agreed-upon determination of net working capital consistent with *past practices in accordance with GAAP*. Such special treatment can range from preemptively deeming certain practices to be in accordance with GAAP, to providing formulas for quantifying certain items, to carving out items from net working capital altogether.

Adjustments are also commonly made to govern or prevent unwanted interaction with other adjustment mechanisms (e.g., carving out cash from net working capital when there is a separate cash adjustment mechanism) or other provisions of the purchase agreement (e.g., to manage overlap between indemnification provisions and the net working capital adjustment mechanism).

Example: Transaction-Specific Adjustment

- The company has warranty exposure for three products: A, B, and C. Product A is the current product. Product B is a legacy product that will be supported by the seller. Product C is another legacy product that will be supported by the buyer at the seller's expense.
- Without an arrangement to the contrary, the parties could end up having a dispute about the recognition and measurement of a warranty obligation as part of the net working capital. Given the circumstances of the transaction, the parties find *past practices in accordance with GAAP* an undesirable methodology for quantifying the warranty obligation as part of the purchase price.
- Instead the parties agree to the following:
  - For product A, the parties agree to a formula to quantify the warranty obligation that incorporates the size and aging of the installation base as of the closing date and an agreed-upon amount per remaining year of equipment warranty.
  - For product B, the parties agree to an indemnification provision and exclude the obligation from the determination of the net working capital.
  - For product C, the parties define the reimbursable expenses and provide for those expenses to be offset against guaranteed and performance-based earn-out payments that will become due under the purchase agreement. The parties contractually exclude both the impact of the warranty obligations and the reimbursements from net working capital.

- As a result, the warranty obligation can potentially result in a post-closing net working capital adjustment, but only in relation to product A and the elements of the formula. A dispute about the appropriate estimation methodology under GAAP is effectively preempted.

We caution the parties and their advisors that if an exception is required to the formula of *past practices in accordance with GAAP*, the exception should be very carefully formulated and should consider the company's accounting as well as the relevant facts and circumstances. As the exception often includes a willful departure from GAAP, the arbitrator cannot necessarily fall back on GAAP to clear up any ambiguities. We discuss some of the complications associated with defining exceptions to and carve-outs from *past practices in accordance with GAAP* in Chapter 7.

NOTES

1. *See* FASB ASC Master Glossary, at Current Assets.
2. *See* FASB ASC 450-20-25-2.
3. *See* FASB ASC Master Glossary, at Current Assets.
4. *See* FASB ASC 210-10-45-3.
5. *See* FASB ASC Master Glossary, at Current Liabilities.

PART Two

Core Concepts and Issues

CHAPTER 4

The Nature of GAAP

This book is not intended to provide general instruction in GAAP and its application. Notwithstanding, the resolution of disputed items in an accounting arbitration commonly requires the application of GAAP concepts and guidance. It is therefore important to highlight several relevant aspects of GAAP. The various GAAP standards are promulgated by the Financial Accounting Standards Board (FASB). Prior to 2009, GAAP guidance was spread across various forms of publications that were authoritative to varying degrees. In 2009, however, the FASB Accounting Standards Codification (ASC) went into effect. Currently, the financial accounting and reporting guidance as contained in the FASB ASC is the sole authoritative source of GAAP for non-SEC registered businesses.[1] For SEC registrants the rules and interpretive releases of the SEC are also sources of authoritative guidance.[2]

BACKGROUND OF GAAP

The FASB elaborated on the specific objectives and concepts that it utilizes in developing GAAP in a conceptual framework that consists of a series of Statements of Financial Accounting Concepts. The first FASB Concept Statement was issued in 1978.

Although the FASB Concept Statements themselves do not establish authoritative GAAP they are useful in understanding the nature of GAAP. GAAP is broadly based on the premise that financial reporting is not an end in itself but is intended to provide information that is useful in making business and economic decisions.[3] For example, financial accounting is not designed to measure directly the value of a business enterprise, but the information it provides may be helpful to those who wish to estimate its value.[4]

The FASB examined the characteristics of accounting information that make that information useful in the context of the FASB's disclosed objectives, such as relevance, reliability, comparability, and consistency. The FASB also recognized that there are restraints applicable, including materiality and cost constraints.[5] The FASB recognized that maximizing the usefulness of accounting information, subject to considerations of the cost of providing it, entails choices between alternative accounting methods.[6] The FASB recognized that accounting choices are made at two levels at least: at the level of the FASB and other standard-setting entities as well as at the level of the individual enterprise. In that context, although the FASB recognizes that GAAP cannot produce optimal outcomes for all users under all circumstances as there is simply too much variation, the FASB—in setting accounting standards—strives to leave as much room as possible for individual choices and preferences while securing the degree of conformity necessary to attain its objectives.[7] The board observed that those who are unfamiliar with the nature of accounting are often surprised at the large number of choices that accountants are required to make.[8]

GAAP IS NOT NECESSARILY NARROWLY PRESCRIPTIVE

The important takeaway from the perspective of resolving post-closing purchase price disputes that rely on an interpretation or application of GAAP is that GAAP is not meant to be a set of narrowly prescriptive guidelines. Rather, GAAP is organized to maximize the usefulness of information—that is largely based on events that have already taken place—that is communicated to economic decision makers. That naturally involves a relatively large degree of freedom and a variety of accounting choices offered to reporting entities. Although both laws and accounting guidance can have in common that they offer choices within a framework of rules, the emphasis on legal certainty that is found in law—which offers those subject to it the ability to regulate their behavior in accordance with the rule of law—does not exist as such under GAAP.

The result is a set of standards and guidelines that leave significant room for management judgment and estimation in the recognition and measurement of financial information included in the financial statements. As a result, the application of GAAP is for many items not single-outcome determinative. Rather, the appropriate application of GAAP can, dependent on the item, lead to different outcomes regarding recognition (e.g., whether an item is included on the balance sheet), measurement (e.g., for what amount an item is included on the balance sheet), classification (e.g., where an item is included on the balance sheet), and disclosure (e.g., whether the item is otherwise discussed) in the financial statements of a company.

Of course, not every accounting item requires judgment or can result in a range of acceptable outcomes. By means of example, the balance of the company's operating bank account is the balance that goes onto the balance sheet. Many items, however, require some level of judgment and estimation. An example of a category of accounting decisions for which GAAP provides substantial freedom is the preparation of accounting estimates and the related application of management judgment. Examples of such items include:

- Collectability of accounts receivable—the actual collection of a company's accounts receivable takes place in the future. Determining what portion of those receivables are collectible requires judgment and estimation.

- Obsolescence of inventory—whether inventory is obsolete or still useful for the company is, in many instances, a question of judgment.
- Probability of contingent liabilities—whether a possible obligation is probable to occur (and for what amount) can require substantial judgment.
- Impairment of fixed assets—there is judgment involved in the projections necessary to determine whether the book value of an asset is recoverable, that is whether the book value is exceeded by the sum of the applicable undiscounted expected future cash flows. Expected future cash flows are estimates by their nature.

The first two items relate to inventory and accounts receivable, two accounts that are at the center of many post-closing net working capital disputes. Both items typically encompass the application of significant management judgment. Contingent liabilities also require the application of significant management judgment.

Impairment of fixed assets can be highly relevant to, for example, EBITDA-based purchase price adjustment disputes. Impairment is separate from depreciation and amortization and without a purchase agreement that specifically excludes it from EBITDA, can lead to significant and unexpected downward pressure on EBITDA. Such issues can be preemptively resolved by using a defined "Adjusted EBITDA" measure on which to base the adjustment.

In line with the FASB's observation included above, GAAP, by its nature, is much more permissive than many people expect. Drafting or entering into a purchase agreement without understanding GAAP's permissiveness and its impact in the context of the target company can be very and unexpectedly expensive.

We have included an illustration here that juxtaposes the common perception against GAAP's actual nature.

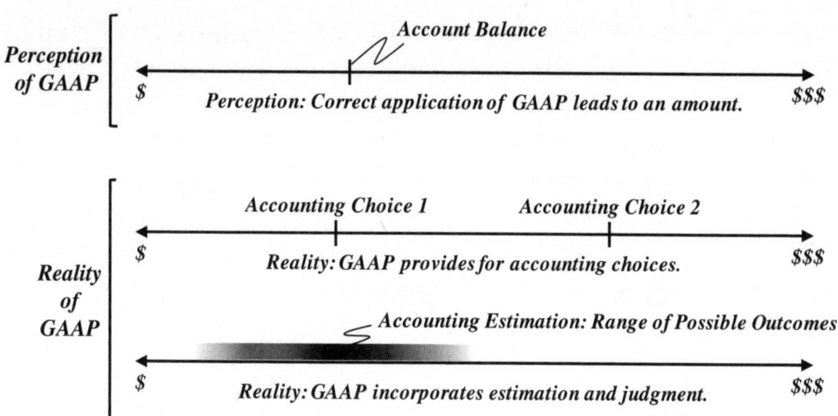

GAAP Is Not Necessarily Narrowly Prescriptive

GAAP IS NOT A FREE-FOR-ALL

Notwithstanding the previous discussion regarding the leeway available to the company and management under GAAP, it is not a free-for-all-do-as-you-wish system. GAAP provides the reporting company and its management with accounting choices that (i) recognize the need to maximize the usefulness of the information provided, given the specific facts and circumstances surrounding a company and (ii) allow the management of the company to apply its judgment as it relates to certain areas as they are typically the most competent people to make those estimates.

Those accounting choices and estimates, however, need to be made within the confines of GAAP. By means of example, dependent on the type of asset or liability, GAAP can allow one or more methods of recognition and measurement, but only those methods are allowed. As it relates to accounting estimates, management is responsible for making the accounting estimates included in the financial statements. Estimates are based on subjective as well as objective factors and, as a result, judgment is required to estimate an amount as of the date of the financial statements. Management's judgment can be based on a variety of qualitative and quantitative factors and observations as well as consideration of what actions management expects to take. That room for judgment can result in a potentially broad range of outcomes. However, that does not mean that everything goes.

Management Judgment Can Be Evaluated for Reasonableness

The accounting arbitrator will evaluate the reasonableness of disputed accounting estimates, including both subjective and objective factors. The accounting arbitrator may conclude that the estimate is reasonable given the facts and circumstances surrounding the business or may conclude that the estimate is inappropriate under GAAP. The estimate can be inappropriate due to errors in the objective elements (e.g., a mathematical error) but also for unreasonableness, whether or not due to bias, in the subjective factors of arriving at the estimate.

Notably, testing of accounting estimates for both objective and subjective factors that go into the estimate, including the reasonableness of management's qualitative and quantitative judgments, is not the exclusive purview of post-closing purchase price disputes. They are also tested in the regular course of performing an audit. The auditing guidance recognizes that given the objective and subjective factors involved, it may be difficult for management to establish controls related to the conception of accounting estimates. The auditing guidance also recognizes that judgment is required. Nonetheless, the auditing guidance states that "[t]he auditor should evaluate, based on the audit evidence, whether the accounting estimates in the financial statements are either reasonable in the context of the applicable financial reporting framework or are misstated."[9]

Limitations on Accounting Changes

GAAP also imposes limits on changing accounting methodologies or estimates in order to maintain consistency across financial statement reporting periods. GAAP's consistency requirements are geared toward the preparation and usage of financial statements. Although GAAPs' consistency requirements may also be useful in the context of purchase price adjustment mechanisms, they are by themselves often deemed insufficiently restrictive in that context. Hence, the common usage of *past practices in accordance with GAAP*. We discuss the limitations that GAAP imposes on accounting changes next.

Changes to Accounting Principles GAAP significantly restricts changes in accounting principles applied by a company. A change in accounting principles can, for example, be a change from LIFO to FIFO inventory accounting. GAAP only allows changes in accounting principles that result from new guidance or if the entity can justify the use of an allowable alternative accounting principle on the basis that it is preferable.[10] In addition, in the event of a change in accounting principle, the entity is required to implement the change in accounting principle through retroactive application unless impracticable or subject to transition guidance to the contrary. Allowing preferable accounting treatment to supplant historical practices is commonly found to be undesirable in the context of purchase price adjustments. It can result in potentially large adjustments relative to the target net working capital without an underlying change in the composition and amount of the company's net working capital. Moreover, retroactive changes to the target net working capital are in many situations, at best, impracticable.

Changes to Accounting Estimates GAAP is generally more permissive of changes in accounting estimates than it is of changes to accounting principles. Changes in accounting estimates result from new information. They can be a necessary consequence of the assessment, in conjunction with the periodic presentation of financial statements, of the present status and expected future benefits and obligations associated with assets and liabilities.

The result can be an adjustment to the carrying amount of an existing asset or liability. Examples of items for which estimates are necessary are uncollectable receivables, inventory obsolescence, service lives and salvage values of depreciable assets, and warranty obligations.[11] A change in accounting estimate should not be accounted for by restating or retrospectively adjusting amounts reported in financial statements of prior periods or by reporting pro forma amounts for prior periods.[12]

Changes to Correct Errors GAAP also recognizes the need to make changes to correct errors. An error in the financial statements of a prior period discovered after the financial statements are issued or are available to be issued should be reported as an error correction, by restating the prior-period financial statements.[13] In accordance with GAAP, restatements in financial statements are effected by adjusting the opening balance of assets and liabilities as well as an offsetting adjustment to retained earnings in combination with adjustments to historical financial statements for period-specific errors. Thus, GAAP safeguards the reporting of the financial results for the period at issue as well as making adjustments to generate consistency. Not surprisingly, if errors are corrected in the closing statement, those corrections may very well impact the ultimate purchase price.

GAAP BY ITSELF IS TOO BROAD FOR CLOSING DATE ACCOUNTING IN MANY SITUATIONS

GAAP provides companies, within the limitations of the GAAP framework, the leeway to make accounting choices that best fit the specific circumstances of the company. It also seeks to protect the user of the information and the consistency of the presented information by limiting accounting choices. GAAP's overall approach ensures that improvements to accounting information are possible while keeping information comparable and limiting the possibility of repeated opportunistic changes to a company's accounting practices. In other words,

GAAP's approach fits the context of the preparation of financial statements.

From the perspective of a purchase price adjustment, however, broadly allowing changes to the company's accounting choices can create uncertainty and significant adjustments without real underlying changes. Such uncertainty is at odds with the fundamental purpose of the post-closing purchase price adjustment process. The post-closing purchase price adjustment process is supposed to, among other things, provide sufficient time to close the books to update the preliminarily determined net working capital. In doing so, consistency is disproportionally important. After all, the final net working capital will be compared against the preliminary net working capital and/or the target net working capital to calculate the purchase price adjustment. Inconsistency in this context can lead to adjustments that find their genesis in theoretical accounting improvements without actual changes to the underlying assets and liabilities.

Example: Consequences of Allowing Accounting Changes

- The company accounts for its inventory using the LIFO (last-in-first-out) method. As of the determination of the target net working capital, the inventory consists of the following items:
  - Tranche 1 (oldest): 1,000 Widgets @ $100 each = $100,000
  - Tranche 2 (middle): 1,000 Widgets @ $120 each = $120,000
  - Tranche 3 (newest): 4,000 Widgets @ $150 each = $600,000
  - Total: 6,000 Widgets @ total of = $820,000
- Subsequent to the determination of the target net working capital, but prior to closing, the company sells 3,000 Widgets and replenishes 2,800 Widgets at $150 each. At closing the inventory consists of 5,800 Widgets. Under the company's historical accounting, the inventory amount would be:
  - Tranche 1 (oldest): 1,000 Widgets @ $100 each = $100,000
  - Tranche 2 (middle): 1,000 Widgets @ $120 each = $120,000
  - Tranche 3 (newest): 3,800 Widgets @ $150 each = $570,000
  - Total: 5,800 Widgets @ total of = $790,000

- Accordingly, the buyer expects to be entitled to an adjustment of $30,000 in its favor for receiving 200 Widgets less.
- If the purchase agreement relied solely on compliance with GAAP and has not limited the accounting to the company's historical accounting practices, the seller could improve the inventory accounting by switching from LIFO to FIFO immediately subsequent to determining the target net working capital. The seller could then claim an adjustment in its favor for delivering less product as follows:
  - Tranche 1 (oldest): N/A
  - Tranche 2 (middle): N/A
  - Tranche 3 (newest): 5,800 Widgets @ $150 each = $870,000
  - Total: 5,800 Widgets @ total of = $870,000
- The result is an adjustment of $50,000 in the seller's favor while delivering less inventory at closing.

In other words, requiring compliance with GAAP is important for the protections it affords the parties, but is by itself often deemed insufficient as the contractual formula for closing date accounting. Simply prescribing *in accordance with GAAP* as the methodology for the proposed closing statement can result in a broad range of potential acceptable outcomes, many of which can be perceived as inequitable or otherwise undesirable. Notwithstanding, under certain circumstances the parties can deem *in accordance with GAAP* as the most appropriate methodology. Although less common, such an approach is encountered in practice.

For many situations, however, the importance of consistency is more appropriately captured in the common concept of *past practices in accordance with GAAP*. We discuss that standard in more detail in Chapter 5.

NOTES

1. *See* FASB ASC 105-10-05-1.
2. *See* FASB ASC 105-10-05-1.

3. *See* FASB Concept Statement 1.
4. *See* FASB Concept Statement 1.
5. *See* FASB Concept Statement 2.
6. *See* FASB Concept Statement 2, at ¶5.
7. *See, e.g.*, FASB Concept Statement 2, at ¶¶17–18.
8. *See, e.g.*, FASB Concept Statement 2, at ¶8.
9. *See* AU-C §540.18.
10. *See* FASB ASC 250-10-45-2.
11. *See* FASB ASC Master Glossary, at Change in Accounting Estimate.
12. *See* FASB ASC 250-10-45-17.
13. *See* FASB ASC 250-10-45-23.

CHAPTER 5

Past Practices in Accordance with GAAP

As discussed in previous chapters, there are three general contractual approaches to determine the amount of net working capital as of the closing date, namely in accordance with (i) GAAP, (ii) the company's historical accounting practices, or (iii) *past practices in accordance with GAAP*. All three methodologies (and a variety of other methodologies) can be encountered in practice.

We also discussed that in many situations the first two approaches have significant disadvantages relative to the application of *past practices in accordance with GAAP*. Excluding past practices from the formula, that is having the closing statement prepared *in accordance with GAAP*, generally provides the parties too much flexibility. That can result in large unexpected adjustments. Excluding compliance with GAAP from the formula, that is having the closing statement prepared *in accordance with past practices,* can result in the seller benefiting from historical GAAP non-compliance issues.

Not surprisingly, purchase agreements routinely provide for net working capital to be determined consistent with *past practices in accordance with GAAP*. That formula has the benefit of requiring GAAP compliance, while narrowing down the broad selection of possibly GAAP compliant accounting choices to those historically made by the company. Utilizing the formula of *past practices in accordance with GAAP* can be a comprehensive and appropriate basis for calculating net working capital in the context of an M&A transaction.

Notwithstanding, utilizing the formula of *past practices in accordance with GAAP* does not guarantee the absence of issues and ambiguities that can occur when determining and evaluating the company's net working capital as of the closing date. In this chapter, we first discuss that—dependent on the circumstances—past practices in accordance with GAAP does not necessarily narrow down the range of accounting treatments that are allowed under GAAP to a single point estimate for every item. We then discuss several issues that can occur dependent on the facts and circumstances and the definition of past practices in the purchase agreement. Thereafter, we discuss the situation that the application of past practices would be in violation of GAAP and the consequences thereof.

We also discuss opportunities for contractual mitigation of some of the issues that can occur when determining net working capital consistent with *past practices in accordance with GAAP*. We cover those opportunities throughout the text and in the final section of this chapter. In addition, an avenue to mitigate issues associated with a particular account (or set of accounts) can be to provide for transaction-specific treatment for that account, while the remainder of the net working capital is determined consistent with *past practices in accordance with GAAP*. Such transaction-specific treatment is discussed in Chapter 7. Finally, we also discuss governing agreements and contractual choices in Chapter 20.

PAST PRACTICES IN ACCORDANCE WITH GAAP DOES NOT NECESSARILY NARROW DOWN THE APPLICABLE ACCOUNTING TO A SINGLE POINT ESTIMATE FOR ALL ACCOUNTS UNDER ALL CIRCUMSTANCES

It is not uncommon for those involved with the transaction to expect that contractually providing for the net working capital to be determined consistent with *past practices in accordance with GAAP* is sufficient to narrowly define the calculation of net working capital for each item and cover all possible circumstances. For some items, however, even the agreed-upon application of the company's own historical accounting practices can still lead to a relatively wide range of possible outcomes dependent on the applicable facts and circumstances. The focus provided by requiring the closing statement to be prepared in accordance with the company's own historical accounting practices is not always as narrow as is sometimes expected. The occurrence of multiple apparently compliant outcomes is especially prevalent in the context of poorly documented accounting estimates.

The Nature of Judgment and Estimation Can Cause a Range of Apparent Past Practices–Compliant Outcomes

Certain accounting items—especially accounting estimates—can require the application of significant judgment. Management's judgment related to accounting estimates is normally based on its knowledge and experience about past and current events and its assumptions about conditions it expects to exist and courses of action it expects to take.[1] In preparing an estimate, management can consider a variety of both objective and subjective factors and their quantitative and qualitative aspects. In other words, the recognition and measurement of those items is often not mechanical or based on easily replicable arithmetic. Even with perfect information/documentation on how an accounting estimate was derived, the amount included in a company's financial statements cannot necessarily be independently reconstituted to the same amount under all circumstances.

The preparation of the closing statement and the implementation of the post-closing purchase price adjustment mechanisms can require the application of the company's historical accounting practices to prepare accounting estimates under more challenging circumstances. The historical accounting practices have to be applied to the facts and circumstances

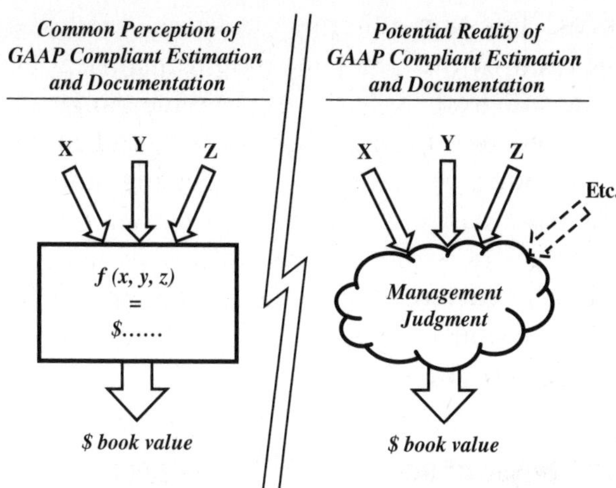

Management Judgment and Estimation

existent as of the closing date. The result is that for certain items the application of *past practices in accordance with GAAP* can lead to diverging positions between the parties that can both appear to be in compliance with that formula.

The Documentation of Historical Management Judgment

An additional complication is that perfect information and complete and unambiguous documentation regarding the derivation of the accounting estimates is not necessarily available. The documentation of past practices is typically not prepared in the context of an anticipated purchase price adjustment dispute or to facilitate the interpretation and application of those practices as of the closing date in that context.

Rather, companies focus on documenting their accounting estimates in a manner that complies with GAAP. Although GAAP contains requirements regarding documentation,[2] GAAP's approach is to show that the financial statements fairly represent the financial performance and position of the company in accordance with GAAP. As the documentation is used in the preparation and audit of the financial statements, the documentation is accompanied by direct and contemporaneous access to the company's management and accounting personnel. Thus, extensive documentation that can be used to unambiguously prepare the accounting estimates as of the closing date is not necessarily prepared in the regular course of business.

Moreover, even if a company wanted to, it cannot necessarily document each of its accounting estimates in such a narrow manner that its documentation only allows arriving at the same conclusion. After all, accounting estimates—by their nature—commonly include an element of qualitative judgment that is not mechanical in nature. Notwithstanding, the problem with accounting estimates can to a significant extent be mitigated by more extensive documentation. Even if the final amount cannot necessarily be quantitatively derived, the seller or company could potentially document the steps taken and considerations employed. That is especially useful when some of the steps are quantitative in nature and can thus be accompanied by dollar ranges that set boundaries on the estimation process. The ranges and the discussions of how an amount is selected from within the range can help support a position and falsify a potential counterparty's position.

Of course, the additional documentation is only useful if it codifies the process as it occurred at the time. Practically speaking, that means that such a documentation approach is often limited to situations in which financial statements are specifically created for the sale (e.g., carve-out financial statements), or situations in which the timing of the process accommodates the preparation of incremental documentation contemporaneous with the preparation of the reference financial statements whether due to long-term planning or fortuitous circumstances.

In preparation for a transaction, it may appear attractive to eliminate the qualitative judgment component from the accounting estimates in order to achieve complete and unambiguous documentation. After all, a purely quantitatively derived estimate can be completely and unambiguously documented. The elimination of qualitative judgment, however, may be in violation of GAAP. In other words, without an accompanying transaction-specific adjustment to the purchase agreement, the accounting arbitrator may have to depart from such a methodology in order to allow for compliance with *past practices in accordance with GAAP*.

The Level of Interpretation by the Accounting Arbitrator

The issues described earlier can be exacerbated by differences in approach among accounting arbitrators. In the absence of the governing purchase agreement providing specificity, there are multiple levels at which accounting arbitrators can interpret consistency with *past practices* in the context of management judgment and accounting estimation. In practice, accounting arbitrators can have very narrow interpretations, very broad interpretations, and anything in between.

Narrowly approached, an arbitrator may consider *past practices in accordance with GAAP* to mean the same "outcome" or the same "applied metric" as it relates to management judgment as long as its application as of the closing date is in accordance with GAAP. On the other hand, in the absence of quantifiable mechanical judgment, an accounting arbitrator may broadly consider the application of management judgment itself in compliance with past practices (as those practices also consisted of the application of management judgment). A more common middle-of-the-road approach is the consideration of judgment that is as much as possible analogous to the management judgment applied in the reference financial statements or other defined basis of consistency in the purchase agreement.

In other words, given the documentation and information available, the accounting arbitrator can attempt to arrive at an outcome as of the closing date that is, as much as possible, equal to the conclusion that management would have arrived at if the circumstances as of the closing date had existed as of the relevant historical date, and vice versa. Either more extreme approach can easily result in a conclusion that management would not have reached in analogously applying their judgment to the changed facts and circumstances.

COMPLICATIONS OF UTILIZING PAST PRACTICES

Purchase agreements vary in their approach to defining the company's past practices as encapsulated in the formula *past practices in accordance with GAAP*. A common approach is to define the past practices by incorporating a reference to one or more of the company's historical financial statements. Other approaches include, for example, a blanket reference to the company's historical accounting or a financial document that was prepared in the context of the transaction.

Gaps and Inconsistencies

A definition that simply defines past practices as the accounting practices utilized in the preparation of one or more reference financial statements appears straightforward. And mostly it is, especially in combination with agreement language that covers the level of interpretation as discussed earlier. Dependent on the company's circumstances, however, the definition may nonetheless result in gaps or inconsistencies.

Accounting Choice Not Covered by Reference Financials There are circumstances that can result in the parties having to make one or more accounting choices in the preparation of the closing statement that are not covered by the reference financial statements.

Expansion of the Company's Activities The company's circumstances in the period between the reference financial statements and the closing statement can have developed in a manner that results in new accounting choices as of the closing date. By means of example, the company may have expanded its business activities and entered into its first international joint venture.

Importantly, the time period between the reference financial statements and the closing statement can easily be more than one year. The reference financial statements are commonly defined as the most recent audited financial statements. For a closing in February 2017, the most recent audited financial statements are likely those as of December 31, 2015. Especially, expanding companies or companies that operate in rapidly evolving industries can be subject to significant business changes in that period.

If there are significant changes to the business between the date of the reference financial statements and the closing date, it could be worthwhile to specifically address any potentially significant items for which historical accounting practices may not exist.

Historical Choices Not in Reference Financial Statements A particular accounting choice can have been historically relevant to the company, but by happenstance or because the item does not occur every year, it may not have been relevant for the reference financial statements. By means of example, the company may not have had ongoing litigation as of the reference financial statement date and thus no associated contingent liability in those financial statements, while the company has been involved in litigation before (and accounted for it) and is again as of the closing date. Of course, such situations are more common when the reference financial statements are defined as a single set, that is, the most recent audited financial statements as opposed to, for example, the most recent three years of audited financial statements.

Accounting Choice Not in Annual Financial Statements The reference financial statements are often the annual financial statements of the company. The closing, however, is typically not at year-end or even at a month- or quarter-end. As a result, it is a relatively common occurrence for the closing statement to require the consideration of cutoff issues that are not relevant as of year-end.

The problem can be mitigated to a certain extent by supplementing the defined past practices with a reference to the quarterly financial statements. The quarterly financial statements, however, are generally less extensive than the annual financial statements and are unaudited. In other words, although a useful supplement, they are generally not more attractive as overall reference financial statements than the annual financial statements. As second-tier financial statements that are used to supplement the annual financial statements for purposes of defining past practices, however, they can certainly be useful. The purchase agreement can, for example, provide for them to be a source of past practices that applies if the accounting for a particular item is not covered by the annual financial statements.

Of course, quarterly finance statements do not resolve all cutoff issues, which can, dependent on the closing date, even include mid-month-driven ones. Fortunately, for most such timing issues the impact is typically limited and the accounting relatively straightforward. Persistent disagreements between the parties on such items are often driven by perceived inequity due to the cutoff issues not having been considered for purposes of calculating the target net working capital.

Possible Resolutions Situations where necessary accounting choices are not covered by the reference financials occur regularly. Those choices are most problematic if the application of GAAP in combination with the relevant facts and circumstances provides for multiple possible outcomes. We further discuss some options for preemptively mitigating that risk throughout this chapter and in Chapter 20.

Inconsistencies in Past Practices A company may have internal inconsistencies in the disclosure and application of past practices across historical financial statements or even within one set of financial statements. Overall, the parties are more likely to be confronted with inconsistencies in past practices in instances where the agreement defines the company's past practices more globally, that is, without designating a single set of reference financial statements or establishing a hierarchy among historical financial statements.

Inconsistencies between Financial Statements There are many legitimate reasons for a company to have inconsistencies from year-to-year between its financial statements. As discussed in Chapter 4, the company could have voluntarily changed one or more accounting methodologies toward "better GAAP." The company could have also implemented a mandatory accounting change in accordance with changes to GAAP or the company's circumstances. The latter generally does not lead to problems under the *past practices in accordance with GAAP* as only one of the potential past practices will be in accordance with GAAP as of the closing date. The former, however, can result in disagreements between the parties.

In addition to formal changes to accounting methodologies, companies also routinely update their accounting estimates. The judgment and qualitative considerations that go into many accounting estimates can result in companies taking a relatively relaxed approach to any changes or improvements in the estimation process and the accounting estimates. Moreover, companies are not necessarily up to date with documenting such changes.

There are often good reasons to incorporate multiple periods of reference financial statements for purposes of defining past practices. An important benefit is that an accounting choice that must be made as of the closing date is more likely to have been covered. The potential downside of increasing the likelihood of inconsistencies can be mitigated by providing for a hierarchy in the purchase agreement. For example, the purchase agreement can provide for three years of reference financial statements and specify that in the event of inconsistencies the more recent financial statements govern.

Internal Inconsistencies There can also be inconsistencies within a single set of reference financial statements. For example, there can be a mismatch in the amount included on the balance sheet and the amount included in the notes to the financial statements. There can also be a mismatch between the narrative included in the notes to the financial statements and the actual calculation of the amount included on the balance sheet. In practice, impactful internal inconsistencies are rare and are addressed by accounting arbitrators based on the specific facts and circumstances of the company and its accounting.

Much more common are disconnects between the amounts included in the financial statements and the supporting documentation, that is, the balance sheet items and the conclusions included in the supporting documentation do not match. Such issues can have a variety of underlying causes. It may be that the company's accounting staff was simply too busy and updated a balance sheet item on-the-fly to reflect the correct amount without contemporaneously updating the supporting documentation. In most regular-course-of-business circumstances this does not necessarily cause any problems.

In the case of a post-closing purchase price dispute, however, it can generate ambiguity, especially if the mismatch is in an area that requires significant effort to get from the general ledger to the balance sheet or is part of an accounting estimate. By the time the dispute is submitted to the arbitrator, there may be multiple versions of the supporting documentation floating around, no documentation of the previous self-evident adjustments, and multiple theories promulgated by the parties. It is therefore critically important for supporting documentation to match the supported accounting entry or account.

Other Causes of Issues and Ambiguities

There are a variety of other circumstances that can lead to problems and ambiguities when interpreting and using the company's historical accounting practices for purposes of preparing a closing statement.

Historical Ties to Group Accounting Complications can arise in situations where, prior to the transaction, the company was part of a larger group of companies. The company may not have had its own accounting department or accounting practices. If there was separate accounting for the company's segments or divisions, the functional accounting structure (for past practices) may not have lined up with the legal structure (for the transfer).

In larger transactions, this effect is often mitigated by the preparation of (audited) carve-out financial statements. Smaller transactions may rely on the slicing-and-dicing of the financial information available to provide historical financial information (e.g., in a trial balance format). Either way, the company-level financials (i) may be based on group-level accounting policies, (ii) may contain significant intercompany transactions, and (iii) may not have previously been closed or subject to top-end closing entries other than at a group level.

Even with professionally prepared carve-out financial statements, those issues can cause ambiguities or in more extreme situations result in violations of GAAP. The extent to which such problems occur depends on the specific facts and circumstances of the case. By means of example, the group's accounting for intercompany transactions can have historically been structured and specific, a complete mess, or anything in between. Even if the group was audited, the intragroup transactions are eliminated in the consolidation process and may thus have received only very limited attention from the auditors.

The Company's Accounting Function There are multiple things that can occur within the company's accounting function that can result in past practices being obfuscated or more difficult to apply. For example, the company may be transitioning to a new accounting or ERP system combined with a new approach to generating bookings, a transition from paper to electronic documentation, and/or a new chart of accounts. Those changes may find their genesis in the company's preparation for the transaction (e.g., the company may be transitioned to its own accounting system to prepare for separation from the group). They can also originate from changes to the accounting function that happen to be occurring in the same timeframe (e.g., the company is transitioning to a new ERP system with integrated fully digital documentation). That change can be part of a long-term plan at the company level that was set in motion prior to the sale, or the target company can be pulled along the waves of change within a much larger corporate group. Either way, such systematic changes can be merely inconvenient, result in delays, or result in errors.

Example: Accounting System Change Results in Error

- As part of the testing of a new accounting system mere months before the closing, a target company enters some dummy inventory items.
- As of the closing date, the implementation is not yet finalized and the dummy items have not been eliminated. In the normal course of business, the timing would not matter as no financial statements are being prepared at the time.
- Between the buyer, who is new to the company, post-closing personnel changes at the target, and remote high-level management, however, the parties only identify the source of the difference when they are well into the accounting arbitration.

Changes to the accounting systems or function can also result in ambiguity on a more granular level. While this may not be an issue for the preparation of financial statements, it can turn out to be problematic in the context of the purchase agreement, the closing statement, and the post-closing purchase price adjustment calculations.

Example: Accounting System Change Results in Ambiguity

- The purchase agreement provides for certain inventory accounts to be carved out from the calculation of net working capital to align it with the nature of the business and the needs of the parties.

- The carve-out is written up in general terms but clarified by a numerical example that shows the carve-out is applied to specific general ledger ("GL") accounts.
- Between the drafting of the purchase agreement, including the example, and the closing date, the company changes its accounting systems and implements a new chart of accounts.
- The new chart of accounts and the old one are not mapped one-on-one. In addition, there is significant movement in the inventory accounts and a clerical error is made in the usage of the relevant new accounts.
- The above issues render the example uninformative for purposes of application as of the closing date. The contractual language is, without the benefit of the example, too vague to be independently implementable.

If feasible, it is advisable to avoid major changes to the accounting function and systems in the period leading up to the closing in order to avoid some of the complications that can occur. Alternatively, it can be helpful (i) to supplement the purchase agreement with side letters to clarify the impact of any significant changes to the accounting system and (ii) to include the closing date and the related accounting requirements on the implementation schedule of any major system changes.

PAST PRACTICES WOULD VIOLATE GAAP

In many disputes that reach arbitration, the buyer has taken the position that the application of past practices as of the closing date would result in one or more violations of GAAP. The accounting arbitrator will have to carefully consider GAAP, the parties' positions, and the relevant facts and circumstances in assessing such disputed items.

In some instances, the seller can take the position that application of the company's historical accounting practices would be in contravention of GAAP. Those types of situations can occur when there have been changes at the company or in the applicable accounting that render the past practices improper as of the closing date. Although much more rare, the seller can also take the position that the company's historical accounting practices violated GAAP as of the date of their application. Purchase agreements do not necessarily always bar the seller from taking such a position. Of course, many agreements contain seller representations that cover the appropriateness of the company's historical financial statements, which can prevent or mitigate the impact of such positions. Notwithstanding, those representations can be formulated in a way that allows the seller to attempt to thread the needle. For example, the seller may argue that (i) the historical accounting practices are partially in violation of GAAP, (ii) the impact on the historical financial statements was immaterial, (iii) the representation only covered that certain audited financial statements are not materially misstated, and (iv) the seller is therefore entitled to a purchase price adjustment in its favor.

The Historical Accounting Practices Were in Contravention of GAAP

The most obvious reason for a buyer to take the position that applying the historical accounting practices would result in GAAP violations, is that the buyer believes those practices were also in violation of GAAP at the time of the reference financial statements.

The historical financial statements can contain violations of GAAP. This can even happen in the case of appropriately audited financial statements. For example, the audited financial statements may contain errors that are not material in the context of those financial statements. Amounts below the materiality threshold from a financial statement perspective may, however, still be significant from a purchase price adjustment perspective. This issue can be exacerbated by the audit having been performed at a group level, which would typically entail a higher materiality threshold. We discuss materiality and various other audit concepts in Chapter 8.

The problems can also otherwise find their genesis in group accounting. The accounting practices as applied by the parent company may be compliant with GAAP on a consolidated basis, but could nonetheless violate GAAP on a subsidiary-only level.

Example: Group GAAP ≠ Company GAAP

- The parent company has multiple subsidiaries that operate diversified businesses. The parent company sets its allowance for accounts receivable using economy-wide measures of creditworthiness combined with its own experience with credit risks and collectability.
- The target company is one of the company's smaller subsidiaries and operates in an industry that is plagued by economic headwinds and a series of client bankruptcies.
- Application of the accounts receivable allowance estimate as calculated by the parent company (for the entire group, including the company) is inappropriate when applied by the target company to only its own receivables.

Past Practices Otherwise No Longer in Accordance with GAAP

There is also the possibility that the application of the company's historical accounting practices as of the closing date can be in violation of GAAP while the historical financial statements based on the same practices are in compliance with GAAP.

Changes to GAAP in the Interim Period GAAP is continuously updated by the FASB. Applicable GAAP can have changed between the reference financial statement date and the closing date. Those changes can render one or more historical practices no longer permissible. Changes to GAAP are typically announced well before their application becomes mandatory. However, the company may not be preemptively aware of those changes, especially not well before the relevant financial statements are due. There can also be a significant period of time between the reference financial statements and the closing of the transaction.

Example: GAAP Changes and Timing

- The company's fiscal year is the calendar year. The reference financial statements are the most recent audited financial statements (FY 2015). There is a change to GAAP that is effective for fiscal years starting on or after December 15, 2016 (FY 2017).
- The transaction closes on January 15, 2017 (during FY 2017). As of the closing date, the company is closing the books and has started preparation of the financial statements for the previous year (FY 2016).
- Assuming the new guidance should be applied, the closing statement can require the company to implement accounting changes that are a year ahead in terms of financial statement preparation.
- Importantly, to prevent disconnects, the target net working capital calculation would have had to be prepared using accounting guidance that was announced but not yet in effect as of the preparation date for it to be comparable.

A potential opportunity for mitigation of this issue is to preemptively identify the changes to GAAP that will impact the accounting of the company as of the closing date. Practically speaking, that requires knowledge of the company's business, the company's accounting, and GAAP as well as a significant effort. A more efficient opportunity for mitigation is to contractually provide for the net working capital to be determined using the version of GAAP that was applicable as of the date of the reference financial statements irrespective of any changes in GAAP that may be applicable as of the closing date.

Changes to the Company's Business and Circumstances The company's business and circumstances can also change significantly in the interim period between the date of the reference financial statements and the closing date. Those changes can require adjustments to the company's accounting practices to remain in compliance with GAAP. It is much harder to prevent a situation in which changes to the business necessitate a change in accounting in order to have the company's accounting remain in accordance with GAAP (given those new facts and circumstances). Possibilities to mitigate the impact are carve-out provisions and defined special treatment for the relevant items.

Of course, the parties—especially the buyer—may not want to have this situation mitigated. Rather, the buyer may take the position that this type of situation falls squarely within the rationale of requiring GAAP compliance to begin with. After all, the buyer will receive the business as impacted by the business changes.

CONSEQUENCES OF THE APPLICATION OF PAST PRACTICES BEING IN CONTRAVENTION OF GAAP

Under the general formula of *past practices in accordance with GAAP*, GAAP trumps consistency. In the event of a conflict between complying with past practices and complying with GAAP, the net working capital should be determined in accordance with GAAP and in contravention of past practices. Better GAAP, however, does not trump GAAP compliant past practices. In other words, if a historical practice is permissible under GAAP, it should not be abandoned in favor of better or preferred accounting practices.

Many purchase agreements specify that the closing statement should be prepared based on *past practices in accordance with GAAP*. Relatively few purchase agreements specify what should happen if application of past practices would result in GAAP violations. In such cases, the parties can—and often do—take different approaches to bringing the accounting into compliance with GAAP.

In the absence of a provision in the purchase agreement that provides guidance to the parties and the accounting arbitrator, the following approaches can be argued by the parties and/or considered by the accounting arbitrator.

Nearest GAAP-Compliant Amount

The parties can argue for the nearest GAAP-compliant amount. In other words, the parties can seek a corrected estimate, the amount of which is as near as possible to the amount the estimate would have been if past practices had been applied, while not being in violation of GAAP. The primary argument for that approach is that it stays as close as possible to past practices. Of course, seeking out the very edge of allowable GAAP is not necessarily practicable or considered desirable by the counterparty.

Nearest GAAP-Compliant Methodology

The nearest GAAP-compliant methodology is an approach that is similar in spirit to the nearest amount approach. A party can argue for a corrected estimate that is conceived in as closely a similar manner as the historical methodology (sometimes by "fixing" the historical approach), but without violating GAAP. The primary argument for such an approach is that it stays procedurally—but not necessarily in outcome—as close as possible to past practices. Again, seeking out the edge of GAAP, albeit in a slightly different matter, may not necessarily be practicable or desirable.

Best/Better GAAP

Replacing past practices in violation of GAAP with the optimal approach under GAAP is regularly argued in such situations. Of course, the parties do not necessarily agree on what best

GAAP means for the accounting of the company. The best or better accounting is not necessarily identifiable as such, because in many cases GAAP does not indicate which method is theoretically or practically optimal. Notwithstanding, a best/better GAAP approach can appear intuitively attractive and objective to many participants. That does not mean, however, that the result is necessarily perceived as equitable. The target net working capital may have been calculated using the noncompliant practices. A switch to best/better GAAP could therefore result in a larger than strictly necessary accounting adjustment without a real underlying difference.

Fall Back to Seller's Approach

Instead of focusing on options under GAAP, a seller may simply argue that its proposed alternative accounting estimate should govern as long as it is in accordance with GAAP. The seller's argument for this interpretation can be that the closing statement is typically prepared as of a moment in time immediately prior to closing. At that time, the company is still under the seller's ownership and the seller could argue that the company (i.e., seller) should have an opportunity to correct its past errors in accordance with GAAP. The result is often the nearest GAAP-compliant amount, but can be an estimate that significantly diverges from past practices in the seller's favor. The buyer will often perceive the latter as an attempt by the seller to opportunistically generate a windfall profit from its own improper accounting.

Fall Back to Buyer's Approach

Similarly, the buyer may argue that its proposed alternative accounting estimate should govern as long as it is in accordance with GAAP. The buyer's primary arguments for this interpretation can be that (i) the final closing statement is prepared after closing and the company (i.e., buyer, which is then in control) should have an opportunity to prepare it in accordance with GAAP and (ii) the error was made under the seller's ownership of the company to begin with. Analogous to utilizing the seller's proposed accounting methodology, a choice for the buyer's methodology is typically viewed by its counterparty as an attempt to obtain a windfall discount on the purchase price.

Middle-of-the-Road/Hybrid Approaches

The arbitrator or the parties (typically as a secondary argument) can also take a compromise approach. That compromise can simply be the midpoint amount between the parties' positions (assuming that such a midpoint is acceptable under GAAP). It can also be a hybrid methodology between components set forth by the parties or a separately derived middle-of-the-road methodology. Although a midpoint approach is not necessarily the summit of elegance from an accounting theory perspective, it can be a pragmatic solution—especially if provided for in advance—to a situation in which both positions are supportable and neither is per se better or wrong.

As may be expected, the approaches reflected earlier and the parties' positions can lead to significantly different outcomes as it relates to the resulting purchase price adjustment. Without a provision that provides for a specific approach or a framework for the parties and the accounting arbitrator in the event that the application of the historical practices would be in violation of GAAP, the parties risk uncertainty in outcome.

PROCEDURAL MITIGATION OF MULTIPLE POTENTIAL OUTCOMES

As discussed in this chapter, the formula *past practices in accordance with GAAP* does not, by itself, definitively handle two situations that can occur. First, there can be multiple possible outcomes for certain accounting items that appear to either comply with the formula or for which the compliance cannot be disproven given the available documentation. Second, there can be no outcomes available that fully comply with the formula, because the application of past practices would result in a violation of GAAP. That can in turn lead to multiple interpretations by the parties on how the violation of GAAP should be addressed.

Although those situations can be mitigated to some extent by, for example, keeping detailed records, they are not necessarily preventable in all circumstances without additional context in the purchase agreement. The parties can take several approaches to providing for those situations in the purchase agreement, some of which we have previously discussed in this chapter. The parties can include provisions that specifically cover certain items or they can more broadly prescribe specific approaches to take in one or both of the previously described situations. For example, the parties can prescribe that the accounting arbitrator select the midpoint in the event of multiple apparently acceptable answers.

The parties can also opt to mitigate the uncertainty associated with potentially having multiple outcomes that ostensibly comply with *past practices in accordance with GAAP* by preemptively selecting a baseline closing statement or by allocating the burden of proof.

Selecting a Baseline Closing Statement for the Adjustment Process

Selecting a baseline closing statement in this context means that the parties preemptively select one of the iterations of the closing statement (that is to be prepared throughout the process) and provide for that statement to govern throughout the closing and purchase price adjustment process unless it fails to comply with *past practices in accordance with GAAP*. The primary benefit of this approach is that it resolves the issue of multiple possible compliant outcomes. However, it does not necessarily resolve the issue of a situation in which the application of past practices would result in GAAP violations. To resolve this, it could potentially be supplemented by one of the choices discussed earlier in this chapter.

There are two readily evident versions of the closing statement that can be selected as the baseline closing statement for *past practices in accordance with GAAP*. The first is the preliminary closing statement, which is typically prepared by seller. The second readily evident alternative is the buyer's proposed closing statement.

Utilizing (Seller's) Preliminary Closing Statement The philosophy behind selecting the preliminary or estimated closing statement can be that the seller's approach should govern because the closing statement should incorporate the company's financial position immediately prior to closing at which time the company was controlled by the seller. Moreover, the preliminary closing statement should be prepared in accordance with the company's past accounting practices, that is, the practices that were utilized under the seller's ownership. The argument here is that the seller—while still in control—would clearly be best positioned to interpret what can be in effect its own practices.

Potential counterarguments to selecting the seller's preliminary closing statement as the baseline can include that the post-closing adjustment process is necessary to begin with because the seller is not able to finalize the necessary financial information prior to closing. Therefore, the seller's preliminary closing statement is, to a certain extent, an approximation by its very nature and cannot be based on a full closing process as there is simply insufficient time. In addition, the buyer could be concerned that the seller would benefit from ambiguity in the company's historical estimation process and the associated documentation. In other words, the seller could potentially benefit from its own poor accounting documentation practices.

Utilizing (Buyer's) Proposed Closing Statement The primary argument for selecting the buyer's proposed closing statement to serve as the baseline is that it will have been prepared after an appropriate closing of the books. The seller could, however, be concerned that the buyer may be at best unfamiliar with the seller's approach, its view on the business, and the nuances thereof. Having the buyer prepare, for example, certain accounting estimates, may require the buyer to step into the shoes, plans, and judgment of the seller's management approach without giving effect to the transaction. The seller may be concerned that the buyer's approach will be impacted by its view on the business whether due to unintended bias or to the willful implementation of what is actually the buyer's judgment as opposed to the company's/seller's judgment.

Moreover, the seller may be concerned that the buyer would benefit from the natural ambiguity in the company's historical estimation process and the associated documentation. After all, the combination of (i) the inherent flexibility in the conception of accounting estimates, (ii) the possibly limited nature of the documentation as the process is not mechanical, and (iii) the buyer becoming in control of the company while the seller loses its information access, can result in perceived leeway for the buyer to "game" the process.

Other Considerations The previous discussion implicitly assumes that the seller is closely involved with the company and that it is responsible for the preparation of the preliminary closing statement. That assumption is not valid in all circumstances as the seller could, for example, be a distant financial investor. Moreover, the buyer could also have been closely involved with the preparation of the preliminary closing statement through, for example, a pre-closing objection procedure.

If the seller and the buyer are truly at arm's length of the company, a third option may be to have the company prepare the closing statement and select it as the baseline. In many situations, however, this would be a distinction without a difference as the parties are often not separated from the company to that degree.

Finally, the selection of the baseline statement can end up swinging the outcome so much that neither of the parties may want to agree to default to the counterparty's closing statement. The uncertainty associated with potentially having multiple outcomes that appear to comply with *past practices in accordance with GAAP* may be overall preferable to increasing the risk of one of the parties being able to game the post-closing process by seeking the very edge of compliance in its preemptively selected statement. In order to have the transaction proceed, the parties may decide to take their chances with the possibility of multiple ostensibly compliant outcomes or use other less overarching avenues of mitigation as discussed throughout this chapter.

Allocating the Burden of Proof

Unlike, for example, civil litigation, accounting arbitrations are not filed by a plaintiff against a defendant to address and remedy alleged wrongful conduct. Rather, the parties jointly submit certain disputed items to an accounting arbitrator for him or her to resolve without allegations of wrongful conduct. As a result, there is also no burden of proof for a plaintiff to meet regarding the occurrence of wrongful conduct in order to obtain a judgment. The accounting arbitrator will utilize the information provided by the parties to determine the correct amounts for any disputed items in accordance with the purchase agreement (i.e., *past practices in accordance with GAAP*).

Notwithstanding, contractually providing for an allocation of the burden of proof can potentially mitigate some of the issues that are encountered in the post-closing purchase price adjustment and dispute resolution process.

Information Asymmetries There exist significant information asymmetries throughout the transaction and dispute lifecycle. Prior to the closing, the seller commonly has direct or indirect control of the company's information and, in many instances, has a history with the business that goes back multiple years.

Prior to closing, the buyer, on the other hand, only has access to publicly available information and information acquired during due diligence. That changes after the sale, when the buyer gains control of the company, gains direct access to its personnel, and comes into possession of the company's accounting records. The seller can to a lesser or greater extent lose access to the company's accounting records as well as the institutional knowledge embodied by the company's personnel.

Of course, the parties should consider the facts and circumstances of the company and the transaction in evaluating informational asymmetries. By means of example, the seller's access to past practices and related information after the sale may vary greatly. On the one hand, in the case of a family-operated business that is purchased by a larger company and for which the management-ownership will be employed by the company subsequent to the closing, the sellers will likely be able to recall the company's past practices. On the other hand, an independently operating division of a major conglomerate may transfer much of its related institutional knowledge with the business and may not have much access to knowledge about the company's past accounting practices subsequent to the closing.

Limited Discovery The accounting arbitration process typically does not involve an opportunity for a significant level of discovery. The parties do not serve discovery requests on each other and typically do not have an opportunity to take depositions. Generally, documentation and information either is submitted by a party to support their position in their initial or rebuttal submissions or is submitted in response to requests by the arbitrator.

Other Considerations The contractual allocation of the burden of proof can independently serve to address some of the issues inherent in post-closing purchase price adjustment disputes or can be combined with other measures—such as the contractual selection of a baseline statement—to mitigate some of the perceived side-effects. Practically, the preemptive selection of a baseline statement and the contractual allocation of the burden of proof can be largely similar in their ultimate effect.

Although the allocation of the burden of proof can resolve some issues, it can also suffer from some of the same disadvantages as the selection of a baseline statement. For example, multiple acceptable outcomes under *past practices in accordance with GAAP* will likely result in the party that does not have the burden of proof having its approach accepted. Similar to the selection of baseline statement, the parties may therefore not be able to reach an agreement regarding which party should have the burden of proof and may decide that some uncertainty in outcome is preferable to opening the door to the counterparty gaming the post-closing process.

NOTES

1. *See* AS 2501.03.
2. *See e.g.*, FASB ASC 310-10-35-4-c.

CHAPTER 6

Target Net Working Capital

For transactions that include a purchase price adjustment mechanism based on net working capital, the final purchase price can be determined based on the closing net working capital as determined after the fact consistent with *past practices in accordance with GAAP*. That purchase price incorporates any differences between the final net working capital determined as of the closing date and the target net working capital as included in the purchase agreement. The buyer is responsible for paying for excess net working capital and the seller is responsible for supplementing in the case of a shortfall (through a post-closing purchase price adjustment or in part preemptively through anticipating some of the difference in the preliminary net working capital as of the closing date).

Because the (combined pre-closing and post-closing) purchase price adjustment is based on the comparison between the final net working capital and the target net working capital, and the target net working capital is generally included as a fixed dollar amount in the purchase agreement, it is of crucial importance to carefully determine the target net working capital. Generally, although as we discuss later, not always, the parties will want to set the target net working capital in a manner that results in the comparison with the closing net working capital being an apples-to-apples comparison. In other words, the parties will generally want the bases for the calculation of the target net working capital and the closing net working capital to be the same.

If they are not the same, the result can be a disconnect that drives an adjustment without an underlying real difference in the amount or composition of the current assets and liabilities available to the company in its operations. By means of a simplified example, in the situation that the quantity of inventory on the company's balance sheet as of the closing date is different than the target quantity or certain inventory items need to be impaired, the parties would typically want that to result in an adjustment. If the quantities, however, are the same and the inventory is unimpaired, the parties would generally deem an adjustment undesirable on an *ex ante* basis. A wedge between the target net working capital and the determination of the closing net working capital can nonetheless potentially result in an adjustment in the latter situation.

In practice, one of the parties may attempt to drive a wedge between the methodologies underlying the target net working capital and the closing net working capital that results in a difference without a distinction and a perceived inequity by the counterparty. Ultimately, such a perceived "gotcha" can end up driving a purchase price adjustment as the accounting arbitrator will focus on the contractually required compliance with *past practices in accordance with GAAP* and not on correcting perceived inequities resulting from perceived issues with the calculation underlying the contractually agreed upon target net working capital.

Besides perceived gaming by the parties, the underlying business dynamics can also cause the target net working capital to be a poor predictor of the "normal level" of net working capital the company should have at closing. We discuss the derivation of the target net working capital and complications that can occur next. We close out the chapter with a further discussion and an example related to the consequences of discrepancies.

APPROACHES TO DETERMINING THE TARGET NET WORKING CAPITAL

There are multiple approaches to determine the amount of target net working capital. The determination of the target net working capital can be an attempt to quantify the amount of net working capital the company needs or should need in order to operate. The parties can use the company's own experience to approximate this amount. For example, they can calculate the company's average historical net working capital and use it as an approximation of the company's net working capital needs.

That being said, the target net working capital is often heavily negotiated as it can essentially have a dollar-for-dollar impact on the purchase price. The outcome may be the result of a negotiation that is driven by a variety of factors other than the amount of working capital the target company needs to operate. The parties can even use the target net working capital as a mechanism to implement a discount subsequent to agreeing on a purchase price, including, for example, in connection with due diligence findings.

Example: A Negotiated Discount through Target Net Working Capital

- The parties negotiated and agreed upon a purchase price. The negotiation required extensive internal procedures, including board approval at one of the parties.
- After agreeing on the purchase price, the buyer identifies an issue during the final phase of its due diligence. The buyer wants a $20 million discount to account for the issue. The seller is willing to provide a discount, but does not want to go through the full approval process again. The seller's negotiators have the freedom to set the target net working capital without any board approvals.
- The buyer and the seller have previously agreed upon a target net working capital of $100 million (based on the company's actual historical net working capital balance). They agree to set the target net working capital at $120 million, effecting the desired $20 million discount.
- *A word of caution:* If the due diligence issue in this example relates to a component of net working capital such as inventory obsolescence, the discount can end up being given twice. The buyer can accept the $20 million discount in the form of a target net working capital increase and then,

post-closing, argue for a $20 million inventory allowance in order to comply with GAAP, effectively double-dipping the discount. In simplified numbers:

The Agreement	
Historical Net Working Capital (100% Inventory)	$100 million
Negotiated Increase to Effect a Purchase Price Discount	$20 million
Target Net Working Capital	$120 million
At Closing	
Seller's Preliminary Closing Net Working Capital (100% Inventory)	$100 million
Target Net Working Capital	$120 million
Shortfall/Purchase Price Discount	$20 million
Post-Closing	
Buyer's Proposed Closing Statement:	
– Inventory	$100 million
– Inventory Allowance (required per GAAP)	($20 million)
Buyer's Proposed Net Working Capital	$80 million
Buyer's Sought Total Discount	
Target Net Working Capital	$120 million
Buyer's Proposed Net Working Capital	$80 million
Total Pre-Closing and Post-Closing Discount	$40 million

The target net working capital can also be set at a negotiated (rounded) amount the parties believe is appropriate based on their experience in the industry or it could simply be set at zero. In certain industries (e.g., companies that provide software as a service on a prepaid annual basis) the target net working capital can even be negative.

CONSIDERATIONS IN DETERMINING TARGET NET WORKING CAPITAL

If the parties seek to approximate the net working capital that should be present as of the closing date in the normal course of business, the target net working capital is often based on the target company's historical net working capital, for example, the average for the trailing 12 or 24 months. The historical net working capital will likely need to be normalized in order for it to be appropriately used as the target net working capital.

Aligning with the Purchase Agreement

Let's assume that the closing net working capital will be based on *past practices in accordance with GAAP*. To be comparable, the target net working capital should be quantified in a similar manner. That means, for example, that if the parties rely on financial information other than the reference financial statements, they should be careful that the information was conceived using the same accounting practices.

It also means that the parties should be careful that the historical accounting practices are GAAP compliant as of the closing date. If they are found to violate GAAP as of the closing date, those violations will be corrected in the closing net working capital calculation but typically not similarly corrected in the target net working capital.

The purchase agreement may also contain transaction-specific adjustments to the application of *past practices in accordance with GAAP*. For example, the purchase agreement may provide for special treatment for certain items or carve-outs from the closing net working capital. The calculation of the target net working capital should also incorporate those provisions to be comparable. A discrepancy in this regard can be very costly. By means of example, if the purchase agreement carves out a specific liability from the calculation of the closing net working capital, that liability should also not be included in the calculation of the target net working capital. Otherwise, the discrepancy will effectively increase the purchase price. This is of critical importance because purchase agreements do not typically provide any mechanism for the adjustment of target net working capital.

Usage of Historical Financial Information

Transaction-related complications aside, the usage of the target company's own historical financial information can appear attractive as a real-world source of the level of working capital the company needs. There are, however, several complications that can impact its usefulness as a yardstick metric.

The usage of historical financial information can be problematic if the target company is part of a larger company that has integrated services and other group relationships. For example, the group may have provided back-office support or centralized inventory management with joint warehousing. If so, the target net working capital may not reflect the target company's actual net working capital needs going forward whether standalone or as part of a differently organized group.

The averaging of historical net working capital can also be problematic if there is volatility over time due to seasonality.

Example: Seasonality and Target Net Working Capital

- The primary business of an agricultural company is growing and selling poinsettias. It also grows other year-round plants.
- The poinsettias are grown during the year and sold to garden centers in November. The company's poinsettias are attractive and predictably sell out every year.
- The company's business is seasonal and results in significant fluctuations of net working capital:
  - During the six-month growing period of the plants, inventory steadily increases to account for the associated direct costs.

  - Upon the sale of the poinsettias the company's net working capital may shoot up. For example, the accounts receivable can be twice as large as the inventory if the company's gross margin on poinsettias is 50 percent of the wholesale price.
  - After collection of its accounts receivable, the company may pay dividends, pay off debt, execute on its capital expenditure plan for next season, or otherwise use the cash.
- Clearly, the historical monthly average net working capital is going to be a poor predictor of the net working capital as of the closing date. To be truly predictive, the determination of the target net working capital should consider when the transaction will be closed and be adjusted accordingly.
- Of course, the parties may not want the net working capital to be predictive of the closing net working capital. If, for example, the closing is scheduled for early December (i.e., immediately after the sales but prior to collection), the target company's economic performance for the past year could then be largely encapsulated in the (target) net working capital. The seller will likely find this undesirable.

Problems related to seasonality may be exacerbated by the closing date not being known at the time of the calculation of the target net working capital. This is especially problematic if the net working capital is expected to fluctuate significantly in the period of the expected closing.

Another set of timing-related complications are cutoff issues. Historical financial information will reflect the net working capital as of the end of the applicable reporting period. The closing, however, generally does not take place on a normal reporting date such as month-end or year-end. The result is that intra-month accruals that may have to be included with the determination of the closing net working capital in order for it to comply with GAAP are not considered for purposes of the target net working capital as derived by averaging end-of-period balances. In practice, it is often not considered worth the effort to preempt this issue or the impact is considered appropriate.

Another issue with using historical financial information is that it may need to be normalized to eliminate, for example, the impact of nonrecurring items or of a historical context that no longer applies. By means of example, if the company closed stores, those stores would no longer need inventory, petty cash, and so forth. If those stores are included in the historical financial information to be used for the calculation of the target net working capital, that financial information would generally need to be normalized prior to using it for the determination of the target net working capital.

Other Complications

It is not uncommon for the parties to rely on the calculation of the target net working capital to illustrate or explain accounting issues throughout the dispute process. One of the benefits of utilizing that calculation can be that the financial information is more granular (e.g., the calculation may contain a trial balance that includes general ledger accounts), which can provide insight that cannot necessarily be gleaned at a financial statement balance sheet level.

Such illustrations benefit greatly from utilizing a target net working capital calculation that matches—directly or with the aid of an uncontested bridging calculation—the agreed-upon target net working capital. In the absence of such a match, the submitted calculation may be one of many drafts that can deviate from the final version for many reasons. In other words, without such matching the calculation can lose much of its illustrative power. It may seem obvious, but if the target net working capital was calculated, the parties can benefit from contemporaneously documenting the specifics of the calculation.

Finally, the focus for purposes of a post-closing purchase price adjustment process is on the net amount of working capital as of the closing date. For operational and other purposes, however, the composition also matters. For example, dependent on the composition, even acceptable overall levels of target net working capital may require cash injections after closing. Although somewhat moot in this context, it is worth considering.

CONSEQUENCES OF DISCREPANCIES

The application of past practices as of the closing date may be found to be in violation of GAAP. As discussed earlier, this may require an adjustment in determining the net working capital as of the closing date. However, a parallel adjustment to the target net working capital typically is not made or even allowed by the purchase agreement. Therefore, if the target net working capital was calculated using those same past practices, a calculated overage or shortfall may result that one of the parties perceives to be without an underlying real difference.

Example: Departures from Target and Closing Comparability

- The historical net working capital, target net working capital, and preliminary net working capital at closing are as follows:

	Historical/Target	NWC at Closing
Cash	$1 million	$1 million
Accounts Receivable	$10 million	$10 million
Inventory	$10 million	$10 million
Accounts Payable	($8 million)	($8 million)
Total NWC	$13 million	$13 million

- Subsequent to closing, the buyer successfully argues that the company should have recognized a portion of its quarterly lease, which is payable in arrears on the last day of the quarter, as a current liability to comply with GAAP. The amount at issue is $2 million for 1 month of accrued lease obligation.

- The company has occupied the same building for a long time and the target net working capital was calculated as the monthly average of a historical quarter. In other words, if the company had always complied with GAAP in its accounting for the lease, the target net working capital would have also been $2 million lower and no post-closing adjustment would have been necessary.
- Without a provision to the contrary, the derivation of the target net working capital is irrelevant as its total simply flows into the arithmetic of the post-closing adjustment. The result is a $2 million discount for the buyer (which the seller likely considers an inappropriate windfall).

On an *ex ante* basis, most parties will agree that the previous example is undesirable both in regards to the existence of a GAAP violation in the company's historical accounting and the outcome. After the fact, however, neither the overall situation and adjustment, nor the parties' internal motivations for accepting the agreed-upon target net working capital are necessarily as clear. For example, the seller may have calculated the target net working capital based on historical financial statements, but the buyer may have only accepted it because it matched industry surveys. Either way, the accounting arbitrator will stay within the four corners of his retention and the purchase agreement and award an adjustment based on the latter part of the agreed upon formula of *past practices in accordance with GAAP*.

Preventing the above perceived injustice is difficult at best and can be worsened by a party's perception that the counterparty is attempting to game the process to purposefully create and exacerbate rifts between the target and closing net working capital. Documentation of past practices and careful evaluation of the target company's books to identify potential GAAP violations and other problem areas can help mitigate some of these issues. Identified issues can potentially be handled in the calculation of target net working capital or through tailored provisions in the purchase agreement.

It may appear attractive to have the purchase agreement include a general parallel application of any adjustments for GAAP violations to the target net working capital. Besides the buyer's likely response that preparing the books in accordance with GAAP would be a better solution, such parallel implementation can easily be more problematic than the problem it is trying to solve. It has the potential of doubling the dispute as the parties start adjusting both closing and target net working capital calculations to reflect *past practices in accordance with GAAP*. Moreover, even target net working capital amounts that are calculated based on the historical financial position of the company tend to utilize averages over a period of time. Accordingly, there is typically not a single set of circumstances at one point in time based on which the included accounting estimates were derived. Rather, there is often a series of such circumstances that were averaged.

CHAPTER 7

Transaction-Specific Adjustments

In certain situations, there may be specific items related to net working capital that warrant special consideration based on the circumstances of the individual transaction, the facts and circumstances surrounding the company, or other needs of the parties. To accommodate this, the parties may agree to partially deviate from *past practices in accordance with GAAP*. Those exceptions take two common forms, namely (i) a defined special treatment for one or more items for purposes of calculating net working capital and (ii) the carve-out of certain items from the calculation of net working capital and/or the post-closing purchase price adjustment process. The defined special treatment can either supplant *past practices in accordance with GAAP* or work within its context.

Example: Options for Handling a Specific Item

- During due diligence, the parties identify the inventory allowance as an item for which they expect disagreement regarding whether the company's accounting treatment is in accordance with GAAP. They have several options for handling this, including:
  - They can do nothing and leave it to be sorted out post-closing based on *past practices in accordance with GAAP*.
  - They can carve out the inventory allowance from the target and closing net working capital calculations.
  - They can contractually deem the company's accounting methodology to be in accordance with GAAP.

- They can agree on an alternative amount or calculation, such as the inventory allowance will be set at $1.1 million or will be calculated as 5 percent of the gross inventory balance as of the closing date.

If the parties agree to an exception to *past practices in accordance with GAAP*, it is important to clearly define the scope of the exception, and the associated treatment, and to make sure that an appropriate analogous implementation is utilized for purposes of determining the target net working capital (or purposefully not). Importantly, insofar as the exception could later be viewed as ambiguous in scope or implementation, the safety net of GAAP—albeit sometimes broad—may not necessarily apply. In other words, the accounting arbitrator will not necessarily be able to rely on GAAP to resolve any ambiguities. As a result, because any such special provisions will typically be non-GAAP and/or inconsistent with past practices, agreement on the specifics of the exception and a detailed contractual implementation can be critical to avoiding a potential post-closing dispute.

POTENTIAL CANDIDATES FOR SPECIAL TREATMENT

Ahead we discuss some situations that potentially lend themselves to being covered by a specifically defined treatment. Of course, for each of those situations the parties would have to reach an agreement on that treatment. Moreover, after considering the potential downside or risk of not having an exception, the parties may decide that the negotiation and implementation of the exception are not worth the effort.

Intersection of Special Treatment and Overall Purchase Price

The target company may have accounts that are known to be problematic either individually or as part of a larger complex of issues at the company. The parties may be well aware of the nature of those problems and the issues may even be a reason for the transaction. To address such known issues, the parties may factor the impact of the issues into the overall purchase price. In such situations, the parties may need to implement a parallel transaction-specific treatment for purposes of the post-closing purchase price adjustment mechanism to prevent any undesirable effects.

Example: Carve-Out to Align with the Overall Purchase Price

- A company uses an outdated methodology to manufacture outdated chips. As a result, it is suffering from decreasing sales and its future is bleak without a substantial turnaround accompanied by an equally substantial capital investment.
- The company has an inventory of spare parts for its current equipment as well as various subassemblies.
- The purchase price reflects the value of the company's knowhow and other assets while recognizing that the existing plant layout and associated equipment is essentially worthless to the buyer.
- If a "normal" net working capital process is included, after closing the buyer may very well claim that the company's manufacturing process was not sustainable and the spare parts inventory is obsolete. As a result, without a transaction-specific treatment, the buyer could potentially get a discount through a post-closing net working capital adjustment that overlaps with the negotiated pre-closing purchase price discount it already received based on the related overall state of the company.

Valid Business Choices and GAAP Risk

At times, GAAP does not fully line up with the strategic or operational requirements of the business. GAAP can require a conservative (e.g., high allowance) accounting treatment that, for example, results in a lower value for an asset while from an economic perspective the asset serves a rational business purpose. In the context of using *past practices in accordance with*

GAAP as a valuation adjustment, that effect can be undesirable. This is often exacerbated by the relevant GAAP treatment being in the proverbial gray area with meaningful arguments for and against while the outcome can be binary (i.e., all or nothing).

Example: Preemptive Handling of Likely GAAP Compliance Disputes

- The company is a service company. The company's value is derived from its client base, its special knowhow and personnel, and the processes it has in place to meet its clients' needs. The price was agreed upon between the parties at 5 times EBITDA or $10 million (including target net working capital based on a historical average).
- In order to provide its services, the company has a large inventory of many obscure parts many of which will become unavailable at some time in the future or will require significant expense to manufacture in-house. From a business perspective the cost of carrying the inventory is small and the inventory ensures the company's ability to operate its business unhampered by part shortages far into the future. The company's inventory is on the books at its historical cost of $4 million. The company's part usage for providing services equates to approximately $200,000 per year. Both the buyer and the seller are aware of this prior to entering into the agreement.
- Although (i) it makes sense from a business perspective to hold onto the inventory and (ii) the price was set based on the company's ability to generate EBITDA, the accounting for inventory is not necessarily driven by those considerations.
- After the closing the buyer may argue that the company needs to recognize a significant inventory allowance in order to comply with GAAP or even argue that some of the preemptively acquired inventory should be considered a long-lived asset. Dependent on the facts and circumstances, and without a contractual measure to the contrary (e.g., a

carve-out or limit), the seller risks that the implementation of *past practices in accordance with GAAP* after the closing to determine the net working capital could potentially result in a downward adjustment to net working capital that is significant relative to the purchase price.

Handling Anomalous Accounting Processes

Over time companies can develop various anomalous accounting practices in how the day-to-day accounting is implemented. Even if those practices do not result in any abnormalities or GAAP violations in the financial statements, the process to get there can sometimes appear opaque and ambiguous. That can be especially true if those practices are used in relation to items that require significant judgment.

Example: Preemptive Handling of Company-Specific Issue

- A car rental company holds most of its cars as fixed assets. Each month the rental car fleet gets evaluated for cars that should be sold. The selection is judgmental and considers the current market for new purchases, rental activity, maintenance expenses, the current market for car sales, and so on. In addition, the company has begun purchasing some used vehicles for resale on its platform. In the event of rental car shortages—for example, in the event of a local hailstorm—those cars can be re-tasked as rental cars (typically for more than a year if it happens).
- The company's accounting distinguishes between cars held for rent (long-lived assets) and cars held for sale (inventory). The distinction between the two, however, is largely dependent on management judgment as of the date of measurement.
- The parties would have to pay careful attention to what is and what is not included in the inventory and to make sure that the comparable inventory is considered for purposes of setting the target net working capital.

- The parties choose to carve out the cars held for sale from the net working capital to be used to calculate the post-closing purchase price adjustment and agree on an approval procedure for the purchase and sale of vehicles in the period between the date of the purchase agreement and the closing date, accompanied by a formula to determine the impact on the purchase price.

Contingent Liabilities, Indemnifications, and Warranties

Accounting for contingent liabilities can be fraught with disagreement related to both recognition and measurement under GAAP. This is often due to the significant judgment involved in arriving at the balance to be recorded, or not recorded, for such liabilities. The same is true from a business perspective as parties can wholeheartedly disagree on the size of various contingent exposures, including environmental cleanup, litigation, taxation, and product warranty obligations. Moreover, the parties commonly view certain contingent liabilities as related to the operation of the company under the seller's ownership for which the seller should remain—at least in part—financially responsible post-closing. Accordingly, contingent liabilities are often the subject of indemnification provisions.

The current part of contingent liabilities can also be captured in the post-closing purchase price adjustment process. The cumulative effect can be both a post-closing dispute on the appropriate accounting treatment for liabilities that results in a purchase price adjustment and also a payment in accordance with an indemnification provision. Notably, even if the purchase price adjustment is imputed on the indemnification payment, the net working capital dispute is not necessarily moot as there can be significant financial impact despite the issue being mere labeling on its face. The financial impact is driven by the typical one-sidedness of the indemnification provision; that is, if the ultimate expenditure is lower than the amount included with net working capital, there is typically no refund, while a shortfall is trued up via an indemnity claim. The amounts at stake can also be very large. Some contingent environmental liabilities can potentially wipe out the value of the entire business.

We discuss contingent liabilities more extensively in Chapter 18 and the interaction between net working capital and indemnification provisions in Chapter 21.

Interaction with Other Adjustment Mechanisms

As we discussed, a purchase agreement may contain multiple adjustment mechanisms that can potentially overlap in scope. For example, one purchase agreement may include three separate adjustment mechanisms for (i) net working capital, (ii) cash and cash equivalents, and (iii) debt and debt-like items.

Without carefully drafted provisions to delineate those adjustment mechanisms, they can partly overlap. The result can be, for example, that the parties provide for the carve-out of certain net working capital liabilities from the contractual definition of net working capital as they are also included in the debt adjustment mechanism.

CONSIDERATIONS IN IMPLEMENTING CUSTOM PROVISIONS

Carving out problematic accounts can appear very attractive as an abstract concept. Implementing such carve-outs can, however, in certain instances negate the benefits of having a post-closing net working capital adjustment based on *past practices in accordance with GAAP*. Moreover, it can potentially lead to serious implementation issues that may only be identified after closing and at that time can lead to a more complicated and contentious post-closing purchase price adjustment process.

Often, the accounts that would most benefit from exclusion are also the accounts that have significant potential for inaccuracy that is unknown prior to closing, especially from a buyer's perspective. A buyer generally wants to be protected from such inaccuracies. Although a seller may argue that the downside can be mitigated by a buyer performing incremental due diligence, a buyer's due diligence is typically already constrained in time and access to documentation. Moreover, the buyer typically has more important issues to focus its due diligence efforts on than the allowance for doubtful accounts or inventory obsolescence. Although those items can have an important and significant impact on the purchase price, identifying large open-ended exposures or issues that hit the core of the operating business are naturally more important prior to closing. That does, however, not mean that the buyer will be amenable to absorbing the shift in economic risk regarding those items that would come with agreeing to a carve-out.

Appropriate Contractual Implementation Is Difficult and Important

Unambiguously defining a carve-out or other special treatment is not as simple as it may seem at first. On an abstract business level, the issue is often easily and intuitively definable. The translation to implementation, however, can be fraught with issues and complexities. For example, the apparent simple demarcation of an environmental exposure may mean considering the isolation of incurred expenses, applicable insurance coverage, legal costs, and other components. This is in addition to attempting to reconcile a contractual implementation with the reality of the company's accounting systems.

In addition, if a carve-out is implemented, it generally needs to be applied to both the contractual calculation of net working capital as of the closing date as well as the target net working capital. Those implementations will ideally mirror each other while appropriately handling changes in circumstances that are not necessarily known when the purchase agreement is drafted and when the target net working capital is calculated.

Going into the dispute phase it is important that any carve-outs and other special treatments are unambiguously codified. For purposes of applying the formula of *past practices in accordance with GAAP*, the accounting arbitrator is primarily focused on the interpretation and application of the company's past accounting practices and the analysis of the GAAP compliance of those practices. In relation to carve-outs and special accounting treatments, however, the arbitrator may have to rely more on precisely understanding and implementing the relevant provisions of the purchase agreement. As the accounting arbitrator cannot necessarily fully fall back on his or her understanding of GAAP in analyzing the purchase agreement, it is important that the purchase agreement is unambiguous in its codification of carve-outs and special treatments.

The Distinction between Balance Sheet Accounts and General Ledger Accounts Is of Critical Importance

In order to appropriately and unambiguously implement the desired special treatment, transaction counsel may need to gain a more granular understanding of some of the accounting of the business than would otherwise be required. Carve-outs or other custom treatments for part of net working capital, whether due to problematic accounting or other appropriate reasons in the context of the transaction, are not necessarily applied at the balance sheet account level. Rather, to carve out a specific issue/asset/liability the parties often have to implement the carve out at a general ledger account level or sometimes at an even more granular level.

General ledger accounts—and below that, sub-ledger accounts—constitute the chart of accounts that the company actually uses for the entries in its accounting system. A balance sheet account, as it appears in the company's financial statements, is at a higher, summary level. As the company prepares its financial statements, it rolls up its many general ledger accounts into its summary-level balance sheet accounts. Each balance sheet account is typically comprised of the sum of multiple general ledger accounts.

Example: Balance Sheet versus General Ledger Accounts

- A company could have a balance sheet with one entry for liquid assets and one entry for accounts receivable while the general ledger may contain many more.
- To illustrate this, here is an accounting entry, which records a payment by a customer, at the balance sheet account level and at the general ledger account level:

	Account Number	Account Description	Debit	Credit
Balance Sheet Account Level	100	Liquid Assets	$1,000	
	200	Accounts Receivable		$1,000
Ledger Account Level	1001131 (Liquid Assets: 100; Petty Cash: 11; Chicago: 31)	Petty Cash Chicago	$1,000	
	20030.103146 (Accounts Receivable: 200; U.S. Trade Clients: 30; Client Number (Sub-Ledger): 103146)	AR-Trade-US-Jones Co.		$1,000

- *Notably*, the general ledger account numbers given in the illustration have been stylized to incorporate the balance sheet account numbers for clarity purposes. That is, of course, not necessarily the case in practice when dealing with a company's accounting system.

The general ledger accounts as included in the illustration above are presented in a manner that intuitively reflects the multiple-to-one general ledger–to–balance sheet account roll up. In practice, however, not every general ledger account necessarily rolls up into only one balance sheet account. Rather, it is not uncommon to encounter situations in which a general ledger account is split across multiple balance sheet accounts, which themselves are an accumulation of multiple general ledger accounts (or parts thereof), as part of the closing of the books and preparing the financial statements.

Such a situation, in which there are general ledger accounts that roll up into multiple balance sheet accounts, is typically not part of the initial design of the chart of accounts or the accounting system. Rather, this and other idiosyncrasies that can be found in a company's day-to-day accounting and its general ledger tend to have grown over time.

Importantly, for purposes of a net working capital carve-out or other agreed-upon special provision that references or (indirectly) relies on general ledger accounts for its implementation, many day-to-day idiosyncrasies and practical patches to the original design of the chart of accounts and its implementation are not necessarily documented in great detail by the company. Small changes and practicalities are often simply remembered and used by the people that work with the system every day. Moreover, even errors relative to that internally known and accepted system are not always fully corrected (if at all) if the error does not result in a financial statement error. Most accounting departments are focused on correct financial reporting and the proverbial making of the sausage does not necessarily have to be pretty or perfect.

Notably, a balance sheet account does not have to consist of a roll up of only accounts with the same sign. In other words, an asset (net debit balance) account on the balance sheet can be the result of a roll up of both general ledger accounts with a net debit balance as well as those with a net credit balance. For completeness, there are also clearing accounts included in the general ledger that generally do not roll up into balance sheet accounts as they are part of a company's internal control system and they should zero out.

Importantly, GAAP offers guidance primarily at a financial statement level and therefore does not generally prescribe how a company should implement its general ledger and day-to-day accounting in order to ultimately be able to prepare those financial statements. In other words, a company's chart of accounts may contain implementation abnormalities that do not result in GAAP violations because those abnormalities do not appear at the level of the company's financial statements. As a result, if there is any dispute on the implementation of the chart of accounts to effectuate, for example, a carve-out that was defined in the agreement using references to general ledger accounts, GAAP may not be helpful in assisting with the resolution of that dispute.

In summary, utilizing the chart of accounts to define a carve-out from net working capital or other special treatment for part of the assets or liabilities can be much less straightforward than it appears. As the carve-out or other special treatment often relates to a specific asset or liability, it may appear attractive to simply refer to the chart of accounts. And that may work if correctly implemented. To make sure that the desired effect will be achieved often means obtaining a sufficient understanding of the accounting that is at the genesis of the desired special treatment. That understanding can then be translated into purchase agreement provisions based on the appropriate accounts, and only those accounts, for purposes of defining the carve-out. Of course, the custom treatment should ideally be codified in a manner that aligns the practical aspect with the true intent of the parties and that can be used to resolve any disputes about what should or should not be included in the general ledger account(s) at issue.

CASE STUDY: Repair Inventory—A Simplified Carve-Out Situation before an Accounting Arbitrator

To illustrate some of the complications that can arise in practice, we have included a simplified case study that covers the implementation of an agreed-upon carve-out.

- A company services high-end computer equipment, leases out high-end computer equipment, rents service time on company-operated computer equipment, and sells computer parts.
- The parties excluded repair parts from the net working capital calculation. Repair parts are defined in the agreement as parts used to maintain and repair the computer infrastructure. None of the terms in that definition are themselves defined in the agreement.
- The company has the following parts-related general ledger accounts:
  - 1001 computer parts magazine
  - 1002 parts on trucks
  - 1003 service part inventory
  - 1004 parts inventory at internal maintenance
  - 1005 retail inventory
  - 1006 miscellaneous parts
- There is a numerical example available that was prepared in the context of determining the target net working capital. The example shows the exclusion of GL account 1004 and part of GL account 1001. Complications are:
  - The total amount of the example does not match the amount of the agreed-upon target net working capital.
  - The split of GL account 1001 was based on an estimated percentage at the time of the example without further explanation or support.
  - At the time of the preparation of the example, GL accounts 1003 and 1006 had no inventory recorded to them. They do at the time of the closing.
  - New retail inventory was accidentally booked to GL account 1001 by a new accounting clerk. GL account 1005 had been largely depleted at the time of closing.
- The parties present the following positions and arguments.
  - *Buyer:* The inventory general ledger accounts 1001–1006 should be excluded in whole from the net working capital. Ultimately, all parts are for the maintenance and repair of computer infrastructure.
  - *Seller:* The company keeps a large inventory of repair parts to keep its computer infrastructure online under all circumstances. The seller recognized that the buyer could have an argument from a GAAP perspective that there is excess repair parts inventory for the seller's own computer infrastructure. The applicable GL account is 1004. It is the only account that should be excluded.

- Throughout the arbitration process, the accounting arbitrator becomes aware that the company routinely utilizes parts for other purposes than the recorded purpose per the general ledger account. For example, retail inventory is routinely used as a source for service parts when the service team needs a part.

Although the previous case may seem like a perfect storm, it is not uncommon for carve-outs to be defined in a manner that appears clear but turns out to be ambiguous when it is time to apply it to the company's accounting after the closing. It is also not uncommon for even tightly controlled companies with well-prepared financial statements to have the underlying process be akin to the proverbial "making of the sausage." Over time, the company's accounting department is confronted with continuous changes to GAAP, translating division reporting into group financial statements, the integration of legacy systems, staff turnover and understaffing, and so on. Indeed, real-world cases can be subject to significant additional factual complications and lengthy and compound arguments from both sellers and buyers.

CHAPTER 8

Audited Financial Statements and Auditing Concepts

The audit of an entity's financial statements is intended to provide the user of those financial statements (as accompanied by an unqualified auditor's opinion) with increased assurance that they are not materially misstated. As such, they can be helpful in the context of a transaction as the availability of audited financial statements may give (i) the buyer comfort regarding the reliability of the company's historical accounting and (ii) the seller comfort with the commonly issued contractual representation that its historical financial statements are materially in accordance with GAAP.

In addition thereto, sellers and buyers commonly attempt to support their positions in the post-closing dispute phase with references to the existence of audited financial statements. For multiple reasons, those references are by themselves often not sufficient to support the parties' positions.

Example: Referencing the Audited Financial Statements as Support

- A transaction closed on May 15, 2016. The buyer performs a count at the end of June 2016 and seeks an adjustment for significant missing inventory.
- The seller argues that the financial statements were audited, that the auditor performed an inventory observation, that no missing inventory was ever identified by the auditor, and

that therefore the adjustment cannot be correct. The company's most recent pre-closing audited financial statements were for the year 2015.

- The buyer argues that the company's financial statements for 2016, which contained the write-off for the allegedly missing inventory, were audited and that the auditor did not object to the write-off.
- The accounting arbitrator considers, among other things, that (i) the financial statements were not prepared or audited as of the closing date, (ii) the auditors' work papers are not available to the arbitrator and the extent of the procedures performed on inventory is thus unknown, (iii) the audits were (likely) performed on a sample basis to obtain reasonable assurance that the financial statements were free of material misstatement.
- Although the existence of audited financial statements provides important situational context and may, for example, provide some comfort regarding the quality of the company's internal controls, the arbitrator may find that neither party's reference to audited financial statements is by itself sufficient to support that party's conclusion.

This chapter discusses the financial statement audit and a variety of auditing concepts and their impact on the resolution of accounting arbitrations in more detail.

THE AUDIT OF FINANCIAL STATEMENTS

The scope of an audit does not encompass providing certainty that the financial statements under audit are completely free of any errors. An unqualified audit opinion is based on the auditor's performance of procedures deemed necessary to support the auditor's opinion. Such procedures are performed to "obtain reasonable assurance about whether the financial statements as a whole are free from material misstatement, whether due to fraud or error."[1]

Dependent on whether a company is public or private, an audit is governed by standards promulgated by the American Institute for Certified Public Accountants (AICPA) or the Public Company Accounting Oversight Board (PCAOB). These two sets of standards overlap to a large degree. For purposes of this book, audit standard references are generally to the AICPA standards (referenced as AU-C). A few references are to PCAOB standards (referenced as AS).

There are distinct differences between financial statement audits and post-closing purchase price adjustment processes. Among other things, an audit incorporates the concepts of materiality and reasonable assurance, whereas an accounting arbitration is concerned with resolving disputed items in order to determine the appropriate amount of net working capital as of the closing date. The latter can impose a more exacting standard in the sense that, for example, an auditor may be willing to accept smaller misstatements in the context of the financial statements (i.e., below the applicable materiality threshold), whereas an accounting arbitrator typically seeks to arrive at the correct amount for each disputed item without considering a similar materiality threshold unless provided for in the purchase agreement. Moreover, an audit is an attestation engagement; serving as an accounting arbitrator is not. An accounting arbitrator is also not issuing an opinion on the financial statements as a whole. Rather, he or she is rendering a determination in resolution of specific disputed items between the parties.

RELEVANCE OF AN AUDIT AND AUDITED FINANCIAL STATEMENTS IN AN ACCOUNTING ARBITRATION

The audited financial statements of a target company can be relevant in an accounting arbitration, including in the context of the accounting arbitrator's consideration of certain arguments proposed by buyers and sellers. While the audited financial statements typically are not sufficient support for a party's position on any particular disputed item, such financial statements can, for example, provide general support for aspects of certain disputed items.

Moreover, audited financial statements that have been audited by a qualified firm or individual can provide a more solid basis for the assessment of consistency with past practices. Some additional comfort may also be obtained from appropriately audited financial statements regarding the internal controls of the target company and the existence of assets, such as inventory as of the financial statement date. These and other factors form the basis of the relevance of audited financial statements in the context of an accounting arbitration.

Timing of the Audited Financial Statements

The transaction closing date generally does not coincide with the end of a financial reporting period. It would be even more unusual for the closing date to coincide with the end of a financial reporting period (to be) covered by a financial statement audit. Moreover, even if it did, the audit for those financial statements will not have been completed on the closing date and may not be completed in time for purposes of the accounting arbitration.

As discussed previously in this chapter, the timing difference between the date of the financial statement audit and the closing date can impact the level of usefulness of the audited financial statements. Notwithstanding, even if audited financial statements were available as of the closing date, they are not as determinative as the parties may expect in arriving at a conclusion on the disputed items. Besides the aforementioned audit concepts, the audit is not designed to test whether the net working capital was prepared in conformity with *past practices in accordance with GAAP*. Rather, the audit provides reasonable assurance that the financial statements as a whole are presented fairly, in all material respects, in accordance with GAAP.

Basis of Comparison for Consistency

As discussed in earlier chapters, consistency with the seller's past accounting practices is a significant element in purchase agreements as it relates to the entire post-closing purchase price adjustment process. Many purchase agreements tie past practices to those used in the preparation of the most recent audited financial statements or other set(s) of reference financial statements. The target company's past practices may also be (in part) separately described and specified in the purchase agreement.

Either way, a full set of financial statements will include footnotes that provide, at a minimum, a high-level description of the target company's significant accounting policies. The footnotes can also contain more detailed information regarding a variety of balance sheet items (e.g., components of net working capital). Such information can include bad debt history, inventory adjustments, inventory turnover, and other information relevant to commonly disputed accounts. As discussed earlier, the (reference) audited financial statements will have been prepared at some date prior to the closing date. Therefore, the actual balances contained in the audited financial statements are typically of limited significance in the context of an accounting arbitration.

The commonly relevant information in the audited financial statements is the information that provides insight into the target company's historical accounting practices regarding classification of items; the recognition, or lack thereof, of items such as contingencies; and the historical accounting practices used to derive the various net working capital items. This can form a basis for comparison, if so provided for in the purchase agreement, in order to assess consistency with the seller's historical accounting practices.

Example: Historical Accounting Practices for Accounts Receivable

- Upon the closing of a transaction, the buyer proposes an adjustment to increase the allowance for doubtful accounts, arguing that it has applied the company's historical accounting practices.

- The seller disputes this fact, arguing that its preliminary closing statement amount is appropriate and was prepared utilizing the company's historical accounting practices.
- On their faces, both parties' descriptions of their methodologies appear to comply with the company's historical descriptions of its process to determine the allowance for doubtful accounts.
- To test the extent of the consistency of the application of the company's historical accounting practices, the accounting arbitrator can, among other things, utilize the audited (reference) financial statements' gross accounts receivable balance, assuming it is available in the footnotes, and apply the allowance methodology proposed by both parties. If either methodology used by the parties results in a different allowance as of the historical test date, the accounting arbitrator can find that methodology not in accordance with historical accounting practices.

Existence of Assets

Notwithstanding the timing difference that may exist, the audited financial statements can, dependent on the facts and circumstances, provide some level of comfort regarding, among other things, the existence of assets. Take, for example, audited financial statements that are dated three months prior to the closing date and related to which the seller can show that an inventory count was performed and observed by the auditor. Due to the time required to perform and finalize an audit, the audit may have only been completed a few weeks prior to the closing date. If an argument is raised by the buyer that \$2 million of the total inventory of \$3 million does not exist, the audited financial statements may call such a claim into question dependent, of course, on the applicable facts and circumstances. In that situation, the audited financial statements, at least, provide support regarding the existence of the inventory not long before the closing date.

Internal Controls and Reliability of Financial Information

The design and effectiveness of an entity's controls over financial reporting impact the reliability of the information reported. The extent of the implemented controls varies greatly and can depend on the size and operations of the company in question. For example, a small family-run business may have limited controls as compared to a heavily regulated, large multinational corporation, which may have numerous and varied internal controls. Internal controls are taken very seriously by regulators and professional organizations alike.

Dependent on the facts and circumstances of the audit, the auditor may rely more or less on his or her testing of the internal controls over financial reporting of the company. If the independent auditor performs an integrated audit, he or she is required to test a company's internal controls over financial reporting and to report on the result of those procedures.

In evaluating the parties' positions in an accounting arbitration, well-documented and tested internal controls can help a party support its position. Notwithstanding, the presence or absence of extensive internal controls are typically not, by themselves, determinative in relation to any particular disputed item.

LIMITATIONS ON THE RELEVANCE OF A FINANCIAL STATEMENT AUDIT IN AN ACCOUNTING ARBITRATION

Although the audit of financial statements serves an important purpose in general, in the context of an accounting arbitration the relevance of the audit can be less than expected due to a variety of differences between an audit and an accounting arbitration. These differences include timing of the audit versus the closing date; providing reasonable assurance versus including the appropriate amount in an arbitration award; audit materiality considerations versus exactness; sample basis versus entire population; the required consistency under the purchase agreement; and others.

An accounting arbitration is solely focused, contractually so, on the disputed items presented to the arbitrator. An audit is much more wide ranging and covers the company's financial statements as a whole. The accounting arbitrator is not being asked to audit the financial statements or to opine on them as a whole. An accounting arbitration is not an audit of financial statements and the accounting arbitrator is not attesting to their correctness. The difference in purpose between an audit and an accounting arbitration limits the comparability between the two tasks and therefore also impacts the relevance of a financial statement audit to the resolution of disputed items.

The reason or reasons why an audit has limited relevance in an accounting arbitration are discussed in the next several sections.

Providing Reasonable Assurance versus Arriving at the Appropriate Amount

A key audit concept is that the auditor is responsible for obtaining reasonable, but not absolute, assurance regarding whether the financial statements are free of material misstatements. In an accounting arbitration, the arbitrator is concerned with getting to the correct amount for each disputed item. The auditor's approach manifests itself in, among other things, the performance of procedures on a sample basis and the consideration of materiality.

Sample Basis versus Entire Population A financial statement audit includes a variety of procedures to test management's assertions contained in the financial statements under audit. These procedures include a variety of techniques to test accuracy, completeness, existence, and other management assertions. Many audit procedures are applied on a sample basis. For example, a sample of inventory items may be selected for valuation or existence testing. Based on the test results for the selected sample, the auditor may draw conclusions about the entire population of inventory.

An accounting arbitration is not performed on a sample basis. An accounting arbitrator is not testing management's assertions; rather the arbitrator is attempting to get to the correct amount for each of the disputed items. In doing so, accounting arbitrators generally do not rely on sample testing as a basis for their award.

Differences in Materiality Considerations An auditor does not provide reasonable assurance that the financial statements are free of all errors. Rather, he or she provides reasonable assurance that they are free of *material* errors. In the context of an audit, an auditor's assessment of materiality "is a matter of professional judgment and is affected by the auditor's perception of the financial information needs of users of the financial statements."[2] Generally, "misstatements, including omissions, are considered to be material if, individually or in the aggregate, they could reasonably be expected to influence the economic decisions of users that are taken based on the financial statements."[3] The auditor considers the materiality threshold in designing the procedures to be performed.[4] As a result, an audit is not necessarily designed to identify immaterial errors.

An amount or error that is not material in the context of the financial statements, however, may very well be a significant amount in the context of an accounting arbitration. For example, the audit materiality for a company may be $1 million. Therefore, any error(s) either individually or in the aggregate below this amount may not be corrected or even identified by a financial statement auditor. In the context of an accounting arbitration, however, the parties may very well feel that a $700,000 inventory shortfall should result in an adjustment.

Materiality considerations can also relate to classification between current and non-current assets or liabilities. An auditor may not conclude that a company needs to reclassify an amount from long-term liabilities to current liabilities because it is immaterial to the financial statements as a whole. That does not mean, however, that it would be inappropriate to propose an adjustment to reclassify that amount from long term to current (i.e., to become a component of net working capital) in an accounting arbitration.

In summary, accounting arbitrators generally do not implement a GAAS-like materiality threshold in the context of the post-closing adjustment process. The parties, however, may find it desirable to implement some sort of analogous limitation on adjustments. We discuss some contractual options available to the parties in Chapter 20.

Lack of Information Regarding the Specific Audit Procedures

Even if an accounting arbitrator wanted to rely on audit procedures performed during the audit of an entity's financial statements, it would in many situations be to a large extent impossible. The accounting arbitrator will typically have limited or no visibility into the specific procedures performed by the auditor, including information as to when the procedures were performed, which items were selected for testing, any immaterial errors that were identified, any adjustments passed on by the auditor, or any other audit procedure details. It would be an exceptionally rare instance in which an auditor would provide its work papers for review by the accounting arbitrator. As a result, regardless of the reputation of the auditor, an accounting arbitrator generally does not solely rely on a company's audited financial statements for purposes of reaching a determination on specific disputed items in an accounting arbitration.

Differences in Assessment of Management Estimates

Management estimates are an appropriate and necessary aspect of the preparation of a company's financial statements. Examples of estimates include collectability of accounts receivable and excess inventory. Such estimates are evaluated by the financial statement auditor as well as the accounting arbitrator.

The basis of the evaluation of such estimates, however, is different between these two.

The auditor evaluates management's estimates and assertions for reasonableness, support, and overall compliance with GAAP. The accounting arbitrator is asked to evaluate whether proposed estimates as of the closing date are in accordance with the company's historical accounting practices as well as GAAP.

THE CONCEPT OF PROFESSIONAL SKEPTICISM

Notwithstanding the limitations of audited financial statements in the context of an accounting arbitration, the parties, as well as would-be accounting arbitrators, can benefit from analogous implementation of the auditor's attitude of professional skepticism. Professional skepticism is an attitude that includes a questioning mind and a critical assessment of audit evidence. The auditor uses the knowledge, skill, and ability called for by the profession of public accounting to diligently perform, in good faith and with integrity, the gathering and objective evaluation of evidence.[5]

Moreover, in applying this attitude prior to the closing, sellers may be able to prevent post-closing surprises that find their origin in an overly optimistic view of the company's business and its accounting in the pre-closing period. In applying this attitude to its own proposed adjustments, buyers may recognize some of its adjustments as overly broad sweeps that lack specific support. The accounting arbitrator can use the concept as a reminder of the need to diligently evaluate the information and supporting documentation provided by the parties.

NOTES

1. *See* AU-C Section 200.06.
2. *See* AU-C Section 320.04.
3. *See* AU-C Section 200.07.
4. *See* AU-C Section 320.06.
5. *See* AU-C Section 200.14 and AS 1015.07.

CHAPTER 9

Subsequent Events, New Positions, and New Information

In the regular course of business, companies' financial statements are prepared and issued after the period they cover. In the time it takes to get the financial statements ready to be issued, events can occur that have an impact on the financial position of the company and that may be considered relevant for purposes of the financial statements. GAAP provides guidance on which subsequent events should be incorporated into the company's to-be-issued financial statements, through recording or disclosure, and to what extent.

Similarly, in the context of an M&A transaction, events can occur after the closing of a transaction that could potentially be considered relevant for purposes of the proposed and final closing statement. Parties to a post-closing net working capital dispute regularly present arguments and/or disagree if and to what extent subsequent events should be considered for purposes of determining the net working capital as of the closing date. In this chapter we discuss subsequent event guidance under GAAP and the analogous application of this guidance to the post-closing purchase price adjustment and dispute resolution process.

In addition to GAAP, the contractual and procedural context of accounting arbitrations also imposes limitations on the parties regarding the adoption of new positions, changes to the support for their positions, and the submission of new information. We discuss the process and a common implementation. We also provide a numerical illustration.

SUBSEQUENT EVENTS

Under certain conditions events that occur subsequent to the financial statement date should nonetheless be incorporated in those financial statements. A subsequent event can have a material impact on financial statements and in the case of an M&A transaction can have a substantial impact on the final purchase price as determined post-closing.

Subsequent Events under GAAP

GAAP, as it is applied to financial statements, generally distinguishes between two types of events that may occur after the financial statement date and prior to the date the financial statements are ready to be issued or are issued (the latter for SEC registrants):

1. Events that provide additional evidence about conditions that existed at the date of the balance sheet, including the estimates inherent in the process of preparing financial statements.[1] Those types of subsequent events are commonly called "Type 1 Subsequent Events."
2. Events that provide evidence about conditions that did not exist at the date of the balance sheet but arose after that date.[2] Those types of subsequent events are commonly called "Type 2 Subsequent Events."

The effects of Type 1 Subsequent Events that occur in the period between the financial statement date and the ready-to-be-issued or issuance date should be recognized in a company's financial statements. The effects of Type 2 Subsequent Events are not recognized in the financial statements of the company, although their disclosure may be required. In certain instances, Type 1 Subsequent Events that occur after the issuance of the financial statements may require the financial statements to be reissued, because they would otherwise be misleading.

Example: Type 1 and Type 2 Subsequent Events

- One of the customers of the company has a lengthy history of being behind in their payments. Two days after the financial statement date of the company, the customer files for bankruptcy. The customer's filings show that it suffered from progressive financial problems over several years, culminating in a bankruptcy that is not expected to result in any recovery of amounts due to unsecured creditors (such as the company). This is a Type 1 Subsequent Event and the company will write off the customer's accounts receivable balance as of the financial statement date.
- One of the company's warehouses gets hit by lightning and burns down two days after the financial statement date. The company loses the uninsured inventory in the warehouse. This is a Type 2 Subsequent Event and the company should still recognize the inventory on its balance sheet, although the company should likely include a disclosure of the event and the resulting loss in the financial statements.

In practice, the distinction between Type 1 and Type 2 Subsequent Events is not always as clear as in the previous example. The distinction may require significant judgment.

The Role of Subsequent Events in the Post-Closing Process

The preliminary closing statement is prepared prior to closing and therefore does not incorporate subsequent events. To the contrary, the preliminary closing statement commonly does not necessarily even include the financial impact of all events prior to closing.

After the closing, the buyer will commonly use relevant information that becomes available prior to the submission of the proposed closing statement in its evaluation of the conditions on which the therein included accounting estimates are based. In other words, the buyer's proposed closing statement can incorporate the impact, if any, of subsequent events similar to the consideration of subsequent events in the preparation of financial statements in the ordinary course of business. Further exchanges between the parties and submissions to the accounting arbitrator may or may not incorporate additional subsequent events. It is not uncommon for the parties to try to bring in new information under subsequent event guidance throughout an accounting arbitration. In addition to the question whether that is appropriate from a GAAP perspective, it may also be barred per the procedures laid out in the purchase agreement and/or the arbitrator's retention agreement.

In an accounting arbitration, parties may explicitly argue for the inclusion of specifically identified subsequent events. The parties can also use post-closing information to attempt to validate their accounting estimates (or even to adjust them). This is especially relevant to arbitrations that go on for extended periods of time as more information will naturally become available. Although both sellers and buyers can argue for the inclusion of subsequent events during the arbitration, subsequent event discussions are commonly initiated by buyers. After all, the buyer typically has more ready access to the information necessary to identify potential subsequent events as it assumes control of the business as of the closing date.

A common example of a party using post-closing information, is the submission and usage of post-closing, actual collection data for the accounts receivable recorded as of the closing date. The submitting party may use that after-the-fact data to attempt to support the amount of its proposed accounts receivable allowance and/or specific accounts receivable write-offs. That information, however, is not necessarily relevant as of the closing date because lower-than-expected collections may well find their genesis in post-closing decisions, events, and/or business priorities. It is also not necessarily allowed under the procedure as set forth in the purchase agreement or the arbitrator's retention agreement. Moreover, it does not necessarily comport with *past practices in accordance with GAAP* or simply with GAAP for that matter. It is not uncommon for the party submitting the information to not address any of those issues and, instead, simply proclaim, "See, we must be right!" Ideally, the submitting party would, among other things, discuss (i) why they believe the information is relevant, (ii) how it relates to the collectability of the accounts receivable as of the closing date, and (iii) why they believe their position comports with *past practices in accordance with GAAP* as well as the broader procedural context.

Treatment May Vary among Accounting Arbitrators

Purchase agreements are often silent on the consideration of subsequent events in the context of the purchase price adjustment process. Although it may be considered as indirectly covered under *past practices in accordance with GAAP*, there is a marked difference with other GAAP guidance. Subsequent event guidance is tied to the issuance of the financial statements (i.e., it is procedurally tied to the financial statements). Thus, although an analogous interpretation under GAAP is possible, it requires identifying a date equivalent to the date the financial statements become available for issuance.

Other contractual limitations notwithstanding, the parties can potentially find arguments for a variety of issuance equivalent dates. On one extreme, a party may argue that the preliminary closing statement equates to the issuance of the financial statements and all subsequent discussions are part of a procedure that is external to the company. On the other extreme, and ignoring other procedural limitations that are commonly included in the purchase agreement, a party may argue that the proposed closing statement and the adjustments thereto only become final with the arbitrator's award and that, therefore, subsequent events should be considered through the date that the award becomes available for issuance. Of course, dates in between those two bookends can also be argued by the parties, dependent on the facts and circumstances of the case.

In practice, especially when subsequent events are explicitly argued and considered, arbitrators may settle on the date of the buyer's proposed closing statement as the earliest date analogous to the financial statement issuance date. The earlier preliminary closing statement is generally prepared pre-closing and, thus, generally not expected to be final. The buyer's proposed closing statement is generally the first closing statement that is prepared after an appropriate closing of the books and it is intended to be complete and correct. Indeed, if it were to be accepted by the seller without objection, there would be no further closing statements and it would become final.

Notwithstanding, there can also be legitimate arguments for later dates. By means of example, a seller may take the position that it should be allowed to incorporate subsequent events through the date of its objection notice. A seller may take the position that the objection notice is its first post-closing opportunity to effectively submit its final version of the closing accounts and that it should, therefore, be allowed to incorporate subsequent events through that date. If the accounting arbitrator agrees, he or she may permit the incorporation of subsequent events through the date of the objection notice.

As discussed earlier, in practice, the parties may attempt to use general post-closing information that becomes available in the regular course of business (e.g., general post-closing date collection information for the accounts receivable as opposed to a specific client bankruptcy) far into the post-closing purchase price adjustment process. Moreover, restraint in the consideration of post-closing information is not necessarily exercised by all accounting arbitrators. That is especially true in the context of such general *ex post* information that becomes available in the regular course of business. In their effort to get to the perceivably "right answer" some accounting arbitrators may reason that more information is better as they grab onto any *ex post* actual financial information submitted by the parties in support of their positions. GAAP, however, does not intend for accounting estimates to be based on actual and complete *ex post* financial information. To the contrary, an accounting estimate is an estimate based on the information available at the time and naturally, largely free from hindsight bias. In addition, as discussed earlier, the after-the-fact financial information is not necessarily informative of the situation as of the closing date. For example, long after-the-fact post-closing accounts receivable write-offs may have well resulted from poor collection practices under buyer's ownership. Moreover, if the parties wanted to rely on the actual financial performance post-closing, they could have easily provided for that instead of for *past practices in accordance with GAAP*. We urge would-be accounting arbitrators to carefully consider the purchase agreement, applicable GAAP guidance, and the facts and circumstances of the case as they evaluate the relevance of any post-closing information submitted by the parties.

The Role of the Purchase Agreement

It is relatively simple to preempt the subsequent event discussion and the associated uncertainty by addressing the issue in the purchase agreement. Contrary to some other transaction-specific deviations from *past practices in accordance with GAAP*, the implementation of such a provision can be relatively straightforward and uncontroversial.

The purchase agreement can, for example, provide that the subsequent event guidance of GAAP shall apply analogously to the proposed closing statement as if it was available to be issued on the date that the buyer's proposed closing statement is due under the agreement. Of course, the parties may pick another date or agree that subsequent events should not be considered. Either way, a definitive subsequent event cutoff date or elimination of subsequent events prevents the uncertainty associated with having the accounting arbitrator decide on the appropriate implementation of subsequent event guidance in the context of an accounting arbitration.

Notably, although purchase agreements commonly do not explicitly address the treatment of subsequent events as such, their implementation is not necessarily a free-for-all. Purchase agreements often provide for procedural limitations that can effectively limit the incorporation of subsequent events after certain dates. We discuss procedural deadlines for new positions and new information next.

PROCEDURAL DEADLINES FOR NEW POSITIONS AND NEW INFORMATION

The contractual and procedural context sets limits on the parties regarding the introduction of new positions, new arguments, and new information. Between purchase agreements, the procedural implementation of the post-closing purchase price adjustment process and the accounting arbitration is often largely similar. Notwithstanding, there can be differences in implementation and even small procedural differences can result in disproportionally large swings in outcome.

Overall Context

The post-closing purchase price adjustment process is aimed at getting to the correct closing date net working capital amount as efficiently as possible. There are arguments for and against allowing new positions and new information throughout the process. On one hand, as the buyer newly owns the company and the seller is piecing together the information received from the buyer (and its own corporate-level records), it should be no surprise that the parties encounter additional information throughout the process that they want to use. On the other hand, the parties will want to prevent a drawn-out process and arbitration by ambush.

This tension field is somewhat mitigated by the nature of the process. As opposed to typical civil litigation, there is no prerequisite condition of wrongful conduct and associated liability. Rather, as the transaction closes, the parties often anticipate some level of adjustments to the preliminary closing statement and therefore the purchase price. Accordingly, the parties are typically willing to accept more procedural leeway especially on an *ex ante* basis as they negotiate the purchase agreement. For example, purchase agreements typically do not impose the application of formal rules of evidence for the accounting arbitration.

The pre-arbitration phase is generally conducted in a friendly and cooperative manner. Even the arbitration process itself can be surprisingly cooperative. At times, the parties simply view their disagreement as an honest difference of opinion and use the process to pose a question to the arbitrator without much advocacy or contentiousness. Of course, other times transactions start out friendly and end up with the parties deeply divided and with accusations of opportunism and gaming the process to obtain improper windfalls flying back and forth.

Finally, it is not uncommon for parties to one-sidedly abandon certain disputed items through the arbitration process. For example, based on the buyer's initial submission in the arbitration phase, the seller may become aware that its accounting for a particular issue contained a clerical error that it was previously unaware of and that has been uncovered by the buyer after the retention of the accounting arbitrator. Of course, the other party will generally welcome the item being resolved in its favor. Theoretically, the timing and context of the one-sided surrender of a disputed item can generate disagreement with respect to the allocation of the arbitrator's fees, which are often inverse proportionally allocated to the parties based on the arbitrator's conclusions. In practice, the parties do not typically present arguments related to the fee allocation. Instead, the arbitrator is mandated by his or her retention letter and the purchase agreement to allocate the fees in a certain way.

The Process

The typical post-closing process, including the arbitration, encompasses a narrowing of the disputed items and of the freedom of the parties to cover new ground over time. The process starts off with the preliminary closing statement based on which the purchase price is calculated at closing.

The next step is the buyer's proposed closing statement, which the buyer submits within a set period after closing. The proposed closing statement typically anchors the buyer to the amounts included therein. Afterwards, the buyer typically cannot change those amounts in its favor. Notably, many purchase agreements provide that any amounts in the proposed closing statement that are not objected to by the seller become final.

The proposed closing statement will typically show the overall difference between the seller's preliminary closing statement and the buyer's position. It is commonly presented at the balance sheet account level and also typically includes a breakout of the individual adjustments and the reasoning behind them. If it is not accompanied by that information, the information is typically provided prior to the seller's objection notice.

Example: Numerical Illustration of the Process

- The table is a summarized version of the information commonly included with the buyer's proposed closing statement, or exchanged shortly thereafter, as well as an illustration of the various levels of information.

	Preliminary Closing Statement	Buyer's Proposed Closing Statement	Difference
Total Net Working Capital	$1 million	$600,000	–$400,000
Balance Sheet Level			
Liquid Assets	$250,000	$210,000	–$40,000
Inventory	$600,000	$550,000	–$50,000
AR	$350,000	$30,000	–$320,000
AP	($200,000)	($190,000)	+$10,000
Total	$1 million	$600,000	–$400,000

Detailed Explanations		
Item 1—Liquid Assets:	Trued up	–$40,000
Item 2—Inventory:	Trued up	+$30,000
Item 3—Inventory:	Missing items	–$10,000
Item 4—Inventory:	Allowance	–$70,000
Item 5—AR:	Trued up	–$20,000
Item 6—AR:	Write-offs	–$290,000
Item 7—AR:	Allowance	–$10,000
Item 8—AP:	Trued up	+$10,000
Total		–$400,000

The next formal step is the seller's objection notice. In practice, however, there tends to be a continuous exchange of information subsequent to the buyer's proposed closing statement as both parties try to get their arms around the numbers and each other's positions. That information exchange and the related discussion can still be in progress as the seller's objection notice becomes due. In such situations, the parties can decide to extend the deadline for the objection notice or the seller may simply object to items for which it believes it has insufficient information to arrive at a final conclusion. Once the objection period has ended, the seller is generally bound by the items it did not object to. In other words, for items not objected to by the seller, the buyer's proposed closing statement becomes final.

The seller's objection notice generally incorporates the seller's responses to the buyer's proposed closing statement at the varying levels included earlier. The seller typically presents its formal response at the item level when possible. The seller's objection notice can also be combined with additional background on the nature of the objection. If it is not included, such information typically follows later on as the negotiations and information are exchanged between the parties continue.

The seller is often limited to two categories of possible objections for each of the buyer's proposed adjustments:

1. The adjustment is not in accordance with GAAP, and/or
2. The adjustment is not in accordance with the company's historical accounting practices

In addition, the seller can be allowed to propose corrected numbers that deviate from both the buyer's proposed closing statement and the preliminary closing statement in its favor.

Example: Numerical Illustration of the Process (Continued)

- We illustrate a situation in which the seller's objection notice can deviate in the seller's favor from both the preliminary closing statement and the proposed closing statement for one of the items included earlier.
- Liquid assets:
  - Seller's preliminary closing statement: $250,000
  - Buyer's proposed closing statement: $210,000
  - Difference: ($40,000)
- The seller objects to the buyer's proposed closing statement as it is (i) not in accordance with the company's historical accounting practices and (ii) not in accordance with GAAP.
- *Explanation:* The seller believes that the buyer has failed to include the petty cash balances held at the company's branch offices.
- *Conclusion:* The seller proposes a liquid assets balance of $260,000.

By the time the seller's objection notice is filed, the list of disagreed upon items is typically a significantly trimmed down version of the earlier list of the buyer's proposed adjustments. The filing of the seller's objection notice is typically also the first time that both parties have taken a position post-closing that limits them going forward. Once the objection notice is submitted, the seller typically cannot revive undisputed items or further change amounts in its favor.

In addition, the parties also tend to take another critical look at their own positions and potentially settle out some (or all) of the items on which they disagree. By the time the arbitrator is retained, the parties typically have trimmed the list of disputed items down further and the positions of each party going into the arbitration are clearer.

Example: Numerical Illustration of the Process (Continued)

- The example is extended here to illustrate how the initial differences between the parties can develop over time.

	Seller Revised	Buyer Revised	Remaining in Dispute
Total Net Working Capital	$1,060,000	$740,000	–$320,000
Balance Sheet Level			
Liquid Assets	$210,000	$210,000	N/A
Inventory	$620,000	$600,000	–$20,000
AR	$330,000	$30,000	–$300,000
AP	($100,000)	($100,000)	N/A
Total	$1,060,000	$740,000	–$320,000

Detailed explanations:

Item 1—Liquid Assets: The seller agreed to –$40,000 after learning that the buyer included the petty cash balances in its calculation.

Item 2—Inventory: The seller agreed to +$30,000.

Item 3—Inventory: The seller located the missing items. The buyer agreed to $0.

Item 4—Inventory: Range narrowed as a result of information exchange. The seller agreed to –$10,000. The buyer seeks an additional –$20,000 for a potential total adjustment of –$30,000 on this item.

Item 5—AR: The seller agreed to –$20,000.

Item 6—AR: No change in positions. In dispute for –$290,000.

Item 7—AR: No change in positions. In dispute for –$10,000.

Item 8—AP: The parties discover a clerical error in the true-up. The true-up is increased to +$100,000.

Total in dispute of $320,000. The seller is at +$60,000 relative to the preliminary closing statement (i.e., increase to the purchase price paid at closing) while the buyer is at –$260,000 relative to the preliminary closing statement (i.e., decrease to price paid at closing) and at +$140,000 relative to its own proposed closing statement.

Dependent on the mandate to the accounting arbitrator—as included in the arbitrator's engagement letter—the disputed items may be included in more or less detail in the retention agreement. After the retention of the accounting arbitrator, the parties submit their initial submissions. Those submissions are typically the last guaranteed opportunity for the parties to provide support for their positions on the disputed items. Typically, the inclusion of additional arguments and documentation/information in support of the parties' existing positions is allowed at this time. By contrast, many purchase agreements that detail the arbitration process provide for rebuttal submissions to the accounting arbitrator that are limited in scope to responding to the initial submission of the other party.

Finally, the parties may get an additional opportunity to provide information in response to specific requests from the accounting arbitrator. If significant new information and documentation is submitted in response to the arbitrator's requests, the arbitrator may issue additional requests in order to give the other party an opportunity to respond.

The Parties

Notwithstanding the limitations on the parties and the agreed upon scope of the parties' submissions, it is not uncommon for parties to seek the edge of permissibility or, in some instances, to attempt to ignore the procedural bounds to some extent.

In extreme circumstances, a party can seek to add a disputed item outside the scope of the previously disputed items. For example, a party can attempt to add an inventory allowance to a dispute that had previously been limited to an accounts receivable allowance. Such additions are uncommon and will typically be rejected out of hand by the accounting arbitrator if their timing is in violation of the provisions of the purchase agreement or the arbitrator's retention agreement.

A party can also seek to increase/decrease the amount of an existing disputed item in its favor throughout the process. A party can argue, for example, an addition to the inventory allowance for axles when the dispute had previously been limited to wheels.

Finally, parties can present new arguments and support for existing positions later in the process. Whether due to finding new information or as a procedural strategy, parties at times attempt to stretch the contractual meaning of *rebuttal* or take a particularly broad approach in responding to an arbitrator's question. In addition, knowing that the disputed items and amounts are fixed, parties sometimes will present a revised amount as supplemental support in an attempt to stay within the procedural boundaries. For example, a party may (i) set forth an argument and (ii) proactively state that they are barred from changing their position, (iii) that they would have been fully justified in taking a more aggressive position if they had only timely discovered the underlying facts, and (iv) that if their support for their original position fails, the new information should result in them maintaining their overall position.

The accounting arbitrator decides on procedural issues and disagreements in accordance with the purchase agreement and/or the arbitrator's retention agreement. Those agreements, however, do not always cover every eventuality. The accounting arbitrator may have to make a decision under contractual ambiguity. In doing so, the accounting arbitrator will often weigh, among other things, two factors in deciding whether to consider additional arguments or information. First, the accounting arbitrator tends to be professionally driven to get to the correct amounts, which by itself errs on the side of considering additional information. Second, the accounting arbitrator does not want to prejudice one of the parties. Although there is no jury to be improperly swayed by inadmissible evidence, the accounting arbitrator will want to prevent an arbitration by ambush that robs one of the parties of appropriately responding to the full position of the other party. The net result can be that in the event of ambiguity, the accounting arbitrator errs on the side of accepting additional information and arguments for existing positions for consideration, while also offering the other party an opportunity to respond.

NOTES

1. *See* FASB ASC 855-10-25-1.
2. *See* FASB ASC 855-10-25-3.

PART Three

The Accounting Arbitration

CHAPTER 10

Mitigation of Post-Closing Purchase Price Disputes

Before we discuss the accounting arbitration process, it is important to discuss certain activities that take place prior to the closing of a transaction that can have an impact on potential disputes. During the pre-closing period there are steps that the parties can take to potentially mitigate the severity and scope of a post-closing purchase price adjustment dispute. Similarly, in the post-closing negotiation phase, the parties can eliminate certain disputed items prior to the retention of the accounting arbitrator.

DUE DILIGENCE

General Context

Due diligence performed in contemplation of the acquisition of a company can be extensive and cover multiple areas of expertise such as financial, environmental, tax, and legal. The overall primary purpose, of course, is to get the proverbial look under the hood prior to acquiring the company to minimize the risk associated with an unexpected negative surprise after closing. There are several competing forces related to due diligence, including:

1. The buyer generally wants to know as much as possible about the company it is buying to prevent or limit undue surprises.

2. The seller wants to set boundaries on the (potential) buyer's quest for information, especially information that is competitively sensitive.
3. Due diligence is typically time and resource restrained. Both parties will want keep the transaction moving.

Subsequent to the signing of the purchase agreement, the information may flow more freely than during pre-signing due diligence, in anticipation of the closing. Interactions with company personnel can evolve from a formal presentation setting to friendlier and more informal relationships through prolonged exposure, and ultimately the recognition that the person requesting the information represents the prospective new owners of the company. By means of example, after signing, the buyer may have a representative go on a roadshow with the CFO of the company to visit potential providers of debt financing. The air of formality may still exist in relation to the potential bondholders, but does not necessarily persist between the buyer and the CFO.

The above relates to what is commonly referred to as buy-side due diligence. In practice, especially in a situation where a large corporation is selling a more remote subsidiary, many sellers perform sell-side due diligence. This helps the seller to (i) prepare a sell-side package to provide to potential buyers, (ii) set and negotiate a price with (potential) buyers, and (iii) identify issues that may also be identified during buy-side due diligence.

Mitigation of Post-Closing Purchase Price Adjustments

Dependent on the provisions of the purchase agreement sellers and buyers can benefit from focusing some of their due diligence efforts on the definitions and mechanics of net working capital–based or other purchase price adjustment mechanisms. In addition, the performance of sell-side due diligence can also benefit the setting of the target net working capital, which we discuss in more detail ahead.

Sell-Side Due Diligence In most instances, it is the seller that can primarily benefit from paying close attention to the potential for post-closing adjustments and disputes in the due diligence phase and even earlier as the company is being prepared for sale. It can use the opportunity to focus on the company's own assets and liabilities and pay particular attention to compliance with GAAP. The same focus can assist the seller with negotiating the target net working capital with the buyer. Importantly, the negotiation of the target net working capital commonly takes place before the execution of the purchase agreement. In other words, in the normal course of events, some of this work is done in a relatively short timeframe and that may be the only time period in which the identification of issues can be translated into adjustments to the target net working capital. As a result, it can benefit the seller to become aware of issues early in the process. For example, a carve-out or special treatment may need to be negotiated as part of the purchase agreement, which may also result in the necessary consideration of such a carve-out for the determination of target net working capital.

In pre-sale preparation for a post-closing purchase price adjustment the seller may want to skeptically review its own accounting practices to identify what could potentially be considered excess optimism in its accounting. Of particular importance are potential judgment areas that may receive limited attention for purposes of the company's day-to-day accounting. The seller can also review its management reporting and other documentation for potential liabilities that have not been recognized and the strength of the arguments for not recognizing such contingent liabilities. A review can also broadly assess past practices for compliance with GAAP in typical problem areas such as accruals and allowances.

If applicable, the review can include comments or proposed audit adjustments from the independent auditor that were not implemented due to lack of materiality, or the identification and review of relevant documentation related to accounting estimates, management judgment, and recognition issues. If lapses in the quality or detail of documentation are observed, the seller can potentially shore up the documentation. If not, the seller may at a minimum benefit from the identification of documentation it may need to keep available for the post-closing phase, given that the seller will most likely lose much of its direct access to company personnel post-closing.

Example: Pre-Sale Self-Assessment

- The company has a relatively large number of older subassemblies in inventory that can be used in switching older computer networks.
- During the normal financial statement close, management has taken only a minimal allowance against this inventory based on possible expansion into foreign markets where those parts are still current.
- The company has used this line of reasoning for three years without expanding to foreign markets, without selling any of the subassemblies, and without translating its general foreign expansion potential into more detailed plans.
- Although the explanation is in isolation not necessarily unreasonable, the buyer will likely point out the context and may receive a post-closing adjustment for past practices that are not in accordance with GAAP as of the closing date.

In the end, a big risk for a seller in the context of a post-closing purchase price adjustment is often a violation of GAAP included in the historical financial information on which the target net working capital is based, that is then identified and eliminated in the post-closing purchase price adjustment calculation, resulting in a perceived windfall for buyer.

Buy-Side Due Diligence The buyer's position is much less precarious than the seller's, because the nature of GAAP and the common link to the company's historical accounting practices tend to naturally prevent large—potentially opportunistic—upward swings in closing date net working capital without an underlying change in the real assets or liabilities of the company. GAAP serves as a *de facto* protection mechanism because its conservatism approach often results in potential gains being deferred while potential losses are more likely to be recognized. The link to the target company's historical accounting practices can also help the buyer as it prevents changes in accounting practices, that are otherwise allowed under GAAP, that could improve seller's position.

Notwithstanding, there is a risk that the seller objects to an amount or amounts included in the preliminary closing statement that is carried into the buyer's proposed closing statement because it is in violation of GAAP. Although commonly mitigated by the seller's representation that the historical financial statements are not materially misstated, the historical practices may become in violation of GAAP or the error may be immaterial in the context of the financial statements as a whole, but significant in the context of a purchase price adjustment. Especially in the last instance, the buyer may experience an adjustment as an unjust windfall. That being said, such issues are typically less common and when they occur the amounts at issue are often significantly less than errors that go the other way.

Example: Seller Objects to Its Own Past Practices

- The seller's preliminary closing statement includes a $2.1 million vacation accrual for which vacation usage for the month prior to closing was estimated.
- The buyer's proposed closing statement is based on actual usage and comes out to $2.2 million.
- The seller, while checking the math for the buyer's true-up of the company's vacation accrual, realizes that the number of vacation days as accrued are not capped by the total number of days that an employee can maximally accrue under the company's HR policies.
- The seller objects to the buyer's proposed vacation accrual and claims the accrual should be $1.4 million. The seller argues that the difference between $2.2 million and $1.4 million is not actually owed by the company and thus should not be included under GAAP.

- If the target net working capital determination incorporates the same error, thc seller can effectively obtain a benefit as a result of its historical accounting inaccuracy. The historical impact may well be immaterial in the context of the financial statements as a whole and may leave the buyer no redress under the language of the related representations in the purchase agreement.

Outside the context of the purchase price adjustment process, the buyer may want to prevent net working capital shortfalls to insure the smooth continued operation of the business without the need for additional capital immediately subsequent to the closing. After all, in the event of a significant net working capital shortfall, the buyer may have to deal with the real-world impact on the business. This can occur even if the net working capital is negotiated based on the historical needs of the company.

Example: Business Impact of Net Working Capital Shortfalls

- The parties calculated the target net working capital based on the historical actual net working capital of the business. In addition, the buyer compared the company's net working capital and inventory levels against commonly accepted industry requirements.
- The company has $25 million of inventory on its books, which is in line with its historical levels.
- After closing, the buyer finds that the company's actual inventory is only $23 million and more importantly largely obsolete. It becomes evident that the proportion of the company's inventory that was obsolete grew over time while the remaining inventory turned faster and faster.
- The buyer successfully argues for a $2 million quantity deduction and a $20 million obsolescence allowance.
- Nonetheless, the (ultimate) financial compensation does not fully cover the effect on the company:
  - The buyer found that the company was behind on its commitments to its clients (robbing Paul to service Peter),

had utilized a significant amount of the useful inventory (i.e., the inventory was not $2 million lower on $25 million—but $2 million lower on $5 million in functional inventory), and was behind on ordering new inventory given supplier lead times.

- The buyer had to get rid of a warehouse full of goods to clean up space, reorganize the existing inventory, and reorganize the warehouse so it could be used as it should.
- The buyer had to invest significant cash into the company to address the inventory issue while waiting for the purchase price adjustment process to be completed.

Insofar as it is possible in the pre-closing phase, the buyer may mitigate some of its risk by assessing the financial statements for completeness and other accounting issues, be alert to any operational red flags and possible side-effects, and otherwise prevent post-closing surprises. Doing so can be well worth the effort and ultimately result in savings of time and money.

DOCUMENTATION OF PAST ACCOUNTING PRACTICES IS CRITICAL

There can be many potential disputes related to what exactly the company's past practices are and whether the proposed accounting as of the closing date is in accordance with past practices. In many transactions, the company's historical accounting practices are not formally documented in the purchase agreement. Rather, the past practices are commonly defined by using reference financial statements. Either way, the documentation by its nature can be incomplete because many accounting practices include estimates, which, in compliance with GAAP, require the application of judgment. This judgment as applied by company management is not always easily documented or communicated even when the seller discloses its various accounting practices and procedures. Any attempt to fully document the seller's historical accounting practices may end up falling short and cannot necessarily be single-outcome determinative for all accounting items. Certain accounting estimates are not necessarily easily documented and not all estimates lend themselves to the level of documentation that would be ideal from a post-closing purchase price adjustment perspective.

Notwithstanding, in an effort to minimize the impact of surprise post-closing disputes and adjustments, the parties can maximize their documentation position in addition to other potential mitigating measures. The parties can pay attention to the documentation issue as part of due diligence. That includes both sell-side due diligence and buy-side due diligence. In the case of the preparation of a sell-side financial package, the company can also disclose some of its accounting practices. In the case of the preparation of carve-out financial statements or a financial package, some of the estimation methodologies can be selected for easy documentation as long as a more mechanical approach is in accordance with GAAP. Ideally, the documentation should be prepared clearly and kept in a manner that ties to the final version of, for example, the carve-out financial statements.

In preparation for the transaction the seller can identify where accounting knowledge resides and what has already been documented. Similarly, post-closing, the buyer can source potentially relevant information from the accounting department's files and other sources. Sometimes past practices may not be clearly codified in the company's accounting department, but documentation exists elsewhere that supports the practices or provides bookends. For example, the sales department may very well track collectability in a manner that the accounting personnel relies on but does not keep in as much detail. Documentation can also exist at a group level.

The parties can also codify unwritten accounting practices that lend themselves to written descriptions and example calculations. The parties can even incorporate a documentation package as part of the contractually agreed upon past practices. An important consideration for the seller can be that it may lose undocumented knowledge after the closing. Even when creating completely buttoned-up documentation is not possible, the parties can benefit significantly by documenting the estimation process and any bookend considerations that narrow the range from all possible outcomes to a smaller set of outcomes. The documentation of a funnel, even if it does not result in single-point estimation, can help prevent an unexpected and broad difference in estimation methodologies that may otherwise drive a significant post-closing adjustment.

Practically, it is not uncommon to see the estimation process be somewhat iterative with multiple people involved and multiple calculations, without the company clearly documenting the calculation of the final amount. After the fact, it can significantly hamper the parties in their presentation to the accounting arbitrator if it is unclear which estimation documentation is final. In such instances, the parties could benefit from at least codifying the institutional knowledge that assists in identifying the support or, even better, taking the final documentation step and clearly tying the final document to the financial statements.

Similarly, in the case of converting the company's historical accounting from U.S. GAAP to IFRS (or vice versa), the process should be carefully documented. Ideally, the documentation should include a schedule that clearly ties original U.S. GAAP amounts to final IFRS amounts. If that transition is clearly documented and supported, the company's historical (original U.S. GAAP) documents can be used as step 1 in a two-step process to establish the historical accounting practices. Again, multiple draft versions that all deviate from the final version without bridge schedules can cause significant problems.

The outcome and conclusions included with the supporting documentation should match the amounts that the documentation is purported to support. This statement is not nearly as self-evident in practice as it may appear on paper. In real life, company accounting personnel who are preparing for a transaction may be very busy. The result is that accounts can get updated on-the-fly with the intent to update the supporting documentation at a later time or not at all in the case of a perceived self-evident update. Of course, accounting estimates tend to be both relatively more iterative in the manner in which they are derived and more likely to result in dispute. By the time the dispute is submitted to the arbitrator, there may be multiple versions of the supporting documentation, no documentation of the previous self-evident adjustments, and multiple theories promulgated by the parties. It can be critically important for supporting documentation to match the supported accounting entry or account.

THE PRE-CLOSING AND POST-CLOSING TEAMS

In many transactions, both the buyer and the seller will designate internal personnel to be responsible for the transaction or to assist with specific issues. In addition, the parties will commonly retain a variety of professionals throughout the transaction lifecycle.

The teams of people included in the pre-closing phase and the post-closing phase may largely overlap or they may be very different. The members of the pre-closing transaction team can include company personnel, investment bankers, transaction counsel, due diligence advisors, and others. The team works together in their various roles to accomplish the task of closing the transaction.

Post-closing, the pre-closing team may remain involved to a greater or lesser extent. The team can be supplemented or (partially) replaced by post-closing financial advisors to assist with the negotiation and any dispute. Litigation counsel may also be retained. Notably, the company may involuntarily lose some of the pre-closing advisors as conflicts of interest may preclude, for example, accountants on the due diligence team from remaining involved throughout the dispute phase.

Parties can disproportionately benefit from making sure that relevant information from the pre-closing phase is available to the team that manages the post-closing phase and the dispute process. For example, ready access to the data room, the identification of relevant side letters and other communications that provide context, and the availability of the relevant people to answer questions can make a real difference.

NEGOTIATION OF DISPUTED ITEMS PRIOR TO THE ACCOUNTING ARBITRATION

Typically, neither party to a transaction wants to be involved in a post-closing purchase price dispute arbitration. The arbitration, while generally less expensive than full-blown litigation, can still be expensive both in monetary terms and in terms of company personnel time.

An important step in attempting to potentially minimize the scope of the accounting arbitration is to resolve as many of the disputed items as possible in the negotiation phase. To get the maximum benefit of the negotiation it is critical to perform an appropriate assessment of each party's position on each potential disputed item.

The Resolution Matrix

A possible tool in objectively evaluating the potential disputed items is a resolution matrix. As a result of the absence of a liability question and the common lack of dependency between many potential disputed items, a resolution matrix can be particularly useful in preparing for a post-closing negotiation and in weighing the cost/benefit of a potential accounting arbitration.

The resolution matrix is used to slot the disputed items, based on the assessed relative strength of argument, along the potential resolution spectrum, ranging, for example, from "Strongly Favors Buyer" to "Strongly Favors Seller." The slotting is based on the assessment of each party's arguments and support for its positions for each disputed item, including accounting records, GAAP, and the purchase agreement. Thus, as the negotiation and the exchange of information progresses, items may move across the range.

The disciplined preparation of a resolution matrix may have the added benefit of allowing the buyer and the seller to see their own positions in an objective light. In preparing the proposed closing statement or objection notice, it is easy to get lost in the detail and lose sight of the core issues and arguments. It also allows the parties to evaluate the potential documentary support they can muster for their positions.

Sellers' (Sample) Resolution Matrix								
	Adjustment Item		Stongly Favors Seller	Favors Seller	Neutral	Favors Buyer	Stongly Favors Buyer	Notes
1	Inventory Existence	($205,000)				($205,000)		Historical shrinkage problems and well-controlled post-closing count.
2	Inventory Allowance	($600,000)		($600,000)				Inventory cleaned out prior year.
3	Deferred Rent	($800,000)	($720,000)				($80,000)	Failure to recognize under GAAP. Only NWC for current portion.
4	Accounts Receivable Allowance	$75,000			$75,000			Preliminary numbers needs updating. Can go either way.
5	*Et cetera*							
6								
7								
Totals		*($1,530,000)*	*($720,000)*	*($600,000)*	*$75,000*	*($205,000)*	*($80,000)*	

Sample Resolution Matrix

The resolution matrix shown here provides a view of the various disputed items with a total for each column that is slotted along the possible resolution spectrum. The adjustments with the lower likelihood of success in arbitration are often the items to try to settle through negotiation prior to arbitration. Another consideration is to attempt to resolve any smaller, less significant items prior to arbitration so that the company is not paying advisors and the accounting arbitrator to resolve items with minimal monetary impact. If both parties pursue this strategy, a narrowly tailored accounting arbitration, if any, can often be achieved.

The inherent limitation of the resolution matrix is that it is, of course, an imperfect estimation of how the disputed items will ultimately be resolved in arbitration. There may very well be surprises as the parties submit their support and the accounting arbitration proceeds resulting in a determination by an accounting arbitrator that may view the disputed items and strength of argument differently than one or both of the parties.

Negotiation of the Disputed Items

Once each of the parties has performed a critical assessment of its positions and those of the counterparty, they are ready to enter into negotiations to attempt to resolve as many of the disputed items as possible. As discussed earlier, if both parties focus on the likely outcomes for the potential disputed items—which may require rising above the resentment caused by perceived windfalls or inappropriate adjustments/objections by the counterparty—the parties can often resolve at least the relatively clear items as well as the smaller issues. Often, the parties may even be able to resolve larger items that are likely to result in an outcome within a relatively narrow and identifiable range.

Moreover, the self-assessment provided by the resolution matrix may provide a party with knowledge that it can use to its advantage. For example, if a party is negotiating an item that its assessment indicates it is likely to lose and it can get the other party to agree to a 50/50 split on the item, it could be considered a pre-arbitration win.

CHAPTER 11

Selection and Retention of an Accounting Arbitrator

Once a post-closing purchase price dispute reaches an impasse in the resolution of one or more disputed items, the parties move to the formal dispute resolution phase as provided for in the relevant purchase agreement (that is, an accounting arbitration—again, therein included for this book, both formal accounting arbitrations and expert determinations). The first order of business in this phase is to identify and engage a neutral/independent accounting arbitrator—the individual that will render a determination regarding the disputed item(s). Notably, accounting arbitrations generally take place before an individual accounting arbitrator as opposed to, for example, a three-member arbitration panel. The selection and retention of the accounting arbitrator includes a variety of considerations for the parties as well as the accounting arbitrator, including the terms of the purchase agreement, the qualifications and experience of the accounting arbitrator, and the terms of the accounting arbitrator's engagement.

TERMS OF THE PURCHASE AGREEMENT

Purchase agreements that include a purchase price dispute resolution provision can provide varying levels of detail regarding the process to be utilized by the parties for selecting and retaining an accounting arbitrator. While some purchase agreements include more procedural detail than others, many agreements include at least (i) a requirement for the parties to agree upon and engage the accounting arbitrator, (ii) a requirement for the parties to provide submissions to the arbitrator with supporting documentation for their positions, (iii) a requirement for the accounting arbitrator to render his determination within a certain timeframe, (iv) a statement that the accounting arbitrator's determination is final, binding, and conclusive, not appealable and not subject to further review, and (v) an allocation of the fees and expenses of the arbitrator. As it relates specifically to the selection of the accounting arbitrator, the parties can take a variety of different approaches in drafting the purchase agreement.

The parties may contractually provide for a specified individual or a list of individuals to serve in the capacity of the accounting arbitrator. The purchase agreement may also specify a firm or list of firms in order of priority. Notably, if the purchase agreement provides for a specific firm, the parties will still need to agree on an individual at that firm to serve as the accounting arbitrator. This often involves the consideration of several candidates from the named firm to narrow it down to an individual that both parties can agree upon to engage as the accounting arbitrator. Importantly, even if a specific firm or individual is named in the purchase agreement, their retention is not guaranteed as that firm or individual may have a conflict of interest and decline the engagement.

The parties may also provide for a procedure to arrive at the individual that will serve as the accounting arbitrator. For example, the parties can provide for a person to nominate five potential accounting arbitrators that meet certain criteria and that the parties can then narrow down through a procedure of vetoes or prioritization.

The parties can also provide for a mutually agreeable accountant to be appointed that is to be jointly selected by the parties post-closing without further detail. As long as the parties are still cordial when that time comes, this can work in practice. In many instances, however, the process has gotten so contentious that working together to select an accounting arbitrator can be difficult.

Either way, whether in advance through incorporation in the purchase agreement or after-the-fact because a specific individual is not directly or indirectly provided for in the purchase agreement, or if the pre-selected individuals are unwilling or unable to serve as the accounting arbitrator, the parties must identify someone to serve as the accounting arbitrator. The following section discusses factors that the parties can consider in evaluating potential candidates.

CONSIDERATION OF THE QUALIFICATIONS OF THE ACCOUNTING ARBITRATOR

The purchase agreement generally provides for the accounting arbitrator's determination to be final and binding on each of the disputed items with only few and narrow grounds available for appeal. Therefore, the selection of an appropriately qualified accountant to serve in the capacity of the accounting arbitrator is critical to the fair and complete resolution of the disputed items.

In evaluating potential accounting arbitrators, the parties may consider a variety of factors. Chief among them is often the selection of a licensed accounting professional (i.e., a certified public accountant (CPA)) who is experienced in resolving post-closing purchase price adjustment disputes. Notably, the role of the accounting arbitrator and the dispute process can be alien to CPAs without this experience as it is in many ways very different from many other accounting engagements. A purchase price dispute arbitration involves understanding both parties' positions and weighing the support for those positions within the bounds of the applicable purchase agreement culminating in an arbitration award. There will typically be various submissions to the accounting arbitrator and potentially a hearing.

Moreover, the accounting arbitrator should be prepared to obtain additional information through clearly formulated document requests and arbitrator interrogatories.

Experience with the role and process may also safeguard the parties against potentially inaccurate outcomes. While a CPA that is not experienced in resolving purchase price dispute arbitrations may have the appropriate accounting knowledge (although that is not necessarily the case), such professionals will most likely not be familiar with the accounting arbitration process, which can result in an inefficient or incomplete process, or in the worst case an unfair process. For example, an inexperienced individual may overstep the scope of his/her engagement or may be persuaded by a flurry of loosely related arguments that are irrelevant from an accounting perspective. In doing so, the result may be a determination that is not firmly founded in the terms of the purchase agreement and/or the accounting arbitrator's retention agreement.

Many buyers and sellers in M&A transactions have never been involved in a purchase price dispute arbitration. Moreover, although they are typically professionally assisted by attorneys and accountants, those professionals themselves may have only limited experience with the process. An appropriately experienced CPA is well suited to knowledgably guide the parties through the process and to reach the appropriate determination regarding the disputed items.

Finally, in many instances, experience in the specific industry of the company is not required. In most post-closing purchase price disputes, the vast majority of the amounts in dispute are those involving a degree of estimation and judgment such as the allowance for doubtful accounts, inventory allowance, and similar items. The accounting guidance relevant to such items is mostly applicable across industries. Notwithstanding, there are certain industries and disputed items that can benefit from specific industry knowledge. For example, oil and gas companies can be subject to unique disputed items and accounting considerations.

ENGAGEMENT OF THE ACCOUNTING ARBITRATOR

Once the parties have identified the individual to serve as the accounting arbitrator, the parties can formally engage him or her. The engagement letter provides the formal written agreement between the parties to the dispute and the accounting arbitrator. Some of the items that can be incorporated into the engagement letter are discussed in the following.

Transaction, Parties, Purchase Agreement, and Scope

The engagement letter, of course, identifies the transaction and the parties. The engagement letter also commonly lists counsel for each of the parties and contains an affirmative statement authorizing the accounting arbitrator to communicate with each party's respective counsel.

The letter also identifies the purchase agreement and commonly references the provisions that govern the purchase price adjustment process and the dispute resolution process. Such references can be limited to the identification of the relevant sections. In other instances, the engagement letter can also include abstracts of the purchase agreement, including, for example, any transaction-specific measures.

The engagement letter may also include a listing of disputed items in greater or lesser detail as well as the arbitrator's mandate in resolving those items. For example, the arbitrator may be constricted to the range as set by the positions of the parties in reaching his determination. Also, sometimes the parties find it useful for context and clarity if all adjustments, including the adjustments already agreed to between the parties prior to the arbitration, are listed in the engagement letter.

Conflict Check and Disclosures

Prior to retention it is very important for the potential accounting arbitrator to perform a conflict check. First identifying a (potential) conflict after the parties have spent a significant amount of resources on the procedures or even after the award is, of course, extremely undesirable. Once the conflict check has been performed, the individual or his or her firm may determine that there is a business or legal conflict and that the identified individual cannot be retained to serve as the accounting arbitrator.

The accounting arbitrator's conflict check may also return relationships or (past) engagements that the accountant does not consider to be direct conflicts that would prevent the acceptance of the arbitration engagement. We urge the accounting arbitrator to err on the side of caution in order to prevent even the perception of a conflict of interest or partiality during the proceedings or after-the-fact. Even in the absence of a legal conflict, certain relationships that were identified but undisclosed to the parties, based on the accounting arbitrator's belief that such relationships are not strictly relevant to the specific dispute, may leave the accounting arbitrator open to later criticism and/or challenge of the arbitration award.

In general, an important consideration for the candidate, his or her firm, and the parties is that the accounting arbitrator should be independent and impartial in appearance and in fact. The potential arbitrator may want to err on the side of caution and disclose the existence of perceivably relevant relationships and engagements to the parties. Those disclosures can be included in the engagement letter. Notwithstanding, the potential accounting arbitrator may have to abide by confidentiality requirements that preclude him from making such disclosures. The combination of erring on the side of caution regarding both potential conflicts of interest and confidentiality requirements may result in the accounting arbitrator passing on an attractive engagement. That should, of course, be both professionally and ethically preferable to even a marginally justifiable claim by one of the parties that the arbitrator lacked independence.

As they should be, post-award claims of partiality are relatively rare in the context of accounting arbitrations. On occasion, however, a party may perceive a lack of independence after-the-fact. In such instances, the arbitrator will have been well-served by his or her professional caution and the vigorous safeguarding of his or her independence and impartiality in the consideration and execution of all accepted arbitration engagements.

Limitation on *Ex Parte* Communications

The accounting arbitrator can also be potentially justifiably accused of improprieties if he or she were to engage in *ex parte* communications with one of the parties to the dispute. There is rarely, if ever, a reason to conduct substantive communications with only one party to the dispute.

Contractually limiting the communications to those that involve all parties for all but mundane administrative items such as, for example, receipt of funds confirmations, avoids misunderstandings as a result of, for example, an indirect relaying of communicated information (because all parties are hearing the same information at the same time). They also prevent the arbitrator from being swayed by arguments set forth by one of the parties that could have easily been rebutted by the other party if only they had been aware of the communication.

Accordingly, engagement letters commonly prohibit *ex parte* communications except for limited administrative issues. Notwithstanding, the protocol for the parties' written submissions often requires the submissions to be sent to the arbitrator by each party without copying the other party. The arbitrator then forwards the submissions when he or she has received them from both parties in order to facilitate simultaneous cross-submission, that is, without one of the parties having the benefit of receiving a submission from the counterparty prior to submitting its own.

The Arbitration Schedule

It is often helpful to include an arbitration schedule in the engagement letter that codifies the various agreed upon due dates for submissions and the overall content and length of the process. A commonly used schedule format may include the start date as the date the engagement letter is signed with all other dates based on counting a specified number of days from the start date. If the engagement letter does not include accompanying calendar dates, the arbitrator can subsequently distribute a list of the calendar dates corresponding to the day counts in order to prevent misunderstandings.

If it is not possible, or desired, to include the schedule in the engagement letter, the parties can perhaps discuss and include the general parameters of the desired arbitration process and anticipated schedule, such as the number and types of submissions, approximate timeframes, and/or whether there will be a hearing.

Generally, an accounting arbitrator will attempt to accommodate the arbitration format and schedule desired by the parties as long as it results in the accounting arbitrator receiving sufficient and timely information to appropriately fulfill the engagement.

Example: Sample Arbitration Schedule

Activity	Timeline
The Parties execute the engagement letter and pay retainers.	Arbitration Start Date
Each Party submits its initial brief to the accounting arbitrator, including all relevant data, reports, correspondence, affidavits, exhibits, and other documentation, in support of its positions.	14 calendar days from Arbitration Start Date
Each Party submits its rebuttal brief to the accounting arbitrator.	28 calendar days from Arbitration Start Date

(*continued*)

Activity	Timeline
The Accounting Arbitrator submits document requests and interrogatories to the Parties (if necessary).	35 calendar days from Arbitration Start Date
Each Party submits its responses to the Accounting Arbitrator's document requests and interrogatories.	45 calendar days from Arbitration Start Date
The Accounting Arbitrator's final award is issued.	60 calendar days from Arbitration Start Date

Separately, the engagement letter can also provide for the consequences of a party failing to timely make one or more of the submissions. For example, the engagement letter may provide that if a party fails to make any submission on a timely basis, the accounting arbitrator may render his determination based solely on the information that has been timely submitted.

Award and Fee Allocation

The engagement letter can provide for the agreed-upon form and content of the final determination of the accounting arbitrator. Such final determinations can be provided at varying levels of detail, ranging from a single-page award letter, to a lengthy, fully reasoned award. The award may also include an allocation of the arbitrator's fees in accordance with the purchase agreement. The arbitration award is discussed in further detail in Chapter 14.

Scope Limitations and the Role and Rights of the Arbitrator

In order to formally safeguard the understanding of the role and rights of the accounting arbitrator in the context of a purchase price dispute arbitration, the accounting arbitrator may include some specific provisions in the engagement letter.

In an abundance of caution, the arbitrator—as an accountant—may, for example, include a provision in the engagement letter that the resolution of the purchase price dispute does not constitute an audit or attestation engagement. Similarly, the independent accountant may include language that the rendering of his or her conclusion does not constitute a legal opinion. The accountant may also preemptively reserve the right to retain counsel to assist him or her at the expense of the parties.

The accountant may also include a provision that formal rules of evidence do not apply and that he or she will determine the weight to be given to any documents or other evidence. Legal rules of evidence are typically not implemented in accounting arbitrations. In practice, that means that the accounting arbitrator can request, receive, and weigh the information and documentation received in his or her sole discretion and need not consider, for example, the legal admissibility or confirm the authenticity of submitted documentation.

Finally, regardless of the purchase agreement's choice for accounting arbitration or expert determination, the independent accountant—who is resolving a dispute between the parties—may deem it prudent to incorporate in the engagement letter that some of the protections that are afforded to arbitrators under the law apply to him or her.

CHAPTER 12

The Parties' Initial Submissions

Once the accounting arbitrator is selected and engaged, the arbitration process can begin. The accounting arbitrator will ultimately render a determination on the appropriate amount for each of the items in dispute and will be looking for documentation and information to be able to establish what that appropriate amount should be considering both the applicable standard, such as *past practices in accordance with GAAP,* and the other pertinent provisions of the relevant agreements.

As previously discussed, the accounting arbitration is governed by both the purchase agreement, which generally sets the parameters of both the relevant post-closing calculations and the dispute resolution process, and the accounting arbitrator's retention agreement, which generally further details the scope of the procedures and the accounting arbitrator's overall retention.

Accordingly, the parties to an accounting arbitration should generally seek to provide documentation and information in support of their respective position(s) in a manner that is aligned with the provisions of the purchase agreement. The number of opportunities to do so is based on the specific process agreed upon between the parties and the accounting arbitrator. A common accounting arbitration process includes the following:

- *Initial Submission*—a detailed discussion of a party's position on each of the disputed items and why that party's position should be accepted.
- *Rebuttal Submission*—a direct rebuttal to the opposing party's initial submission, discussing why the opposing party's positions are incorrect.

- *Accounting Arbitrator Interrogatories and Document Requests*—after receiving the initial and rebuttal submissions the accounting arbitrator may, and typically does, have several clarifying questions and/or requests for additional documentation from the parties.
- *Responses to the Accounting Arbitrator Interrogatories and Document Requests*—the parties' opportunity to respond to the arbitrator's interrogatories and document requests.
- *Arbitration Award*—the report from the accounting arbitrator providing the final and binding determination for each of the disputed items.

While this schedule is very common, the process can be altered in any reasonable manner desired by the parties that results in the accounting arbitrator receiving the information necessary to reach a conclusion on the disputed items. Ultimately, the process is the parties' process.

The sample arbitration process above does not include a hearing. An in-person hearing is a part of some accounting arbitrations, but hearings are generally not the norm due to the time and expense involved in conducting a hearing. In many situations, the parties will be able to adequately discuss and support their positions in their submissions and a hearing may not add new information for the arbitrator to consider. Moreover, in many situations, the accounting arbitrator will be comfortable deciding the issues based on the information received through the parties' submissions. Notwithstanding, there are accounting arbitrations for which a hearing may be advisable (e.g., unusually complex disputed items) or may be desired by the parties for other reasons. In such cases, the hearing would typically be scheduled for a date after the parties provide their responses to the accounting arbitrator's interrogatories and document requests. Hearings are discussed later in Chapter 13.

After receiving the information and documentation from the parties, the accounting arbitrator will review and analyze it and, ultimately, formalize determinations on each of the disputed items. It is important for each of the parties to appropriately educate the arbitrator on their respective positions on each of the disputed items. It is, of course, also crucially important that the accounting arbitrator appropriately considers the information and documentation received, the relevant purchase agreement provisions, and the relevant accounting guidance in rendering a determination on each of the disputed items.

Therefore, the parties should generally aim to provide sufficient discussion and support for their positions in the various submissions to the arbitrator. The importance of this is further highlighted by the fact that many disputed items are of a nature that involves some level of subjective judgment and estimation, which often require detailed discussion and support. As a result, success or failure on certain disputed items in an accounting arbitration may end up being directly related to the level of discussion and support provided by each party for its respective positions. In summary, the importance of the quality and content of the various accounting arbitration submissions cannot be overstated.

INTRODUCTION TO THE INITIAL SUBMISSIONS

The initial submissions are critical to educating the arbitrator about each party's positions on the disputed items. Each party should endeavor to fully discuss and fully support its position on each disputed item in the initial submission. The more complex and/or the more qualitative the accounting for the disputed item is, the more discussion and support are generally necessary to adequately educate the arbitrator regarding a party's position.

On occasion, some parties may implement a strategy of holding back information until the rebuttal submission in an attempt to gain a procedural advantage. Many purchase agreements limit the rebuttal submissions to rebuttal responses, and accompanying documentation, to the other party's initial submission only. Thus, the party holding back the information may, dependent on the counterparty's initial submission, not have an opportunity to present the information. If a party ends up submitting information in the rebuttal submission that may be considered outside of the appropriate scope, it risks, although rare, that the accounting arbitrator deems the information inappropriate in the context of a rebuttal and excludes it from consideration. Moreover, even if the accounting arbitrator considers the additional information, such a strategy will typically be ineffective. By means of example, the accounting arbitrator can use the interrogatories to solicit a reaction from the counterparty on the additional information.

Following are several items that are typically included in initial submissions across a variety of accounting arbitrations and disputed items:

- Background information on the transaction, the entities involved, and the dispute
- A discussion of unique accounting or business considerations regarding the company and its industry
- A discussion of the individual disputed items
- Supporting documentation, including transaction documents and exhibits
- References to authoritative literature

It is important to note that the accounting arbitrator will reach a determination on each disputed item individually. Therefore, no single disputed item should be ignored or addressed incompletely.

Initial submissions may also be accompanied by expert reports. We discuss the usage of expert reports and affidavits in Chapter 13.

BACKGROUND OF THE TRANSACTION AND THE DISPUTE

The initial submission is the first time the accounting arbitrator will be receiving detailed information about the transaction and the post-closing purchase price dispute that led to the arbitration proceeding. The parties have been involved in the transaction since pre-closing negotiations began, typically many months ago, through the post-closing purchase price adjustment phase and now into the purchase price dispute phase. It is easy to forget that the accounting arbitrator most likely knows very little, if anything, about the company involved, the purchase agreement, and the dispute. Therefore, it is advisable to provide some general background on the transaction and the dispute that led to the arbitration.

Examples of information to provide in this context include:

- A discussion regarding the basics of the transaction—was it a carve-out, did it involve an earn-out, and/or is there any other important information specific to the transaction? In fact, anything the parties would like the accounting arbitrator to know or understand about the transaction generally should be discussed in the initial submission. It is generally advisable to err on the side of providing more background information rather than less. This is each party's opportunity to tell their side of the background story.
- A discussion of the post-closing purchase price adjustment provisions of the purchase agreement and any unique aspects, such as any agreed-upon non-GAAP measures or any other unique purchase price adjustment provisions. Much of this information, while most likely available in the purchase agreement, is relevant to discuss in the initial submission.
- A discussion of any relevant information regarding the purchase price adjustment process leading up to the dispute. For example, the initial submission should generally describe the process followed by the parties, the objection notice issued, proposed adjustments resolved prior to the dispute, and other relevant information regarding adjustments to the purchase price. Often, the party proposing the adjustments to the purchase price (normally the buyer) proposes several adjustments for consideration by the other party (normally the seller). Certain adjustments may be

very straightforward and fact driven (e.g., the gross balance of the accounts receivable) rather than judgment driven (e.g., the allowance for doubtful accounts).

The transaction and dispute background is generally not ultimately determinative of a disputed item. The benefit of providing this information is that it sets the stage for the arbitrator. It provides what is often useful background information to more fully understand the company, the transaction, and the background of the various disputed items. This background section generally does not comprise an overly large portion of the initial submission, but sufficient, relevant information in this regard can be important to include.

UNIQUE ACCOUNTING OR INDUSTRY CONSIDERATIONS

The arbitrator may not have significant experience in the specific industry of the acquired entity. While this generally does not impede the accounting arbitrator's ability to appropriately resolve the dispute, in arriving at a determination the accountant will benefit from receiving industry-specific information that aids his or her understanding of the business and its accounting. It is therefore advisable to educate the arbitrator on any industry-specific, company-specific, and transaction-specific information that can impact the accounting.

GAAP contains some industry-specific accounting guidance, but in general, GAAP seeks to be broadly applicable by all companies. To achieve this, it provides significant freedom to companies to make accounting choices that best fit their circumstances. Thus, the facts and circumstances of the business and the company can be very important to the resolution of the disputed items. GAAP guidance may be general in nature, but there can nonetheless be unique considerations for each company. Such considerations can be as straightforward as information on the type of customers and their industry, which may provide background information on the methodology used by the company to determine the amount to be recorded for the allowance for doubtful accounts. There is generally more than one acceptable methodology for determining this contingency, including various iterations based on the aging of receivables and others based on alternative stratifications of the accounts receivable to quantify potential collection issues. Other unique accounting items can be much more complex. Whether straightforward or complex, the relevant accounting should be discussed in the initial submission either on an overall basis or related to specific disputed items if that is more appropriate.

Example: The Impact of Business Information on Accounting

- A company maintains a large inventory of older parts, equivalent to five to ten years of use based on recent usage history, to support certain equipment.
- Subsequent to closing, the buyer proposes a purchase price adjustment claiming that the acquired inventory included quantities of older items that should be considered excess and obsolete. Without further context, this may appear to be a textbook case of excess and/or obsolete inventory.
- The seller may, however, discuss the following background information in its initial submission:
  - The company sells and services (decades old) legacy equipment that is still used by large institutional companies and government entities to postpone or avoid conversion.
  - The parts kept in inventory by the company are no longer generally available in the market. When they are available the price is up to ten times the cost carried on the company's books for similar items.
  - If the company runs out of a specific part and it is no longer available from any source, the part must be custom made at significant cost, including costs to create the mold and then manufacture the parts.
  - Importantly, the company's service contracts require it to provide customers with replacement parts for the contractual service period. If the company does not have the part

in stock and must have it custom made, it has no way of recouping the increased costs under the service contract. In addition, if the part cannot be made or purchased, the company will be in breach of its service contracts and will need to refund a portion of the service contract fee.

- Sellers' discussion of the circumstances can put the company inventory in a different light for the accounting arbitrator. Is the inventory of parts actually excess and/or obsolete based on the unique considerations of the company? If so, to what extent? Without discussing such unique characteristics, the arbitrator may not be aware of the underlying business issues that should be considered.

DISCUSSION OF INDIVIDUAL DISPUTED ITEMS

After the parties have provided some background on the transaction and discussed any unique transaction or company characteristics, it is time to deal with the heart of the matter—the specific disputed items. In deciding how detailed of a discussion to present regarding the various disputed items in the initial submission, keep in mind that the initial submission is the accounting arbitrator's first introduction to the disputed items. Therefore, providing more detail is generally advisable, including a full discussion of each disputed purchase price adjustment component.

Fully discussing each disputed item should generally include fully communicating the information that each party feels is persuasive and supportive of its position. The information should, at least, be sufficient to support the accounting arbitrator ruling in the submitting party's favor. That generally means providing the accounting arbitrator with sufficient information to understand each disputed item, including:

- A description of the specific item in dispute
- The proposed amount for the specific disputed item
- References to accounting guidance (e.g., specific GAAP references) relevant to the specific disputed item

- References to any purchase agreement provisions relevant to the specific disputed item
- A discussion of why, from a factual, accounting, and contractual perspective, a particular party's position is correct and, perhaps, pre-emptively why the opposing party's position cannot be correct
- Supporting documents for the respective party's reasoning and position on the specific disputed items
- A conclusion that ties back to the requirements of the purchase agreement (e.g., *past practices in accordance with GAAP*)

For most disputed items, the above information will provide a well-rounded and supported discussion. By failing to provide such information, the parties may be, intentionally or not, leaving it up to the arbitrator to identify the relevant accounting guidance, the relevant purchase agreement provisions, and necessary supporting documentation. While it is not advisable to omit potentially relevant information from the initial submission, it is also not advisable to go with an everything-but-the-kitchen-sink approach. Information that is not directly related to the appropriate accounting for, or calculation of, the disputed items or relevant to providing the accounting arbitrator a clear understanding of the transaction and other relevant context should generally be avoided. The submission of large swaths of apparently unrelated data without providing context is generally counterproductive. This is not intended to suggest that the parties should hold back information from the initial submission as a cost-saving measure or with the expectation that such information could be brought into the rebuttal submission if needed. Again, the rebuttal submission is generally intended to rebut the issues raised by the other party. It is generally not an opportunity to more fully discuss and support a party's own arguments.

Although factual context and the documentation to support it can be highly relevant, the supporting documentation may not be available to one of the parties. Notwithstanding, the party lacking the supporting documentations can still broach the topic. If a party cannot fully support its statements, because it does not have access to certain documentation, it can simply say so and discuss why it anticipates the documentation supporting its position. The accounting arbitrator may request the documentation from the other party. We discuss the supporting documentation in more detail ahead.

An accounting arbitration can involve parties with very strong feelings about the counterparty and its post-closing behavior. Despite the souring of the relationship, derogatory comments about the counterparty that appear to serve no other purpose than allowing the party an opportunity to vent are generally not productive. An accounting arbitrator seeks to make an independent determination on disputed accounting items in the context of a purchase agreement. The accounting arbitrator is not a court of equity that finds liability and assigns damages related to a variety of causes of actions and allegations.

Also, the inclusion of extensive case law is generally unnecessary. For example, a party does not need to support its interpretation of GAAP with a cite to case law. Rather, it can simply rely on GAAP. The dispute is being brought before an accounting arbitrator for a reason—because it is related to the appropriate *accounting* for the disputed items.

Finally, the accounting arbitrator performs his/her analysis in the context of the provisions of the purchase agreement. It is generally important that the parties include a conclusion on each disputed item that ties back to that agreement. By means of example, a party can conclude its discussion of a particular disputed item with a statement that its interpretation deviates from historical accounting practices because those practices do not comport with GAAP.

SUPPORTING DOCUMENTATION

The parties are often very familiar with the available population of supporting documentation for the disputed items. Each party should generally attempt to proactively provide sufficient documentation with its initial submission to support its position on each of the disputed items.

For example, for a disputed item related to excess inventory, typical supporting documentation might include historical sales or usage information for the inventory items in question. Of course, there may be information in addition to the historical usage data that would provide the arbitrator with a better understanding of the current and future expected usage given the specific company, such as documentation regarding product improvements or a new sales channel. If that information is not provided, the accounting arbitrator may make a determination that, unbeknownst to the accounting arbitrator, is not fully informed. Moreover, if the accounting arbitrator is not made aware of such factors altogether, he or she is unlikely to spontaneously request that additional, specific supporting documentation. In such a situation, the party or parties may have lost the opportunity to provide relevant documentation for consideration by the arbitrator. Again, in such situations, the accounting arbitrator may unknowingly end up making a determination that is not fully informed.

The previous scenario is but one example of the importance of supporting documentation. It is one thing for a party to explain why its position is correct; it is another to provide an appropriate level of documentation supporting that position. The parties should strive, when possible, to include both. Supporting documentation or calculations that result in an amount that is supported by the purchase agreement and the relevant accounting guidance are very persuasive.

Examples of supporting documentation vary greatly and depend on the specific disputed item as well as the facts and circumstances of the case. Supporting documentation can include, for example:

- Documents reflecting the company's accounting policies
- Disputed item and purchase price adjustment calculations

- Trial balances and other accounting detail
- General ledger printouts providing specific transaction detail
- Information from human resources showing vacation day accruals and usage
- Accounts receivable aging and subsequent collections
- Inventory sales or usage history
- Inventory purchase history
- Inventory count sheets and procedures

Such information can be critical to supporting a party's position on each disputed item. This is not to say that providing more information is always desirable. The supporting documentation should be relevant to the specific disputed items being resolved by the accounting arbitrator.

Although, an accounting arbitration is not an audit and therefore GAAS standards do not generally apply, the GAAS concept of audit evidence can provide helpful context. AU-C 500 *Audit Evidence* discusses that audit evidence should be both sufficient and appropriate, with *sufficiency* being the measure of the quantity of evidence and *appropriateness* being the measure of the quality (relevance and reliability) of evidence.[1] In deciding on the volume and type of supporting documentation to provide in the initial submission (and in any submission to the accounting arbitrator), each party should consider the sufficiency, relevance, and reliability of the information to be provided.

As an example, providing a 50,000-line Excel file exported from the general ledger may provide a large quantity of general financial information about a company, but it is not necessarily relevant to a disputed item or items without an explanation. There should be a rationale for the supporting documentation being provided to the accounting arbitrator. Does the accounting arbitrator need such information to understand a party's position? How does the party intend for the accounting arbitrator to use such information? How does such information support a party's position on a particular disputed item? All of these questions are relevant considerations for supporting documentation. In the general ledger Excel file example, if it is relevant to a disputed item, it will generally serve a party well to explain to the accounting arbitrator how the information is relevant and how it should be applied.

REFERENCES TO AUTHORITATIVE GUIDANCE

Parties can disagree on the correct application of GAAP, especially in areas requiring subjective judgment. It is therefore important for each party to clearly discuss its application of GAAP, including how the proposed application complies with the terms of the purchase agreement. References to specific GAAP literature are also advisable and can assist the accounting arbitrator in reviewing and understanding a party's position. Chapter 5 discusses the formula for quantifying the net working capital as of the closing date that is contained in many purchase agreements (i.e., *past practices in accordance with GAAP*). That provision, or the alternative included in the purchase agreement at issue, should guide each party's references to GAAP guidance in support of its positions. Notably, in addition to references to the authoritative guidance included with the ASC, there are also, for example, interpretative guides issued by the AICPA on various industry topics and complex accounting topics. Those are also good resources to use as references, if relevant.

If the purchase agreement requires the determination of the net working capital to comport with *past practices in accordance with GAAP*, all included items are required to be in accordance with GAAP unless otherwise agreed to by the parties through, for example, a transaction-specific measure. As discussed in Chapter 5, an important concept to remember in the context of many purchase agreements and that formula is that GAAP trumps consistency. In other words, consistently wrong from a GAAP perspective is still wrong and an inappropriate basis for a purchase price adjustment. A non-GAAP accounting estimate will not be acceptable simply because it was consistently applied in the years leading up to the transaction (again, unless such treatment is accepted through a purchase agreement provision). Again, the parties should support their conclusions and tie them back to the purchase agreement. So in the situation that a party believes a historical practice is not compliant with GAAP, it should generally state this belief and explain how the practice violates GAAP as opposed to simply submitting a calculation that deviates from the company's historical accounting practices.

After all, under the formula of *past practices in accordance with GAAP* an argument that boils down to preferred or better GAAP cannot support a deviation from past practices unless those past practices are not compliant with GAAP. If the purchase agreement is silent as to consistency, which is relatively rare, the ultimate determination can be much more difficult for the accounting arbitrator. Without a consistency requirement, the accounting arbitrator is left to determine which position is better GAAP, or otherwise preferable, dependent on the provisions of the purchase agreement. Such a determination can also benefit from sufficient and appropriate supporting information provided by the parties.

Barring a GAAP noncompliance issue, consistency can be a primary issue in dispute, especially when there is more than one GAAP compliant application. Consistency is a critical component for the consideration of disputed items involving GAAP with more than one acceptable application, such as, for example, establishing the allowance for doubtful accounts or inventory reserves. Nonetheless, disputes often arise related to such items due to a party's preference for one GAAP compliant methodology over another GAAP compliant methodology. Those disputes can take various forms. In some cases, a buyer arguing against the methodology consistently applied by the seller is doing so because it believes its proposed approach results in a more accurate estimate (i.e., "better GAAP") of future activity (e.g., accounts receivable collectability or inventory usage). In other cases, the buyer arguing against the methodology consistently applied by the seller is doing so simply out of preference for the methodology it uses across its company. For example, the buyer may argue that the seller's consistent use of a three-year usage limit to identify excess inventory is too long and it prefers a two-year usage limit, which it uses throughout its group, claiming that limit is more conservative and more reflective of changing technology. Both approaches may be perfectly acceptable under GAAP, and if so, the consistency requirement would be in favor of the seller's use of the three-year usage limit.

The terms of the relevant purchase agreement are critical in such cases. If the purchase agreement requires consistency in the application of GAAP, the notion of "better GAAP" may support the permissibility of a change in accounting under GAAP, but it cannot support a departure from *past practices in accordance with GAAP*.

GIVE THE ARBITRATOR OPTIONS

One final topic regarding initial submissions (which also applies to rebuttal submissions) is that for certain disputed items it may make sense to give the arbitrator options in reaching a determination. As the accounting arbitration does not involve a liability/damages two-step in front of a jury, the parties generally need to be less concerned that an extensive discussion of the counterparty's implementation of its approach on a particular disputed item, including perhaps an alternative calculation, will be viewed as an admission that the counterparty's approach is correct. It is often perfectly acceptable for a party to argue, for example, that (i) the counterparty's approach is in violation of GAAP and that (ii) if it were not in violation GAAP, which it is, the outcome of the calculation should be $1 million and not $2 million as calculated by the counterparty. Moreover, in a situation where the accounting arbitrator concludes that the approach at issue is in accordance with GAAP but the implementation of the calculation is not correct, the arbitrator will generally not—as may be the case under certain circumstances in civil litigation—conclude that the appropriate amount has not been provided and that therefore no amount can be awarded on that disputed item. Rather, the accounting arbitrator, who is an accounting expert, may simply arrive at the appropriate amount—within the boundaries of the governing agreements—through analysis of the provided documentation or request supplemental information. Indeed, providing the accounting arbitrator with information on various alternative scenarios across disputed items can be a beneficial strategy.

Moreover, let's assume, for example, a matter in which one party believes that the inventory allowance should be $1 million and the other party believes the inventory allowance should be $5 million. Neither party, if their own approach were to be found incorrect, would want the arbitrator to rule totally in the opposing party's favor because that would result in a $4 million loss. Thus, if there is an alternative position that may mitigate the impact of an adverse ruling, such as if a party has secondary arguments for a $3 million inventory allowance, it can be beneficial to explicitly provide such an alternative to the accounting arbitrator. Importantly, even both parties arguing $3 million secondary positions does not mean that the accounting arbitrator can or will simply default to that outcome.

In the example, the dispute may relate to excess inventory. The party arguing for a $1 million inventory allowance may not have included any amount for excess inventory and can take the position that there is none (note: the $1 million allowance could be for obsolescence). That party can secondarily argue that if the counterparty's position of excess inventory has merit, which it does not, the counterparty implemented it incorrectly. It can then proceed to perform an alternative calculation that shows that even in the event the arbitrator finds excess inventory, the appropriate inventory allowance would only be $3 million. Such an argument can be helpful in minimizing the loss in the event the accounting arbitrator does not agree with a party's primary position.

Notwithstanding, the accounting arbitrator still has to fully consider the disputed item, including the parties' primary positions, and arrive at the appropriate conclusion. In the example, the conclusion may be an allowance of $1 million, $3 million, $5 million, or some other amount in accordance with the purchase agreement.

CONCLUSION

Prior to receiving the initial submissions, the accounting arbitrator will know little, if anything, about the company involved or the specific disputed items being submitted by the parties for resolution. The initial submission is each party's first and potentially only opportunity to fully discuss and support its positions on the disputed items. The initial submission should be well organized and thorough in its presentation of the information, and sufficient to educate the accounting arbitrator regarding the relevant aspects of the transaction, the business, and the disputed items.

NOTE

1. *See* AU-C Section 500.05–.06.

CHAPTER 13

Further Submissions, Proceedings, and Considerations

Subsequent to the initial submissions, the parties typically have an opportunity to send rebuttal submissions, which we discuss here. In addition, this chapter will discuss other aspects of the parties' submissions and the arbitration process including the use of experts by the parties, the accounting arbitrator's requests and the responses thereto, and the possibility of a hearing.

REBUTTAL SUBMISSIONS

The initial submission is each party's opportunity to affirmatively state its position; the rebuttal submission is each party's opportunity to tell the accounting arbitrator why the positions presented by the opposing party are incorrect. In the initial submission, each party explains why it is correct on each of the disputed items and provides support for its positions. The parties are also educating the arbitrator about the transaction, the company, the industry, and any unique entity or transaction considerations. In the rebuttal submissions, there is normally no need to provide background on the transaction, the industry, the company, and so forth. On occasion, the rebuttal will need to include additional detail regarding the transaction, the company, or the industry, if necessary to fully develop the rebuttal arguments.

Content of the Rebuttal Submission

The primary caveat with the rebuttal submission is that it should typically be limited to direct rebuttal arguments to the positions presented in the opposing party's initial submission. In other words, the rebuttal should not be used as a forum to raise new affirmative arguments for a party's own positions on the disputed items—that is the purpose of the initial submission. There is an element of fairness in providing for such a limitation in the purchase agreement. There is not necessarily an opportunity to rebut the rebuttal and, therefore, if one party introduces completely new proactive arguments for its own positions in its rebuttal submission, the opposing party is potentially unfairly precluded from responding. A rebuttal submission should also not be viewed as an opportunity to re-present a party's initial submission, although some of that will naturally occur in rebuttal to the opposing party's initial submission.

The rebuttal submission is commonly intended to be focused on why the opposing party is incorrect. So, for each disputed item, the rebuttal submission should explain and support why the opposing party's positions are wrong, including any documentation and references to relevant GAAP guidance and purchase agreement provisions supporting such conclusions. If fully and appropriately developed, rebuttal submissions can be as lengthy as the initial submissions because of the need to fully address the issues with the opposing party's positions.

The Rationale for Rebuttal Submissions

Rebuttal submissions provide the accounting arbitrator insight into relevant counterarguments to each party's positions on the disputed items. The rebuttal submission provides each party the opportunity to address the opposing party's arguments and to clarify or correct any identified errors in the opposing party's initial submission. Without rebuttal submissions, and for items the parties chose not to include, the parties would be effectively relying on the accounting arbitrator to spontaneously recognize the weaknesses in the initial submissions of the counterparty. Although such confidence can be justified in many instances as it relates to, for example, technical accounting guidance outside of the factual context, the parties would generally be well advised to err on the side caution and to provide rebuttal arguments.

In the rebuttal phase, it is advisable to include specific arguments and support for the rebuttal positions. The rebuttal arguments should generally be a direct rebuttal to the opposing party's positions. The accounting arbitrator is interested in receiving the opposing arguments to each party's positions, including appropriate supporting documentation. The rebuttal arguments should be just as well developed, thorough, and organized as the affirmative arguments in the initial submission. Taking the time to explain to the arbitrator why the opposing party is incorrect can be well worth it. The successful rebuttal of the other side's positions can greatly assist in prevailing in the accounting arbitration.

EXPERT REPORTS AND AFFIDAVITS

Depending on the complexity or nature of the disputed items, there are a few additional items the parties could consider including with the initial and/or rebuttal submissions. Some transactions, companies, and/or disputed items are sufficiently unique and complex that the parties' submissions could benefit or be further supported by specific information from company personnel, industry professionals, or others with relevant expertise including retained experts.

In addition to choosing which information to include in support of their position, the parties also have a choice as it relates to the form in which the information is submitted. The parties have more freedom in this regard in an accounting arbitration than, for example, in civil litigation as legal rules of evidence generally do not apply. By means of example, the parties generally retain accounting advisors who are experts in the application of GAAP, but who do not necessarily submit expert reports. The parties can incorporate opinions from the accounting expert in the body of their initial submission or they can submit expert reports as exhibits to those submissions.

Affidavits

In an accounting arbitration, affidavits or sworn statements of fact can be used to provide background information and support for a party's position on any number of issues, including historical accounting practices, management's plans for the business, and similar items. Of course, those items should be relevant to the proceedings at hand. The accounting arbitrator is focused on the scope of his engagement pursuant to the purchase agreement and his or her retention agreement. In other words, the accounting arbitrator seeks to arrive at the appropriate accounting treatment for the disputed items as opposed to, for example, weighing evidence to decide on liability. Although the content of statements of fact can be helpful, the form (e.g., affidavit versus summary exhibits) is in many situations of lesser relevance.

Affidavits that are factual and supported can be helpful in providing some level of additional information as well as information specific to the accounting for the disputed items. This type of information can be especially helpful to an arbitrator if it identifies and discusses verifiable information regarding the proposed accounting treatment or other factors relevant to the disputed item(s).

Affidavits that explain the process or context of, for example, accounting documentation or other issues discussed by a party are often most helpful to the accounting arbitrator. Such affidavits often take the form of a road map to a set of the target company's business records. An affidavit that is primarily conclusory in nature without any corroborating supporting documentation may in many situations be of limited relevance (even when signed). After all, the accounting arbitration process generally does not offer the counterparty the benefit of, for example, cross-examination and the accounting arbitrator will view it through a lens of professional skepticism.

In summary, affidavits can be used to provide some explanatory information regarding the company, the transaction, the disputed items, or other relevant topics. Affidavits from company personnel or others with direct knowledge of the company and/or the transaction can be a good source of complementary information that can be relevant to one or more of the disputed items. In practice, affidavits are rarely presented as or sufficient as standalone determinative support for specific disputed items.

Expert Reports—Accounting and Industry

The parties may retain one or more subject matter experts to assist them with the accounting arbitration. Commonly retained experts include accounting experts and industry experts. In utilizing the analysis by their experts, the parties generally have a choice between incorporating the information into their submissions or attaching expert reports as an exhibit. Again, the legal rules of evidence do not typically apply to accounting arbitrations, and expert reports are generally not a required part of submission in an accounting arbitration.

Accounting Experts Each party to an accounting arbitration typically engages an accounting expert/advisor to assist in formulating arguments, navigating the arbitration process, assisting in preparing submissions, and other tasks. The parties may also request of that accountant, or engage an additional accounting expert, to prepare an expert report on the application of relevant GAAP in general or in relation to specific disputed items.

As the accounting arbitrator is himself an accounting expert, including an expert report versus incorporating a GAAP discussion in the body of the submission is often a distinction without a difference. The arbitrator will generally focus on the merits of the GAAP arguments in the context of the issues at hand. In practice, the GAAP aspects of the matter are commonly included in the body of the party's submissions.

Notwithstanding, the preparation of an expert report may be attractive, for example, from a logistical perspective as it allows counsel to focus on the presentation of the facts and arguments of the parties while the accountant can work on the GAAP implications in parallel. The parties can use, for example, an initial submission format that consists of two separate reports: (i) an overview report prepared by the party and/or its counsel that provides the transaction background, the company information, and any relevant purchase agreement provision discussion and (ii) an expert report prepared by an accountant discussing the accounting aspects of the disputed items. The reports can be submitted together as a single initial submission with the company/counsel-prepared report making reference to the accounting expert's report. This is not necessarily common, or efficient as there will be some overlap, but it can be desirable to some parties because it results in the two parts being separately prepared by those most knowledgeable and experienced about the specific subject matter.

Industry Experts A report from an industry expert can add real value when it is related to a unique industry or technical topic that is relevant to a disputed item and not normally within an accounting arbitrator's area of expertise. The energy industry would be an example of an industry that has some unique industry aspects that can be explained by an industry expert. Similarly, a technology company may use an industry expert to explain its products or services and their market. Industry experts often provide information necessary for the accounting arbitrator to more fully understand specific industry issues that can impact the accounting.

For example, there is normally no need to have an accounting expert provide a report discussing general GAAP guidance related to inventory obsolescence. On the other hand, if there is some facet unique to either the company or industry that may impact the usefulness of the inventory in question, an industry expert report may very well be beneficial.

Analogous to the previous discussion, the parties may decide to include the information provided by the industry expert in the body of the initial submission or have him or her prepare a separate expert report. In the case of industry experts, there can be more of a distinguishable benefit derived from submitting a separate expert report as an exhibit to the initial submission, as opposed to simply incorporating the information in the initial submission.

INTERROGATORIES AND DOCUMENT REQUESTS

After receiving the initial and rebuttal submissions, the arbitrator and his or her team review and analyze those submissions to gain an understanding of the disputed items and the parties' positions and arguments. A typical accounting arbitration schedule provides a period for this review to be performed, after which the accounting arbitrator may submit interrogatories and/or document requests to the parties to attempt to gain further information or additional clarity regarding the disputed items. Such requests are submitted to the parties in written form and, if not already provided for in the schedule, provide for a deadline for the parties' responses to such requests.

In accounting arbitrations involving numerous and/or very complex disputed items, there can be more than one round of interrogatories and document requests as the accounting arbitrator and his or her team review the information provided by the parties. For example, the arbitrator may submit the first round of interrogatories and document requests and, depending upon the information and support provided, additional questions and needs for documentation may be identified.

Notwithstanding, the accounting arbitrator is generally not obligated to issue requests for additional information. As a result, it is not advisable for the parties to hold back information from their initial and rebuttal submissions in anticipation of forthcoming interrogatories and/or document requests from the accounting arbitrator, which may never materialize.

Arbitrators Should Carefully Craft Their Questions/Requests

In preparing the document requests and the interrogatories, an accounting arbitrator should proceed carefully. The arbitrator's requests may be the first significant communication that the parties receive from the arbitrator. As such, the parties can be tempted to over-analyze the language used by the arbitrator to glean insight into the arbitrator's thought process. Another reason to carefully craft the requests is to prevent ambiguity in the questions that can result in the parties providing other information than the arbitrator was seeking. This may result in the need for iterative requests and inefficiency.

The arbitrator should also generally make sure each party has an opportunity to weigh in on issues for which it has relevant information. For example, the arbitrator may ask a question regarding the post-closing sales and usage of inventory, which is most likely only answerable by the buyer. Notwithstanding, the arbitrator may still ask the seller, or at least give it an opportunity to respond to such a question.

That is not to say that the accounting arbitrator should not direct questions to a specific party. In fact, a typical list of interrogatories and document requests includes questions/requests to both parties as well as questions/requests to each party individually. Even in those instances, however, the instructions accompanying the interrogatories and requests commonly invite either party to respond to the questions/requests directed to the opposing party if the other party has information or an explanation responsive to the arbitrator's questions or requests. In doing so, both parties are provided an opportunity to respond to all interrogatories and document requests from the arbitrator. If a party believes a request by the arbitrator has been partially or in whole addressed in its previous submissions, the party can of course refer to those submissions.

The Parties' Responses to the Arbitrator's Questions/Requests

The parties should generally strive to answer the arbitrator's questions as completely and clearly as possible. The questions typically reflect areas where the arbitrator is not clear on a party's (or the parties') positions, the support provided, or both. In many accounting arbitrations, the responses to the arbitrator's interrogatories and document requests will be the final opportunity to provide information to the arbitrator. Submitted responses should therefore be as complete and comprehensive as possible. Of course, a party may not be in possession of certain requested information. There is nothing wrong with stating that fact. If known, it can be useful to the arbitrator to distinguish between information that does not exist and information that is not, or no longer, in the possession of the party.

Notwithstanding, the responses should also be narrowly focused on the specific question or request. The parties should not view the responses to interrogatories and document requests as an opportunity to bring in unsolicited new arguments for a party's position or against the opposing party's position. The accounting arbitrator is asking the questions of the parties because he or she is seeking additional information to more fully understand the disputed items or the parties' positions on the disputed items.

The arbitrator is also typically not asking the parties to re-argue their positions through the reiteration of previous arguments. If an argument has already been presented, the accounting arbitrator should be aware of the argument and consider it in his or her analysis.

HEARINGS

The example arbitration schedule discussed at the beginning of the previous chapter did not include a hearing because most accounting arbitrations do not include a hearing. This is generally because of the time and expense required to conduct a hearing and the lack of perceived benefit of hearings in most accounting arbitrations. A hearing can be expensive due to travel costs for the arbitrator, advisors for the parties, and the parties themselves. Also, if the initial and rebuttal submission are fully developed and supported, there is rarely a need for a hearing. Most post-closing purchase price disputes include accounting issues that are very familiar to an experienced accounting arbitrator. In most situations, the accounting arbitrator will be comfortable deciding the issues on the papers.

Notwithstanding the previous paragraph, accounting arbitrations can include hearings on occasion, most commonly at the request of the parties. In more limited circumstances, an accounting arbitrator may request a hearing. While an accounting arbitration hearing can be very formal and include common courtroom procedures, it is typically very different from, and much less formal than, one conducted in a courtroom. It typically does not include the normal courthouse trappings of court reporters, swearing in of witnesses, and other courtroom formalities.

A typical accounting arbitration hearing will generally last one day or less and will provide each party the opportunity to present their information and an opportunity to respond to the information presented by the opposing party. After the parties' presentations, there is commonly a period of time allocated for the accounting arbitrator to ask questions of the parties about the information presented during the hearing or in the parties' initial or rebuttal submissions. Once the question-and-answer session is concluded the hearing is ended. There are typically no determinations or resolutions communicated at the conclusion of the hearing. The hearing is typically intended to be an information presentation and gathering session; it is generally not intended to result in an immediate resolution of any disputed items.

Including a Hearing in an Accounting Arbitration

A hearing is generally not a required part of an accounting arbitration. There are three common ways in which a hearing becomes included in an accounting arbitration: (i) the parties request the hearing (either at the outset or at some point during the arbitration process), (ii) the accounting arbitrator requests a hearing, or (iii) the purchase agreement and/or retention agreement provide for a hearing as part of the purchase price dispute resolution procedures. Most commonly a hearing is included in the accounting arbitration process at the request of the parties at the outset and is incorporated into the anticipated arbitration schedule.

Even if the purchase agreement includes a provision that allows for a hearing as part of the purchase price dispute resolution process, the parties are not necessarily required to actually conduct it. In accordance with such a provision, however, a hearing will generally be held if only one of the parties desires one. That is not necessarily the case without such a provision.

If the purchase agreement does not provide for a hearing, the parties or the accounting arbitrator can often still request one. If the parties jointly request that the arbitrator schedule and conduct a hearing, the accounting arbitrator will normally agree to the hearing. After all, the parties likely have good reason to want a hearing in the context of their specific dispute. The hearing will allow for the presentation of information in a live format and a question-and-answer session that the parties apparently believe will be useful in deciding on the disputed items. If the accounting arbitrator requests a hearing, the parties will also typically agree. The right of the accounting arbitrator to request a hearing is often included in the engagement agreement with the parties.

Common Format of an Accounting Arbitration Hearing

As noted earlier, an accounting arbitration hearing is not generally held in accordance with the formal rules of a courtroom hearing. The arbitrator and the parties are generally free to create the format that best suits the needs of all involved. Some hearings are more formal proceedings; some are more like a meeting. This is not to say that accounting arbitration hearings are free of structure; it simply means that the parties and the arbitrator can set up the hearing procedures in a manner best suited to accomplish the goals of the meeting.

Creating the hearing format can be an iterative process between the parties and the arbitrator giving consideration to the desires and needs of all involved. The parties often defer to the experience of the arbitrator for the general format of the hearing, unless the parties (or their representatives) have strong feelings regarding the content or formality of the hearing.

In practice, many accounting arbitration hearings allow for presentations by each party, possibly followed by rebuttal presentations from each party, which are then followed by questions from the accounting arbitrator. In some instances, accounting arbitration hearings are very formal and include court reporters, swearing in of witnesses, and so on. Such formality is almost always at the request of the parties and is rare in practice. Regardless of the format or the formality of the hearing, legal rules of evidence generally do not apply.

In presiding over the hearing, the accounting arbitrator is generally responsible for keeping the hearing moving in the right direction and on schedule. The arbitrator can discuss hearing guidelines prior to the start of the hearing that include, for example, basic presentation parameters such as time limits, prohibition of interrupting the opposing party's presentation, and scheduled breaks and other housekeeping items.

Information Typically Presented in an Accounting Arbitration Hearing

The general scope and content of the presentations at an accounting arbitration hearing are typically agreed upon between the parties and the arbitrator in advance. For example, the parties may request a hearing before the accounting arbitrator to provide an opportunity to discuss the unique characteristics of the business and how that impacts the inventory valuation in dispute. Another example could be a case where the arbitrator has requested a hearing to hear arguments from the parties regarding certain disputed items that are very complex or involve unique provisions of the purchase agreement.

There is most often very little, if any, additional documentation provided at the hearing beyond a PowerPoint presentation or information requested by the accounting arbitrator. If documents are presented, the accounting arbitrator should guard against arbitration by ambush. Often, any additional documents are exchanged beforehand or, at the very least, exchanged in full afterwards. Finally, the hearing may result in additional interrogatories or document requests by the accounting arbitrator especially if new documentation is provided.

The hearing is generally not a forum for the accounting arbitrator to arrive at and share his conclusions on any of the disputed items. The hearing is an information presentation and gathering session for consideration by the arbitrator in reaching an ultimate determination on one or more of the disputed items. In other words, upon ending the hearing, the parties and the arbitrator go their separate ways pending the arbitrator's award at a later date.

CHAPTER 14

The Arbitration Award

The accounting arbitrator's determination or award can take various forms based on the wishes of the parties engaging the arbitrator. In addition to the form of the determination ultimately delivered to the parties, there are several considerations or expectations related to the arbitrator arriving at a determination on each of the disputed items that are discussed in more detail in this chapter, including that the arbitrator will:

- Perform his or her duties in a professional manner
- Follow the provisions of the purchase agreement
- Consider all evidence submitted by the parties
- Resolve all disputed items submitted
- Avoid partiality and a lack of independence

The role of the accounting arbitrator in rendering a determination on each of the disputed items should not be taken lightly. The amount in dispute is often significant to the parties; otherwise, the parties would not go through the trouble of engaging an accounting arbitrator to resolve the dispute. Rendering such a determination is not simply a matter of applying the accounting arbitrator's best judgment to each of the disputed items. It should involve the careful consideration of documentation and information submitted to the accounting arbitrator as well as the framework and provisions set forth in the purchase agreement and the accounting arbitrator's engagement agreement.

It is important for the arbitrator to be free of bias and independent of the parties. Actions of an arbitrator that call his or her independence into question or reflect an inappropriate bias can create highly undesirable results, potentially resulting in the overturning of an arbitration award.

This chapter discusses the approach the arbitrator can take in reaching a determination on the disputed items in a professional manner. We also discuss the various ways in which those conclusions can be communicated.

PROFESSIONAL STANDARDS

The accounting arbitrator and accounting advisors involved in the accounting arbitration are generally certified public accountants. As such they can be subject to various professional standards, including those promulgated by the AICPA (other professional standards may also be applicable). For example, the AICPA Statement on Standards for Consultancy Services No. 1 (CS Section 100) includes standards that are broadly applicable to, among other things, transaction services.

CS Section 100 includes standards for:

- *Professional competence.* Undertake only those professional services that the member or the member's firm can reasonably expect to be completed with professional competence.
- *Due professional care.* Exercise due professional care in the performance of professional services.
- *Planning and supervision.* Adequately plan and supervise the performance of professional services.
- *Sufficient relevant data.* Obtain sufficient relevant data to afford a reasonable basis for conclusions or recommendations in relation to any professional services performed.[1]

None of these standards should come as a surprise to the accounting arbitrator—the accounting arbitrator should be competent, perform the role with due professional care, appropriately plan the engagement and supervise any staff, and reach a reasonable supported determination. Anything less can sell the parties and the profession short.

APPLICABLE AGREEMENTS

The general procedures that govern the arbitration are commonly set forth in the purchase agreement (in varying degrees of detail) and the engagement letter. Many purchase agreement provisions in this regard are very similar, especially those related to the engagement of the accounting arbitrator, the submission of information to the arbitrator, and the requirement for the arbitrator to render a final and binding determination on the disputed items. Notwithstanding, the rendering of a determination may be precluded by issues that arise during the arbitration. For example, the accounting arbitrator's engagement letter may contain a provision that he or she may resign from the engagement under certain circumstances, such as a conflict of interest that arises or is only identified after acceptance of the engagement.

In addition to the procedural context, the purchase agreement also sets the contractual framework based on which the arbitrator should evaluate the parties' positions. Besides the common procedural requirements, a purchase agreement may include unique provisions related to the applicable GAAP and consistency requirements and/or non-GAAP measures to be used to determine net working capital as of the closing date. By means of example, the purchase agreement may require the various closing statements to be prepared based on *past practices in accordance with GAAP* and may also contain a non-GAAP transaction-specific adjustment that provides for an upper limit on the inventory allowance. The purchase agreement and engagement letter can also otherwise impose restrictions on the arbitrator. For example, the mandate of the arbitrator can be limited to deciding the disputed items within the range of values presented by the parties' opposing positions.

Using the previous example of the requirement to resolve the disputed item(s) within the range of the parties' positions, if the arbitrator's analysis were to show that the appropriate amount for a disputed item is outside this range, the arbitrator would nonetheless render a determination at the amount in the contractually permissible range that is closest to his determination as opposed to the amount that the arbitrator's analysis shows.

Transaction specific purchase agreement provisions can add an extra layer of complexity to the resolution of disputed items because they often deviate from GAAP. Some purchase agreements even include a detailed listing of specific adjustments or other calculations of components of the purchase price that should be considered if the disputed items are related to any such provisions.

It is therefore important that the accounting arbitrator be aware of the relevant provisions of the purchase agreement. To do so, the accounting arbitrator generally needs to carefully examine the purchase agreement for any provisions that are relevant to the resolution of the disputed items. While the specific purchase price adjustment and dispute resolution provisions are relevant, they are not necessarily the only relevant provisions. In fact, the purchase agreement may only devote a paragraph or two to the purchase price adjustment and dispute resolution process. Other sections of the purchase agreement, however, can also be relevant, such as, for example, the definitions, transaction-specific measures, and exhibits that present example calculations.

An accounting arbitrator should become well versed in and comfortable with the application of all of the provisions of the purchase agreement that have a bearing on the determination of the disputed items. Failing to appropriately consider the provisions of the purchase agreement can create a basis to challenge the accounting arbitrator's award. The provisions of the purchase agreement are generally a critical aspect for an accounting arbitrator to consider in arriving at his or her determination.

CONSIDERATION OF SUBMITTED INFORMATION

The parties rely on the accounting arbitrator to resolve their disputed items in a professional manner that results in a final and binding determination of such items, to be utilized in calculating the final purchase price and any resulting purchase price adjustment. The accounting arbitrator should recognize the significance of this process and the trust placed in him by the parties to render such a determination. The parties often expend significant effort and incur significant expenses both in preparing the information for the accounting arbitrator as well as in having him or her evaluate that information. The accounting arbitrator should at least endeavor to understand and assess all the arguments set forth by the parties and the documentation provided in support therefore.

That can be a straightforward task in a dispute with a limited scope and limited documentation. In many arbitrations, however, it is not uncommon for the information provided to be substantial in volume and detail, requiring a significant effort to review and analyze. Nonetheless, the accounting arbitrator should endeavor to appropriately review and analyze the submitted information, and not rely on inappropriate assumptions or preconceived notions to reach a determination on the disputed items. The accounting arbitrator should diligently resolve the disputed items presented and not take an inappropriate shortcut by, for example, applying inappropriate generalizations based on past engagements. Transactions and disputes often have unique elements that the accounting arbitrator should appropriately consider.

INDEPENDENCE AND IMPARTIALITY

Prior to the engagement, the arbitrator should perform a conflict check. Moreover, the arbitrator should maintain his or her independence and impartiality for the duration of the engagement. Indeed, the avoidance of inappropriate bias and conflicts of interest are important throughout the arbitration process both in fact and in appearance.

Maintaining freedom from conflicts of interest throughout the accounting arbitration may, of course, mean that the arbitrator has to refuse another engagement while the arbitration is going on if accepting that engagement would result in a conflict of interest. In addition, the arbitrator may become aware of relationships during the engagement that require disclosure to the parties in accordance with his or her engagement letter. In certain circumstances, the arbitrator may even have to resign from the engagement in accordance with his or her retention agreement.

Maintaining formal independence is not necessarily sufficient by itself. The arbitrator should also be free of inappropriate bias. The arbitrator should analyze the issues presented and render a determination in an impartial manner. Of course, the fact that the arbitrator ends up awarding one party significantly more than the other party is in itself not evidence of bias or partiality.

Notably, a lack of independence and the presence of inappropriate bias constitute two of relatively few ways in which an arbitration ruling can potentially be successfully challenged. Failing to maintain independence and/or introducing inappropriate bias into the arbitration can have significant consequences for the accounting arbitrator and the parties.

RESOLVE ALL DISPUTED ITEMS

It may seem obvious, but all disputed items submitted to the accounting arbitrator for resolution should generally be resolved by the accounting arbitrator. Indeed, even if the arguments and support presented by the parties are less than optimal, the accounting arbitrator is typically still contractually charged with resolving all of the disputed items. Again, the parties have brought their dispute to the accounting arbitrator for resolution, not for partial resolution. Portions of the dispute should generally not be left unresolved if at all possible.

In this regard, the accounting arbitrator will generally also need to separately analyze and reach a determination on each of the disputed items, which are typically to a large extent independent of each other, while avoiding incorporating any inappropriate preconceived notions into the process. Reliance on general notions or a lazy split-the-baby approach do not do the parties or the process justice. After all, if the parties would be satisfied with a 50/50 split of the disputed items, they could easily accomplish that result without an accounting arbitrator. In other words, the arbitrator should not normally attempt to arrive at an equal splitting of the award, nor should the arbitrator seek to apply more lenient judgment to a particular disputed item because he has ruled in favor of the other party on other disputed items. The goal of the accounting arbitration is to render a determination on each of the disputed items in accordance with the purchase agreement and the engagement agreement, not to appease one or both parties to the dispute or otherwise avoid ruling more in favor of one party.

Notwithstanding, an appropriate analysis of disputed items can, of course, by happenstance result in a near 50/50 outcome. There is nothing wrong with that per se, if it is arrived at as a consequence of the accounting arbitrator's analysis and determination on each of the disputed items. Unless the facts and circumstances of the case dictate otherwise—sometimes certain disputed items are intertwined—the arbitrator should generally resolve each of the disputed items independently of the others and on its own merits. Of course, the same standard of analysis and boundaries as set forth in the purchase agreement is likely applicable to each of the disputed items and the relevant facts may overlap.

That being said, many accounting arbitration awards end up somewhere in between the overall positions of the parties as a byproduct of the nature of the dispute. First, many disputed items are not "all or nothing" items. Rather, they are accounting estimates that are determined across a range and for which both parties may have taken positions beyond the opposite ends of the range. The answer arrived at by the accounting arbitrator is often somewhere between the two positions, but not necessarily in the middle. Moreover, in many situations the disputed items are relatively independent from each other, which often results in each of the parties being (partially) correct on at least some of the items. Again, the ultimate goal is an appropriate resolution of the disputed items. If that ends up being a near 50/50 split of the total amount in dispute, that should be a consequence of the process and the arbitrator's analysis, not his or her pre-meditated intent.

THE WEIGHT GIVEN TO EVIDENCE PROVIDED

The accounting arbitrator is generally the sole evaluator of the weight to provide to the information and documentation submitted by the parties as well as the arguments presented. Indeed, the accounting arbitrator's engagement letter may include, for example, a statement that he or she will be the sole judge of the weight given to any evidence submitted.

The documentation and information provided by the parties to the accounting arbitrator typically comprises the body of his or her knowledge on the specific facts and circumstances surrounding the disputed items in the matter at hand. In addition to such information, the accounting arbitrator may, of course, also consider overall documentation and information relevant to the matter, such as the purchase agreement, and other information such as relevant accounting literature (e.g., the FASB Accounting Standards Codification) in arriving at a conclusion on a disputed item and the overall dispute.

Notably, the two primary sources, information provided by the parties and the relevant guidance, comprise the vast majority of information considered by the accounting arbitrator. For example, many purchase agreements specifically restrict the accounting arbitrator from considering alternative sources of information. Purchase agreements can document such a restriction through a statement such as: "The Accountant's determination shall be based solely on (written) materials submitted by Buyer and Seller ... "

The information provided by the parties can be divided into three major categories:

- Initial and rebuttal submissions, including the various exhibits thereto (which may include affidavits and expert reports)
- Responses to the accounting arbitrator's interrogatories and document requests
- Information obtained at hearings including from presentations or statements by, for example, company personnel and retained experts

In analyzing the information received, the arbitrator will be required to determine the significance and applicability of that information to the disputed items and the impact on the resolution of the disputed items. Every accounting arbitration is different and there are no mechanical rules to apply in assessing the information provided. It is nonetheless the arbitrator's responsibility to make such determinations.

ALLOCATION OF THE FEES AND EXPENSES OF THE ACCOUNTING ARBITRATOR

If the purchase agreement calls for a 50/50 split of the arbitrator's fees and expenses (collectively, "fees" for purposes of this section), there is generally no need to include an allocation of fees in the arbitrator's report. If the purchase agreement calls for anything other than a 50/50 allocation, however, such as an inverse proportion calculation, the arbitrator's ruling will typically include the accounting arbitrator's determination of the disputed items as well as the allocation of fees between the parties.

Example: Inverse Proportion Fee Allocation

- The seller and the buyer go into the accounting arbitration with the following positions:
  - The seller claims buyer owes it a post-closing adjustment in an amount of $1 million.

  - The buyer claims seller owes it a post-closing adjustment in an amount of $10 million.
- The purchase agreement provides for the allocation of fees in inverse proportion to the party's success in the proceedings.
- The accounting arbitrator awards an adjustment of $9 million in the buyer's favor.
- The accounting arbitrator incurred fees of $250,000. The accounting arbitrator can calculate the allocation of fees:
  - The parties had $11 million in dispute ($10 million minus –$1 million).
  - The seller lost $10 million ($9 million award and loss of original –$1 million position) and is thus responsible for ($10 million/$11 million) * $250,000 = $227,272.73.
  - The buyer lost $1 million ($9 million award relative to original position of $10 million) and is thus responsible for ($1 million/$11 million) * $250,000 = $22,727.27.
- Assuming the fees of the accounting arbitrator were billed to and paid by the parties over the course of the arbitration on a 50/50 basis, the fee allocation is:
  - The seller has paid $125,000 (1/2 * $250,000) to the arbitrator, is responsible for $227,272.73, and should thus pay $102,272.77 to the buyer.
  - Upon receipt the buyer will have paid $22,727.27 ($125,000 to arbitrator minus $102,272.73 received from the seller).

If the purchase agreement calls for an allocation of fees on a basis other than 50/50, it also commonly calls for the fee allocation to be calculated by the arbitrator and presented in the award to avoid any disagreement between the parties.

TYPES OF ARBITRATION AWARDS

Thus far this chapter has focused on a variety of items relevant to an accounting arbitrator reaching an appropriate determination on the disputed items. Once the accounting arbitrator has reached an appropriate determination on each of the disputed items, the determination needs to be documented in a report to be delivered to the parties. The general form and content of the award varies greatly in the level of detail included, depending on the type of award desired by the parties. There are three common forms, or levels of detail, for an accounting arbitration award:

1. Fully reasoned award
2. Summary reasoned award
3. Summary award

The parties and the arbitrator generally will have agreed on the type of award to be provided during the engagement process. It is not necessary to have done so, but in doing so it ensures that all parties are on the same page as to form of the ultimate award to be delivered. There are a variety of reasons for selecting one form of award over another. Some are based on future needs, such as the potential need for more detail in the award because it may be helpful in anticipated follow-on litigation. Some are practical, such as a desire to just have the dollar amount of the award without any rationale, because the dispute is fairly straightforward. The formal difference between an expert determination and an accounting arbitration may also play a role in the selection of the type of award. Those and other considerations can be considered by the parties in deciding which form of award to request from the accounting arbitrator. In this section we will discuss various pros and cons for each form of award as well as some of the reasons certain types of awards are selected.

Fully Reasoned Award

A fully reasoned award is the most extensive of the three forms of arbitration awards and also generally the most expensive. This type of award will typically include a full discussion of the rationale behind the arbitrator's determination for each of the disputed items. Common sections in a fully reasoned award include:

- A brief discussion of the engagement of the arbitrator
- A summary presentation of the award, which is normally a table presenting the amounts proposed by each party for each disputed item, the arbitrator's determination for each disputed item, the award for each disputed item, and the overall award
- A brief (or longer if needed) discussion of the transaction background and any impact it has on the dispute and/or the determination of the disputed items
- A discussion of the various purchase agreement provisions that were relevant to the accounting arbitrator's engagement and the analysis and determination of the disputed items
- A very detailed discussion of each of the disputed items, typically including a description of the disputed item, a summary of the significant position/arguments put forth by each party regarding each of the disputed items, a discussion of the GAAP guidance and/or purchase agreement provisions relevant to the disputed item, a discussion of the rationale behind the arbitrator's determination, a discussion of the factors the arbitrator found relevant in reaching a determination, and a summary of the award for each disputed item
- An allocation of fees, if necessary
- An overall conclusion that may also include, for example, appropriate caveats restricting the use of the award
- Exhibits with calculations prepared by the arbitrator regarding the determinations on the disputed items

Clearly, this is a very detailed report that requires a significant amount of effort that is in addition to analyzing the submitted information in order to reach a determination on the disputed items. After all, for each disputed item, this form of award commonly provides a summary of the parties' positions as well as a detailed discussion of the rationale behind the arbitrator's determinations.

There are various reasons why this form of award may be selected by the parties. One of those reasons might be that the matter involves disputed items that are particularly complex or very significant in dollar amount. The parties may want to have a fully reasoned award to better understand and provide clarity regarding how the determination on each disputed item was reached.

In other instances, the accounting arbitration is only the first dispute to be resolved. There could be planned follow-on litigation related to representations and warranties or indemnities that may be impacted or supported by the determinations in the accounting arbitration. The additional detail provided by a fully reasoned award can be helpful in such cases.

Finally, the parties may believe that the requirement of a fully reasoned award forces the arbitrator to carefully think through all the issues involved as he or she prepares the award. The parties may want the arbitrator to prepare the fully reasoned award to reap the benefit of the disciplined process that must go into such an extensive documentation of the dispute resolution.

Summary Reasoned Award

The summary reasoned award is a very common form of award in accounting arbitrations. The summary reasoned award can be a good compromise between the fully reasoned award and the summary award, which undoubtedly contributes to its frequent selection. The fully reasoned award provides a significant level of detail that most parties do not require, while the summary award provides too little in the way of detail for many parties.

A typical summary reasoned award can include the following:

- A brief discussion of the engagement of the arbitrator
- A summary presentation of the award, which is normally a table presenting the amounts proposed by each party for

each disputed item, the arbitrator's determination for each disputed item, the award for each disputed item, and the overall award

- A brief discussion of the various purchase agreement provisions that were relevant to the accounting arbitrator's engagement and determination of the disputed items
- A summary-level discussion of each of the disputed items, typically including a description of the disputed item, a listing of the significant position/arguments put forth by each party regarding each of the disputed items, a brief mention of the GAAP guidance and/or purchase agreement provisions relevant to the disputed item, a listing of the factors the arbitrator found relevant in reaching a determination, and a summary of the award for this specific disputed item
- An allocation of fees, if necessary
- An overall conclusion that may also include, for example, appropriate caveats restricting the use of the award
- Exhibits with calculations prepared by the arbitrator regarding his determinations on the disputed items

This list looks very similar to the fully reasoned award, because the summary reasoned award is a condensed (i.e., summary version) of the fully reasoned award. The primary differences generally include the elimination of the discussion of the background of the transaction and the summarization of much of the award including the discussion of the disputed items. For example, the discussion of the disputed items is commonly reduced from a full, detailed discussion to a bullet point list. Moreover, in a fully reasoned award the arbitrator will typically discuss the factors he/she found relevant in reaching a determination. In a summary reasoned award, the arbitrator will simply list the factors most relevant to the determination. In addition, the summary reasoned award does not include a full discussion of each party's position on each disputed item; rather a summary (often a bullet point list) of the key positions/arguments from each party are included in the discussion of each disputed item.

The summary reasoned award is often an attractive option to the parties because of the cost savings and because it typically provides a sufficient level of detail for the parties to understand what factors underlie the arbitrator's determination of each disputed item, albeit at a summary level.

Summary Award

The summary award is the most basic form of an arbitration award. This form of award rarely exceeds a couple of pages and typically only includes a summary presentation of the award, such as a table presenting the amounts proposed by each party for each disputed item, the arbitrator's determination for each disputed item, and the overall award. This type of award also includes any necessary allocation of fees.

A summary award normally does not provide any discussion of the factors the accounting arbitrator found relevant in reaching a determination on the disputed items. In fact, the summary award often does not provide any discussion at all. It can literally be a table providing the award, an allocation of fees, and a caveat paragraph restricting the use of the award.

The parties often perceive a true summary award as not providing enough information. The parties generally have some level of interest in understanding how the arbitrator arrived at the determinations of the disputed items. This form of award is typically utilized or requested for accounting arbitrations having a very few, straightforward disputed items that are less significant in dollar amount.

NOTE

1. *See* AICPA Statement on Standards for Consulting Services No. 1, CS Section 100, at ¶.06.

PART Four

The Disputed Items

CHAPTER 15

Overview of Disputed Items

In this chapter, we provide an overview of common categories and causes of disputed items. Again, given the prevalence of net working capital–based purchase price adjustment mechanisms and disputes, the discussion is primarily focused on net working capital related disputed items. As is common in practice, we assume for purposes of our discussion that the underlying purchase agreement utilizes the formula of *past practices in accordance with GAAP* as the standard for quantifying the net working capital as of the closing date.

NET WORKING CAPITAL UNDER GAAP

We first discussed net working capital in Chapter 1 as the difference between its current assets and current liabilities. Net working capital is formally defined in the FASB Codification as:

> *Working capital (also called net working capital) is represented by the excess of current assets over current liabilities and identifies the relatively liquid portion of total entity capital that constitutes a margin or buffer for meeting obligations within the ordinary operating cycle of the entity.*[1]

The GAAP definition of net working capital incorporates the concepts of current assets and current liabilities, which are also defined in GAAP:

> *Current assets is used to designate cash and other assets or resources commonly identified as those that are*

reasonably expected to be realized in cash or sold or consumed during the normal operating cycle of the business.

...

Current liabilities is used principally to designate obligations whose liquidation is reasonably expected to require the use of existing resources properly classifiable as current assets, or the creation of other current liabilities.[2]

The operating cycle is defined as follows under GAAP:

The average time intervening between the acquisition of materials or services and the final cash realization constitutes an operating cycle.[3]

GAAP further provides that if a company has multiple operating cycles per year, a one-year period shall be used for the segregation of current assets.[4]

The definitions above relate to net working capital under GAAP. Purchase agreements often use their own—albeit largely similar—definitions of net working capital, current assets, and/or current liabilities that can be adjusted to reflect the circumstances of the transaction. For example, a transaction for which the base purchase price is determined on a cash free/debt free basis may contain separate definitions for cash and debt and carve-out potentially overlapping items from net working capital.

Notwithstanding, the starting point for such customized definitions is generally still the equating of net working capital to current assets minus current liabilities. Before we discuss common causes of disputes, we first further discuss current assets and current liabilities under GAAP.

Current Assets

Assuming a GAAP definition, or equivalent, of net working capital, GAAP lists several categories of assets that are generally included with current assets.[5]

Current Assets Generally Include:

a. Cash available for current operations and items that are cash equivalents
b. Inventories of merchandise, raw materials, goods in process, finished goods, operating supplies, and ordinary maintenance material and parts
c. Trade accounts, notes, and acceptances receivable
d. Receivables from officers, employees, affiliates, and others, if collectible in the ordinary course of business within a year
e. Installment or deferred accounts and notes receivable if they conform generally to normal trade practices and terms within the business
f. Marketable securities representing the investment of cash available for current operations
g. Prepaid expenses such as insurance, interest, rents, taxes, unused royalties, current paid advertising service not yet received, and operating supplies.

Prepaid expenses are not assets in the sense that they will be converted into cash but in the sense that, if not paid in advance, they would require the use of current assets during the operating cycle.[6] Also, the list of items in the previous table is not limitative. Other items, such as, for example, an overfunded pension plan, can also be a current asset.[7] Both the GAAP definition of current assets and the broader guidance should be utilized in assessing whether an asset should be classified as a current asset or not.

GAAP also provides that the concept of the nature of current assets contemplates the exclusion from that classification of certain resources including, but not limited to, restricted cash, investments in securities that have been made for a continuing business advantage (even if those securities are marketable), receivables arising from unusual transactions that are not expected to be collected within 12 months (e.g., related to the sale of capital assets), depreciable assets, and long-term prepayments that are fairly charged to the operations of several years.[8]

The classification of an asset as current or noncurrent can be very significant in the context of an accounting arbitration. Assuming that the definitions in the purchase agreement align with those under GAAP, the asset would only be included in net working capital if it is properly classified as current.

Current Liabilities

Under GAAP, current liabilities generally include obligations for items that have entered into the operating cycle. A prime example of such obligations are accounts payable for the acquisition of materials and supplies to be used in the production of goods to be offered for sale. They also include collections received in advance of the delivery of goods or the performance of services by the company unless, of course, the underlying obligation represents a long-term deferment (e.g., the sale of a long-term warranty). In addition, such obligations include debts arising from operations directly related to the operating cycle, such as accruals for salaries and commissions.[9]

Importantly, the concept of current liabilities includes estimated or accrued amounts that are expected to be required to cover expenditures within the year for known obligations for which (i) the amount can be determined only approximately or (ii) the specific person or persons to whom payment will be made cannot as yet be designated.[10]

Current liabilities also generally include other liabilities whose regular and ordinary liquidation is expected to occur within a relatively short period of time, usually 12 months, such as short-term debts arising from the acquisition of capital assets and serial maturities of long-term obligations.[11] Various transactions may also result in current liability classifications, including due-on-demand loan agreements, callable debt agreements, and short-term obligations expected to be refinanced.[12]

Again, the purchase agreement definition of current liabilities can be customized and may depart from a pure GAAP-based classification of liabilities.

COMMON DRIVERS OF DISPUTED ITEMS

From an accounting perspective, there are three common drivers of post-closing purchase price adjustment disputes related to net working capital items: (i) estimation and judgment, (ii) the nature of accrual accounting, and (iii) non-GAAP transaction-specific measures.

Driver: Estimation and Judgment

The use of estimation and judgment are necessary to arrive at a conclusion on the appropriate amount to be included in net working capital, if any, for multiple accounts. For example, many companies have valuation allowances related to their accounts receivable and inventory on their books. As we discussed, the implementation of estimation and judgment are generally not solely mechanical in nature. In addition, changes in the underlying conditions result in estimates changing over time. Moreover, estimates used and judgment applied at one date may not be documented in sufficient detail to allow for a repeated identical implementation at a later date.

Not surprisingly, sellers and buyers commonly disagree on the implementation of accounting estimates. The valuation allowances for inventory and accounts receivables are prime examples of such disagreements. The existence of such valuation allowances is ubiquitous in practice and so are post-closing disagreements on their sufficiency.

Sellers commonly take the position that the accounts receivable and inventory are of high quality and that any valuation allowances that should be included to comply with *past practices in accordance with GAAP* have been included. Buyers, on the other hand, commonly take the position that those allowances are understated and need to be increased to appropriately account for credit risk (accounts receivable) and obsolescence and excess (inventory). We discuss inventory and accounts receivable in more detail in Chapters 16 and 17, respectively.

Valuation allowances for inventory and accounts receivable are not the only source of estimation-related disputes. Another common category of disputed items includes those related to contingent liabilities. Accounting for contingent liabilities incorporates estimation and judgment related to both the recognition and measurement of the relevant obligations. Again, a mechanical approach is nearly impossible for many contingent liabilities. We discuss contingent liabilities in more detail in Chapter 18.

Driver: Accrual Accounting

A company's balance sheet reflects its financial position as of the financial reporting date while a company's income statement reflects its financial performance over the reporting period. The balance sheet and income statement are to a certain extent communicating vessels. That is especially relevant in the context of the matching of a company's revenues and expenses to the correct reporting period, which is at the heart of accrual accounting.

The income statement recognition of revenue and expenses does not necessarily line up with the timing of the cash receipts or outlays. The timing differences are processed using the balance sheet. On the balance sheet, this can result in the recognition of various amounts, including (i) unbilled amounts for services performed, (ii) deferred revenue for services to be performed, (iii) prepaid expenses for services not yet utilized, and (iv) accrued liabilities for services utilized but not yet paid.

Example: Balance Sheet Accruals

- A company provides software services under one-year contracts. It subcontracts with other companies to perform some of the services. The company's fiscal year is the calendar year.
- Some of the company's customers prepay their one-year contracts. A $10,000 contract running from July 1 to June 30

of the next year can have the following income statement and balance sheet consequences.

- The income statement for fiscal year 1 includes revenue in the amount of $5,000 for the first half of the contract.
- The balance sheet as of the end of fiscal year 1 includes deferred revenue (liability) in an amount of $5,000 for the second half of the contract.
- In the second fiscal year, the second half of the contract is included with the company's revenue ($5,000 on the income statement) and the deferred revenue is removed from the balance sheet as the contract is performed.

- Some of the company's customers only get invoiced at the end of the annual contract period.
  - The income statements for fiscal years 1 and 2 are the same whether the contract is prepaid or postpaid. Revenue in an amount of $5,000 is recognized in both years.
  - The balance sheet as of the end of fiscal year 1, however, contains unbilled revenue (asset) as opposed to deferred revenue (liability) in an amount of $5,000.
- One of the company's vendors charges the company $2,500 for its part of the work in support of the contract, which it performs ratably during the contract year. The work is prepaid by the company.
  - The income statement for fiscal year 1 includes an expense in an amount of $1,250.
  - The balance sheet as of the end of fiscal year 1 includes a pre-paid expense (asset) in an amount of $1,250 for the second half of the vendor contract.
  - In the second fiscal year, another $1,250 in expenses is included on the income statement and the prepaid expense is removed from the balance sheet.
- Another vendor, which otherwise provides similar services at a similar expense, invoices the company at the end of the service period.
  - The income statements for fiscal years 1 and 2 are the same whether the vendor is prepaid or postpaid. An expense

(income statement) is recognized in both years in an amount of $1,250.

- The balance sheet as of the end of fiscal year 1, however, contains an accrued liability as opposed to a prepaid expense (asset) in an amount of $1,250.

Revenue and expense accruals can end up in dispute under a variety of circumstances. The recognition of revenue is not always as straightforward as in the previous example. It is not uncommon for revenue recognition–related items to end up in dispute because the buyer believes the company's historical revenue recognition practices were not in accordance with GAAP.

A company will typically have a host of accruals to properly match expenses to the period to which they relate such as payroll, vacation days, health insurance, bonus accruals, and many others. It is very common for there to be adjustments to the various accruals during the post-closing process. Mostly, those are the adjustments that would normally happen subsequent to the balance sheet date to close the books and true up the amounts of the accruals to arrive at the correct amounts as of the financial statement date. Not surprisingly, although often adjusted, proposed adjustments to accruals are often either accepted by the seller when proposed or resolved prior to the arbitrator's involvement. That is understandable given that many such proposed adjustments are simply true-ups of verifiable accruals.

Notwithstanding, there are also many disputes related to expense accruals. They commonly relate to the measurement of the amount that should be included on the balance sheet or whether an accrual should be included at all. It is not uncommon for cutoff issues that find their genesis in differences between the timing of the closing and the regular date as of which the books are closed to result in disputes between the parties. We discuss revenue recognition and expense accruals in more detail in Chapter 19.

Driver: Non-GAAP Transaction-Specific Measures

Transaction-specific measures represent another common source of disputes. In the context of post-closing purchase price adjustments, these are agreed upon adjustments that impact the inclusion with, exclusion from, and/or measurement of one or more net working capital components. Such measures can run the gamut from carve-outs to a variety of contractually agreed-upon special treatments. They can include deviations from the seller's past accounting practices and/or deviations from GAAP. The parties can also agree on transaction-specific measures that have a more general application. For example, the parties may agree that adjustments to the closing accounts below a certain dollar amount will not be implemented, regardless of whether such an adjustment would be recorded in the normal course of business.

Even with good intentions from the parties, transaction-specific measures can turn out to be ambiguous after the closing, creating the opportunity for disagreement and disputes. Properly implementing transaction-specific measures can be complicated and may require a thorough understanding of the company's underlying accounting processes. Moreover, contractual provisions that seemed perfectly clear as of the signing of the purchase agreement can turn out to be a source of dispute as the parties attempt to apply them under changed circumstances (and in their favor) after the closing.

Although some transaction-specific measures are relatively common and straightforward, for example, the carve-out of cash from net working capital, there are many possibilities and varying degrees of complexity. We discuss transaction-specific adjustments in more detail in Chapter 7.

THE IMPACT OF OTHER CIRCUMSTANCES

During the post-closing period, it is not uncommon for many net working capital accounts to be adjusted based on differences between the seller's preliminary closing statement (at closing) and the buyer's proposed closing statement (after closing). Many such adjustments are resolved between the parties without the need for a formal dispute resolution before an accounting arbitrator. For other items, the resolution is not so easy. The likelihood of disputes can vary, depending on the circumstances, and can be due to factors other than the previously discussed common drivers.

Timing Issues

The timing of the closing can have a real impact on the occurrence of post-closing purchase price adjustments and disputes between the parties. A longer period between negotiation of the purchase agreement and the closing can drive adjustments and disputes because the facts and circumstances relevant to the company's operations and its accounting can progressively change over time.

The timing of the closing can also determine to what extent cutoff-related issues occur. Financial statements are typically issued as of the end of a year, quarter, or month. The closing, however, can occur on any day of the month. The result is that the company may be confronted with intra-month accruals that have to be recognized as of the closing date, but are not normally necessary as of the date of the financial statements.

(Perceived) GAAP Violations

The (perceived) existence of past practices in contravention of GAAP also drives proposed adjustments and disputes. The parties may disagree on the application of GAAP. Even if they agree that the application of the company's past accounting practices would result in a violation of GAAP as of the closing date, the parties may still disagree on what should be the appropriate accounting treatment or the amount of the adjustment.

At times, the existence of known uncorrected immaterial errors in the financial statements can exacerbate this situation.

The buyer will likely want them corrected while the seller may argue that such a correction is not necessary because the adjustments are immaterial and were known prior to closing.

Finally, one or both parties can at times simply misunderstand GAAP. For example, it is not uncommon for even licensed accountants to believe that *current* always means one year, while for the company at issue a longer period may be appropriate and GAAP compliant due to the existence of a longer operating cycle.

Perceived or actual GAAP violations are at the heart of many disputed items, which makes sense in the context of accounting arbitrations. In addition, the GAAP issues often overlap with other dispute drivers discussed in this chapter, such as judgment and estimation. For example, a buyer may argue that the seller's accounting for the allowance for doubtful accounts is not GAAP compliant due to an inappropriate estimation of collectability.

Factual Surprises

Post-closing changes in facts and circumstances can potentially drive large adjustments dependent on whether and to what extent subsequent events should be incorporated. Such circumstances can easily lead to disputes. The seller may have the perspective that the economic risk of the business has transferred to the buyer while the buyer may argue that the issue should be regarded as new information that should be incorporated into the preparation of the proposed closing statement, and therefore the purchase price adjustment.

Factual surprises can also be of a non-subsequent-event nature. For example, the buyer may be surprised by the state of the inventory, or the absence thereof, as it gains full access to the company's facilities and books and records after closing. Such fact-based adjustments are often presented as adjustments to accounting items such as proposed increases to allowances or write-offs.

Transaction due diligence, both buy-side and sell-side, can be a mitigating factor that can preempt certain post-closing disputes. An appropriate level of due diligence can prevent some, but not all, surprises or perceived misrepresentations or omissions. Of course, if the buyer is provided an opportunity for extensive due diligence that can also result in or exacerbate disputes as the seller may take the post-closing position that the buyer performed extensive due diligence and knew exactly what it was getting (or should have known).

Some factual surprises are not knowable prior to the closing date, while others may be identifiable at some level prior to the closing date. Either way, the parties may disagree regarding the need for, or amount of, any necessary adjustment, which can drive post-closing disputes.

Pragmatic Factors and Procedural Posture

There are a variety of other factors that can otherwise contribute to the progression from post-closing purchase price adjustment negotiation to a full blown dispute. One straightforward factor can be the magnitude of the amount in dispute. The accounting arbitration process is generally relatively quick and inexpensive as compared to typical commercial litigation. Notwithstanding, the decision to proceed to a formal dispute may not make sense if the economic interest is simply too small. On the other hand, in the case of large disputed amounts, the expense of the procedure can easily be relatively insignificant.

The perceived procedural posture of the counterparty can also matter. For example, if a party believes that the counterparty is attempting to game the post-closing purchase price adjustment process to get a discount or maximize its return from the transaction, a dispute becomes more likely. Similarly, if a party perceives that the counterparty is trying to reinterpret a perceivably clear contractual provision to uncover ambiguities in order to gain an unwarranted advantage, negotiations can break down.

MISCELLANEOUS DISPUTED ITEMS

Notwithstanding the common occurrence of disputes related to valuation allowances and common accruals, proposed post-closing adjustments to many other items can end up in dispute between the parties. There can be adjustments and disputes related to cash, fair value, current vs. long-term classification, and so forth. Disputes can occur related to items unique to the facts and circumstances of the company or the transaction as well as in relation to common items that rarely end up in dispute despite their ubiquitous presence. This book does not intend to cover all potential disputed items that can arise related to post-closing purchase price adjustment mechanisms. Nonetheless, to further illustrate the types of disputes that can occur, we next discuss five additional sources of disputed items that occur in practice with a lesser degree of frequency. We discuss certain commonly disputes items, such as inventory and accounts receivable, more extensively in the next few chapters.

Cash and Cash Equivalents

Cash and cash equivalents, whether part of the net working capital adjustment mechanism or not, are typically trued up to the correct balance as of the closing date. Although adjustments occur regularly, disputes generally do not because the closing date cash balance is typically readily determinable.

Notwithstanding, disputes can occur both related to the physical existence of the cash as well as the appropriate accounting treatment. An example of the former is a buyer who inventories petty cash across locations, finds there is a significant amount missing, and seeks an adjustment. The seller may disagree as it believes that its controls are sufficient, such an issue has never previously occurred, and the problem is with the buyer's count.

An example of an accounting treatment dispute can be whether cash is restricted from a GAAP perspective. Evaluation of such a dispute may involve considering the reasons for the perceived restriction. As discussed earlier, restricted cash may not be a current asset under GAAP and the cash at issue may, therefore, not be included in net working capital if it is found to be restricted cash in accordance with GAAP.

Fair Value, Derivatives, and Hedge Accounting

The company may be a party to derivatives contracts or other financial instruments that need to be recorded at fair value without readily available pricing data. The valuation of such over-the-counter instruments may become a source of dispute between the parties.

The contracts may also be part of business practices to hedge some of the company's business exposures, such as price hedges for portions of the existing inventory. The accounting treatment for those instruments may depend on whether the contracts are treated as hedges under GAAP. Moreover, that treatment may be impacted by management's intent and/or nuances of the positions that can be adjusted. In such cases, the parties may disagree on the appropriate accounting treatment.

Current Portions of Long-Term Liabilities

Balance sheet classification distinctions between current and noncurrent liabilities can also be a source of disputes between the parties. An example of such classification disputes is the recognition of current portions of certain types of long-term liabilities. The parties may disagree on the amount, if any, that should be separated from the long-term liabilities and accounted for as a current liability. For traditional debt, adjustments can occur due to the timing of the closing, but such adjustments are often not disputed. Other separations between current and long-term, however, can result in disputes because of perceived non-GAAP compliant past practices of the target company, such as those related to deferred rent.

Classification driven disputes can be exacerbated by the perception of an unjust windfall. For example, a company may not have historically segregated the current portion of its deferred rent as a current liability or did not recognize deferred rent at all (deferred rent can be the result of ratably accounting for a beneficial lease concession over the lease term). The seller may focus on the absence of a real difference between the historical net working capital and the net working capital at closing, its historical practices, and the calculation of target net working capital. The buyer may argue that the company's historical treatment violates GAAP and needs to be corrected in accordance with the purchase agreement requirement to comply with GAAP, regardless of past practices.

Transaction Costs

Purchase agreements often explicitly address the consideration of the seller's as well as the buyer's transaction costs for purposes of the preparation of the preliminary closing statement, the proposed closing statement, and/or the purchase price calculation. By way of example, in the case of a carve-out transaction, the purchase agreement may preclude the seller from pushing down costs associated with the sale to the target company. In addition, the purchase agreement may explicitly provide that the determination of any post-closing purchase price adjustment will not include any costs associated with the transaction either paid or accrued as of the closing date.

Another contractual exclusion could be for any transaction costs or other costs allocated or obligated for by the buyer. For example, while not common, there can be transactions that are very near closing for which the buyer begins incurring costs on behalf of the company before the closing date, for example, in relation to the anticipated refinancing of the company's debt. Those costs can result in accounts payable to a vendor or to the buyer for reimbursement.

Transaction costs can be significant and can result in disputes.

Intercompany Accounts and Allocations

In some transactions, the company may have been part of a larger corporate group prior to the sale. Although intercompany balances are often extinguished as of the closing date, there can be ongoing relationships with the parent or other group entities, at least temporarily. For example, the company may continue to receive certain services from or through the former group for a defined period after closing.

The related accruals can lead to disputes between the parties related to the recognition of such accruals, or the lack thereof. The purchase agreement commonly includes specific provisions related to intercompany transactions, but such provisions may not cover all (perceived) post-closing issues.

NOTES

1. *See* FASB ASC Master Glossary, at Working Capital.
2. *See* FASB ASC Master Glossary, at Current Assets and Current Liabilities.
3. *See* FASB ASC Master Glossary, at Operating Cycle.
4. *See* FASB ASC 210-10-45-3.
5. *See* FASB ASC 210-10-45-1.
6. *See* FASB ASC 210-10-45-2.
7. *See* FASB ASC 210-10-45-2.
8. *See* FASB ASB 210-10-45-4.
9. *See* FASB ASC 210-10-45-8.
10. *See* FASB ASC 210-10-45-6.
11. *See* FASB ASC 210-10-45-9.
12. *See* FASB ASC 210-10-45-7.

CHAPTER 16

Inventory

Among the most commonly disputed post-closing purchase price adjustments are those related to inventory and the inventory allowance. Such disputes can relate to the existence of inventory and/or the valuation of inventory. Inventory valuation disputes are not all that surprising given that the valuation of inventory often requires the use of estimates and the exercise of judgment.

Inventory existence disputes may arise based on an inventory count performed by the buyer after the transaction closing. The buyer may seek to write down the inventory for items that, according to the buyer's count, do not exist in inventory. The seller, on the other hand, may argue that the items were transferred at closing and either the buyer counted wrong or the company lost them after closing. Existence disputes are often, but not always, less significant than valuation disputes and are frequently resolved without the need for an accounting arbitration.

Post-closing inventory valuation adjustments and write-offs for excess and obsolete inventory are very common and are often included as disputed items in accounting arbitrations. In considering the various valuation adjustments, certain company-specific factors come into play. Inventory is not only a commonly disputed item, it is also often a significant disputed item in terms of the dollar amount at stake. This chapter will seek to answer several questions regarding inventory-related disputed items, including:

- How can such disputes be minimized or avoided?
- How should the parties present their positions regarding inventory?
- How should an accounting arbitrator assess and resolve inventory-related disputed items?

GAAP GUIDANCE RELATED TO INVENTORY

The GAAP guidance related to inventory is primarily contained within FASB ASC 330—Inventory. Generally, inventory can be much broader than goods that are purchased and held for resale. It commonly includes items that are:

> *a. Held for sale in the ordinary course of business*
> *b. In process of production for such sale*
> *c. To be currently consumed in the production of goods or services to be available for sale.*[1]

The GAAP definition of inventories "excludes long-term assets subject to depreciation accounting, or goods which, when put into use, will be so classified."[2] Beyond the definition of what is inventory, we must also consider the classification of inventory and more importantly the valuation of inventory. GAAP provides guidance for both of those concepts.

Balance Sheet Classification of Inventory

Inventory is generally a current asset and a part of net working capital. As previously discussed, there is a common misconception that the cutoff for classification of an asset (or liability) as current is always one year. GAAP describes current assets as assets that are reasonably expected to be realized, sold, or consumed during the normal operating cycle of the business.[3] For companies that have multiple operating cycles per year, GAAP prescribes a one-year time period for the segregation of current assets.[4]

Classification issues can be complex, but in the context of inventory are not explicitly brought up as such very often. If classification arguments are raised, the accounting arbitrator will need to carefully assess the basis for the arguments in light of the relevant GAAP guidance, the purchase agreement, and the unique characteristics of the company and its inventory.

Valuation or Measurement of Inventory

In the context of a purchase price dispute related to inventory, the more commonly disputed issue is the valuation/measurement of inventory. GAAP discusses two measurement or valuation points for inventory: initial measurement and subsequent measurement. The initial measurement is most commonly a cost-based measurement, which in its simplest form is the purchase price paid to acquire an item or the costs incurred to make an item ready to sell. The subsequent measurement involves an assessment of the inventory based on the lower of cost or net realizable value test (or market – dependent on timing and the applicable facts and circumstances).[5] This measurement is normally performed for each financial reporting period, or at least once each year. As discussed ahead, the subsequent measurement of inventory is the valuation commonly at issue in accounting arbitrations.

Currently, FASB ASC 330 states that "[a] departure from the cost basis of pricing the inventory is required when the utility of the goods is no longer as great as their cost."[6] The related pending content for the measurement of inventory using any other method than LIFO or the retail inventory method, involves an evaluation of inventory using the lower of cost or net realizable value test.

The mechanics of assessing the lower of cost or net realizable value or market for inventory items, if applicable, can appear straightforward:

- Determine the cost basis of the inventory, which is normally readily available in the accounting system. Notwithstanding, the amount of the cost basis can depend on various accounting choices made by the company. Such choices can include the flow of cost factors (LIFO versus FIFO) and choices that have been made regarding the distinction between period costs and costs that are booked to inventory in a production environment. The former choice is typically not the subject of dispute. The latter choice, however, may very well result in a dispute about what the cost of inventory should be under GAAP.

- Dependent on the timing of the transaction and the type of inventory measurement (LIFO, retail inventory, or other):
  - Determine net realizable value, which is the estimated selling price in the ordinary course of business, less reasonably predictable costs of completion, disposal, and transportation.[7]
  - Determine market, which is current replacement cost as long as market does not exceed net realizable value and is not less than net realizable value less a normal profit margin.[8]
- Compare net realizable value or market to cost and use the lower amount as the inventory value.[9]

A departure from the inventory's cost basis is generally only captured in the event of a decrease in the value or utility of inventory. In accordance with FASB ASC 330, it is a very limited circumstance in which an increase above cost in the value of inventory would be recognized.[10] Disputed items related to inventory increases above cost would also be a rare occurrence.

A decrease in the perceived utility or value of the inventory can have a variety of causes. FASB ASC 330 includes potential causes such as damage, deterioration, obsolescence, changes in price levels, or other causes.[11] Other than obvious damage, how does a company determine if the value or utility of its inventory has decreased? And if it has decreased, what is an appropriate reduction in the value of inventory based on damage, deterioration, obsolescence, changes in price levels, and other causes? These two questions are the source of many disputed items related to inventory.

Notably, the utility of inventory may have decreased, but it may still not be below cost. Moreover, based on the guidance in FASB ASC 330, in cases where the cost plus a normal profit will be recovered based on the sales price in the ordinary course of business, no loss may have to be recognized.[12]

FASB ASC 330 includes several other considerations related to the subsequent measurement of inventory, including considerations as to whether the inventory should be evaluated in its entirety, in subsets, or per item. It also provides guidance for specific situations such as purchase commitments and sales incentives. The bottom line is that the subsequent measurement of inventory involves judgment and estimation in assessing the value of the inventory on hand. In the context of an acquisition, the seller and the buyer can have vastly different conclusions regarding the utility or value of certain categories of inventory, and these different conclusions often involve the assessment of excess or obsolete inventory.

BUYERS AND SELLERS CAN HAVE DIFFERING VIEWS REGARDING THE VALUE OF INVENTORY

Buyers and sellers often disagree regarding the value of the inventory transferred in a transaction. A primary reason is that the subsequent measurement of inventory can require significant estimation and judgment regarding the value of inventory and the differing perceptions of the buyer and the seller can result in vastly different conclusions. The seller may be optimistic about the value of the company's inventory, while the buyer may be more pessimistic. While wholly unrealistic adjustments are sometimes proposed, the buyer and seller may simply be relying on different perspectives, or otherwise have a difference of opinion regarding how certain categories of inventory will be used going forward, which impacts the resulting assessment of the value of that inventory (i.e., the assessment of inventory as excess or obsolete). The seller may see value in some older, lesser used inventory items based on anticipated future usage, whereas the buyer sees that as unrealistic and has no intention of ever using those items. Either or both views can be in violation of GAAP dependent on the facts and circumstances.

Notwithstanding, either approach can also be in accordance with GAAP. If a company has a verifiable basis and rationale for continuing to carry slower moving inventory items at some amount, GAAP could support such treatment. If a company has no intention of ever using older inventory items, GAAP could support writing off such items, or at least reducing the carrying amount to a scrap value, if applicable. Viewed separately, neither position is necessarily in violation of GAAP.

The two conclusions may simply represent each party's assessment of the value of the inventory to the respective owner of the company—the seller prior to the closing and the buyer after the closing. In other words, the different conclusions may be due to a different approach for running the entity in question. For example, the buyer may have a plan to shut down certain unprofitable business lines in order to focus on the more profitable aspects of the acquired business. As a result, the inventory of the business lines to be shut down may have no real value to the buyer, outside of possibly scrap value. In such a situation, it would generally not be appropriate to obtain a purchase price reduction related to inventory solely based on the buyer's future plans for the perceivably unprofitable business lines. Purchase agreements commonly provide for the net working capital to be determined immediately prior to the closing without giving effect to the transaction. Notwithstanding, the buyer's future plans may well result in it assessing the inventory supporting the unprofitable business lines much more critically in a post-closing purchase price adjustment process than the seller.

Without considering buyer's post-closing plans, buyer could still argue that the inventory value has decreased due to, for example, obsolescence. In such instances, the measurement of the inventory will have to be considered under *past practices in accordance with GAAP* in accordance with the purchase agreement.

DISPUTED ITEMS RELATED TO INVENTORY

Given the discussion thus far regarding the subsequent measurement of inventory, it should be no surprise that the value of inventory is a commonly disputed component of net working capital. Transactions involving companies for which inventory is the most significant asset are even more likely to involve inventory-related disputed items. In practice we have encountered inventory-heavy businesses where the requested adjustment was not only a significant amount in isolation, but a double-digit percentage of the purchase price.

Disputes can arise due to competing perspectives of the parties. The seller may have an optimistic view of the value of the company's inventory, possibly overly optimistic, and the buyer may have a more pessimistic view of the valuation of certain categories of inventory, possibly overly pessimistic. As an example, a seller of a computer company may recognize some modest reductions in the value of older technology equipment based on the conclusion that, at a minimum, the parts of the older equipment can be sold as replacement parts, resulting in the recouping of a significant portion of the inventory cost. The buyer, on the other hand, may conclude that all such equipment is excess and obsolete and should be written off completely.

In that example, the appropriate value may be somewhere between the two positions. Resolving such disputes will typically involve an appropriate assessment of the value of the inventory in question based on the facts and circumstances of the case. The parts could have some value as replacement parts, but what if the equipment in question represents a ten-year supply of replacement parts? What if the demand for such replacement parts has been rapidly declining due to replacement technology? On the other hand, what if the company was the only supplier, or one of a very few suppliers, in the world of replacement parts for older technology? These and other questions are considerations in the evaluation of the value of the inventory in the normal course of business as well as in the context of a transaction dispute.

The most common bases for disputed items related to inventory are allegedly excess and/or obsolete inventory. Those are not the only causes of disputes related to inventory value. There can also be disputes related to, for example, physical deterioration of the inventory. For purposes of this book, we focus on excess inventory and obsolescence as the related disputes are very common. Before discussing those valuation issues further, we first discuss inventory existence disputes.

Inventory Existence Disputes

Existence disputes can be more common in transactions involving entities that have numerous locations with higher levels of inventory, or entities that have poor inventory management systems. Many buyer-proposed adjustments for nonexistent inventory end up being resolved between the parties without a dispute. In some cases, however, the parties do not agree regarding the amount of nonexistent inventory. Such disputes commonly arise based on an inventory count performed by the buyer at some point after the closing. Based upon the count, the buyer may propose an adjustment claiming that a certain amount of inventory is not present at various locations. The seller may object to the adjustment, claiming that the inventory, or some portion of the inventory in question, was present as of the closing date.

These can be difficult disputes to resolve because in many transactions a physical count is not performed by the seller (or the buyer) near or on the closing date. This could be because the seller has a perpetual inventory system and does not perform regular counts, or it could be that the seller does not have a history of inventory adjustments when it does perform counts. Either way, a count was not performed *as of* the closing date. So, without a verified count the question remains, was the inventory there as of the closing date?

For companies that do not have a perpetual inventory system, the lack of a closing date (or near-closing date) count can make it difficult to prove the inventory was present. Further complicating the resolution of such disputes is the timing of the count performed by the buyer that resulted in the claim of missing inventory. Even if the buyer's count was performed a few weeks or a month after the closing date, there is still no closing date count. The period between the closing date and the count may also be longer. The length of time between the closing and the count may leave the nonexistent inventory claim open to question because anything could have happened to the inventory in, for example, the month following the closing. In such situations, a helpful factor for the buyer could be a reconciliation of the count it performed with the sales since the closing date to arrive at its proposed closing date inventory combined with a discussion of internal controls. Although this does not prove that the inventory claimed by the buyer as nonexistent was not actually present as of the closing date, it can help the buyer build a more solid foundation for its position especially in combination with other relevant information about the interim period and the timing of the count.

Existence-related disputes, especially those with competing or disputed counts, tend to result in the exchange of significant quantities of documentation.

Excess and Obsolete Inventory Disputes

Excess inventory and obsolete inventory can be similar in nature and often overlap (e.g., obsolete inventory is often also excess inventory), but they are two separate concepts. Excess inventory relates to inventory in excess of what will be sold or utilized by the company in the course of its operations in the sufficiently near future, whether obsolete or not. Applying that concept can require judgment and depends on the nature of the inventory and the facts and circumstances. For example, items that spoil have a short shelf-life as compared to steel, which can have a long shelf-life. Obsolete inventory may not be excess in quantity, but it may be older versions or older technology that have been surpassed by new technology and therefore may have a greatly reduced value.

Buyers and sellers can disagree regarding the likelihood of selling excess or obsolete inventory and any impairment of that inventory due to excess quantities or obsolescence. They can also disagree regarding alternative uses for such inventory to achieve future sales or uses of inventory. In a purchase price adjustment process, those differing opinions (i.e., judgment and estimation) regarding the utility of inventory frequently result in buyer-proposed adjustments that are objected to by the seller.

The subsequent measurement of many types of inventory can be subject to the exercise of some level of judgment and estimation by the seller before the transaction closing and then by the buyer after the closing. The judgment exercised by either party can be challenged by the opposing party (an adjustment proposed by the buyer, or an objection to the adjustment by the seller) regardless of the type of inventory transferred in the transaction. Just about any type of inventory can be involved in a post-closing dispute, but certain types of inventory appear to be more commonly involved in purchase price disputes that end up in accounting arbitrations. Examples of these types of inventory include rapidly or constantly changing technology items (e.g., computer hardware, data storage devices, and cable TV equipment), and commoditized industrial products, such as steel tanks.

Technology-Related Inventory Disputes The valuation of technology-related inventory is more likely to be adjusted and/or disputed because of the high rate of obsolescence that can occur in this industry. Think of how quickly our smartphones change to add newer, better, and faster technology, capabilities, and applications. Once replaced by a newer and better technology, the older technology inventory may be reduced in value (or at least in sales price) because most consumers seek out the latest technology or because the existing technology is no longer new. Also, consider LED TVs and how the prices have decreased over the last few years, even for the very large screens. Smartphones, TVs, computers, video game systems, and any other type of changing technology can be subject to rapid decreases in value as we move further away from the product launch date. Of course, the same is also true for rapidly evolving technology other than consumer products. In other words, the value of this type of inventory generally decreases as technology changes and advances.

The decrease in utility and value is due to obsolescence and possibly excess inventory levels. The GAAP question is whether the cost is lower than the net realizable value or market as of the measurement date. For example, a 65″ LED TV may have been reduced in sales price from $1,500 to $750, but if the recorded cost of the TV is $500, there may be no inventory valuation impact of the price reduction (depending on inventory levels). It is only when the value is below cost that an adjustment to inventory may be required by GAAP. Notably, net realizable value is not necessarily the same as the offering price or price included in the company's standard price list. An item may not sell at that price. The actual net realizable value or market is the real question, not simply the standard price set by a manufacturer or reseller.

A common theme in technology-related inventory disputes is that of alternative uses for older inventory as replacement parts or spare parts. That could be a very regular practice for some companies and therefore easily supported; for other companies it may be a possibility, but one never actually utilized in the normal course of operations. Often the frequency that such parts are actually used in that capacity and in what volumes and what value can be realized from such usage is indicative, rather than the hypothetical possibility that the company could employ such alternatives.

Example: Failed Product Launch

- A company developed a new router that offered additional Internet speed by bundling ISDN connections.
- By the time the product was fully developed, faster DSL and cable Internet had become widely available. The product launch did not live up to expectations. The company had preemptively produced sufficient routers to supply a successful nationwide launch.
- The buyer argues that the inventory is impaired. The seller argues that the routers may be used in other countries that follow a different technological roadmap, without any plans or specificity.

Industrial Product Inventory Disputes Industrial products such as steel products have different valuation considerations than technological products. For the most part, steel and other non-spoiling industrial products are not subject to rapid obsolescence. Of course, new forms of steel are developed over time or for specialized uses, but in general steel is a fairly stable commodity in terms of its usefulness. Rather than obsolescence, the dispute-related issues regarding this type of inventory are often: (i) a large supply of miscellaneous parts (nut, bolts, etc.) and/or (ii) a large supply of older products. In other words, excess inventory is a frequent driver of adjustments and disputes related to certain commoditized industrial products.

Example: Manufacturer of Steel Products

- The company has been in business for many years and the owners decide to sell to a private equity firm in order to retire. The inventory consists of a variety of plate steel, steel tanks, and numerous steel parts. The majority of inventory is carried at cost.
- Upon acquisition the buyer proposes adjustments to write off many of the older steel tanks that are allegedly rusting in the field out back as well as a significant amount of the steel spare parts, primarily boxes of thousands of nuts, bolts, and

valves that have little recent use. The buyer's position is that this inventory is excess in quantity and has no value above scrap value.

- The seller's position is that the old tanks can be easily restored to like-new quality and can be further modified to different sizes as needed based on customer order specifications. In addition, the seller believes that the boxes of nuts, bolts, and valves have actual value regardless of the quantity.

The types of arguments included in the preceding example are very common regarding all manner of industrial products.

PRESENTING AND RESOLVING INVENTORY-RELATED DISPUTED ITEMS IN AN ACCOUNTING ARBITRATION

Inventory disputed items can often be the most significant disputed items in an accounting arbitration. The presentation of each party's position and the arbitrator's resolution can thus be disproportionally important. It is typically not sufficient for a buyer to simply state that the inventory is a bunch of old junk or for a seller to comment that its inventory was audited by a reputable firm and is therefore appropriately valued. Sufficient supporting information is often critical for disputed items requiring detailed documentation such as inventory.

Presenting Positions on Inventory Disputed Items

The basic concepts of presenting each party's arguments to the arbitrator were discussed in Chapters 12 and 13. In this chapter we will discuss more specifically how to present arguments related to inventory disputed items from the perspective of both the buyer and the seller. The sufficiency and relevance of the information provided to the arbitrator can impact the success on any disputed item, and inventory disputed items are no different. The accounting arbitrator will likely benefit from detailed information on which to base a conclusion regarding each disputed item and, outside of general GAAP guidance, that information can typically only come from the parties.

Valuing inventory requires judgment and estimation. The judgment and estimates utilized by each party for their positions must be supported by information provided to the accounting arbitrator. The appropriate evaluation of the judgment exercised and the estimation utilized requires context and related factual information. Each party should support their position to the arbitrator, including how it complies with the relevant accounting guidance and the terms of the purchase agreement.

Advice Relevant to Both Buyers and Sellers Generally, there are several elements of the presentation of inventory disputed items that both buyers and sellers should address:

- Discussion of the inventory and any unique characteristics
- Discussion of the relevant accounting guidance
- Discussion of the relevant purchase agreement provisions

Remember from the Chapter 12 discussion that the accounting arbitrator has very little in the way of detailed knowledge, if any, regarding the target entity or its inventory when he or she is retained. It is therefore very important to discuss the nature of the inventory in general and more specifically the inventory items in dispute. For example, if the seller wants the accounting arbitrator to understand why a perceivably high volume of older inventory still has value at or above cost, or at whatever carrying amount the seller believes is accurate, the seller will need to first provide a description of the inventory and its possible uses. If the buyer wants the accounting arbitrator to understand why the allegedly obsolete inventory has no alternative uses, and therefore greatly reduced utility, the buyer will need to first provide a description of the inventory and why its use is limited.

The parties also need to discuss the relevant accounting guidance and perhaps interpretative guidance relevant to the specific inventory in dispute. Each party should describe how the guidance is being applied and how it supports the position being presented. This is an accounting arbitration and the determination should be based on the appropriate application of the relevant accounting guidance, as provided for in the relevant purchase agreement. In other words, the parties can provide the arbitrator with a roadmap of this guidance and its application to the case at hand.

Finally, each party should highlight and briefly discuss the purchase agreement provisions relevant to the inventory disputed item. The applicable provision in the purchase agreement may be a general provision, such as *past practices in accordance with GAAP*. Even in such cases it is important to point out the provision and how the position being presented complies with the purchase agreement. Some purchase agreements include very specific provisions regarding inventory, such as minimum or maximum inventory levels for certain products, or non-GAAP provisions such as reclassifications or exclusions of certain types of inventory. In many transactions the purchase agreement includes a listing of *excluded assets*, which can include certain categories of inventory. It is important to discuss those specific provisions and to explain how the position being presented conforms to them.

These three general discussion items are not necessarily the primary argument for or against either party's position. Rather, they set the stage for the discussion of why the position that will be presented is in compliance with the relevant accounting guidance and purchase agreement provisions. This information, however, can be critical to the accounting arbitrator's understanding of the support for each party's position on the inventory disputed item(s).

Advice to Sellers

The seller of a company often knows more about the historical usage and context related to the inventory in question than the buyer. After the closing, however, the buyer will generally be the party with access to the detailed accounting records and institutional knowledge related to the inventory that is in dispute. This can put the seller at a documentation disadvantage, at least initially. As will be discussed, this can be remedied, or at least mitigated, in a couple of ways. Regardless, the seller may have retained relevant historical knowledge of the company and related accounting records.

Hypothetical versus Actual Markets for Inventory Sellers can often benefit from basing their position and arguments on tangible activity related to the inventory items at issue. Hypothetical scenarios are often more difficult to support. As an example, consider a seller's argument that some of the older technology products can be sold to developing countries that are somewhat behind in technology. This could possibly be true, but if the company has never done so with any of its products nor has any concrete plans to do so, such an argument can ring hollow. FASB ASC 330 generally requires subsequent measurement of inventory to be based on its value as supported by evidence. The GAAP guidance is the lower of cost or net realizable value (or market). If there is no viable market that is realistic for the company to tap into to sell the inventory in question, the inventory may not have much actual value, at least in the context argued by the seller. It can be difficult for sellers to successfully argue against excess and obsolete inventory based primarily on alternative uses or sales markets that the company has no history or experience employing. As opposed to unsupported hypothetical markets, sellers could show what has historically been done with older/excess inventory or discuss the viable plan developed to sell older/excess inventory, including the actual or expected volume of usage and the prices to be obtained. This information can sometimes be for similar products within the company. Such support gives the arbitrator information and insight into the potential utility or value of the inventory.

There are other situations where higher levels of inventory (possibly alleged excess by the buyer) can be sufficiently and appropriately explained. One example would be the pre-rollout production of a new product line. The company may have a new product coming online in a new market. The company could have produced inventory to support an expected level of sales in this new market, but as of the closing date, sales have not yet commenced or were only commenced a few months prior to the closing date. Notwithstanding, the buyer may argue that the lack of pre-orders or the slower sales activity immediately prior to the closing date indicates that the product is, or may be, a failure and the inventory has little if any value.

A common argument from sellers is that it would be unfair if the inventory is written down because then the buyer gets it for free or too cheap. Such arguments are generally not compelling as the accounting arbitrator will focus on the applicable standard as provided for in the purchase agreement. Perceived fairness is not a decisive factor; rather, the appropriate balance sheet value of the inventory is the determining factor. Moreover, the simple existence of inventory does not mean that it has value at or exceeding its historical cost.

Overcoming Seller's Documentation Disadvantage As noted earlier, after the closing the buyer will generally gain access to the detailed accounting records of the company and seller may lose that access. To overcome this documentation issue, there are things sellers can do to get the necessary information to the arbitrator including the following.

First, assuming this is contractually allowed, the seller could maintain a copy of the detailed accounting records used to prepare the reference financial statements, the target net working capital, the preliminary closing statement, and other calculations. This can include detailed inventory listings that add up to the amount in the preliminary closing statement used to derive the purchase price. By doing so, the seller at least has a detailed record as of the closing date. The seller can also maintain a copy of the data room files and a record of all information provided to the buyer during due diligence, which would include historical accounting information.

Second, the seller can often obtain much or all of the relevant information in the post-closing adjustment phase as documents are exchanged between the buyer and the seller. The buyer will generally supply documentation to support its position and respond to document requests by the seller.

Third, if inventory becomes a disputed item and there is additional information the seller needs to support its position, the seller can proactively specify in its initial submission that the buyer is in possession of the relevant detailed accounting records necessary to fully support certain of the seller's arguments. If advised in this manner, the arbitrator may request the information through the arbitrator interrogatories and document requests. Thus, even if the seller does not have access to the information to include in its submissions, the accounting arbitrator will end up having the information available for analysis of the disputed item.

We discussed earlier that existence disputes related to inventory are not necessarily as common, but they do occur. To attempt to avoid existence disputes, the seller, possibly in conjunction with the buyer, can perform a physical count near the closing date. By doing so, the seller will have a record of the inventory at or near the closing, thereby potentially significantly limiting the possibility, or significance, of any inventory existence dispute.

If a pre-close inventory count is not feasible, the seller could maintain records of the most recent physical inventory count and any necessary adjustment, which can be provided as support for the historical inventory levels and accuracy. This can be provided as support in the event of an inventory existence dispute. With respect to any physical inventory count, the supporting documentation should ideally be of a quality that will be well received by an accounting arbitrator. For example, if count sheets are used, the count sheets should generally be numbered, complete, dated, and approved. It can be difficult to refute such supporting documentation.

Presenting the Seller's Position to the Accounting Arbitrator At its core, the seller's argument against a purchase price adjustment is that its accounting for inventory as of the closing date complies with *past practices in accordance with GAAP* while the buyer's does not. To be successful this is what the seller's submissions to the arbitrator should present and support. Whatever the nature of the inventory dispute, the accounting arbitrator will be seeking sufficient supporting documentation to rely on in reaching a determination. Historical usage and sales information can be strong sources of supporting information regarding inventory, especially as it relates to inventory alleged to be excess and/or obsolete. Similarly, any closing date or near-closing date physical inventory count results can support the existence of inventory.

This type of documentation, supported by discussions of the inventory and its characteristics, the relevant accounting guidance, and the relevant purchase agreement provisions will provide a well-rounded argument to the arbitrator, resulting in the best opportunity for success.

Advice to Buyers

The post-closing purchase price adjustment process provides the buyer with the opportunity to assess what was purchased and whether the closing date accounting complies with the purchase agreement. Inventory is a part of this assessment and can be subject to careful review by the buyer.

For any target company that produces or sells products, odds are that inventory is a significant component of the transaction. This being the case, the buyer is typically interested in assuring that this inventory exists and is in good useable or saleable condition. This assessment often requires some effort on the part of the buyer.

Confirm the Existence of the Inventory Does the inventory exist in the quantities included in the detailed accounting records of the acquired entity and in the preliminary closing statement presented by the seller? This is generally an important question and can lead to an adjustment even before the buyer starts considering the valuation of inventory as of the closing date. Of course, any existence issues identified may impact the valuation, but that is a separate determination from the subsequent measurement of the existing inventory. If certain inventory items do not exist, their value for accounting purposes is, of course, zero.

A physical count is the best way to confirm the existence of inventory, even if the acquired entity has a perpetual inventory system. If there was no physical count performed near the closing date or if there was one performed but the buyer did not participate in the physical count, the buyer may choose to perform a physical count, ideally as near the closing date as possible. The longer after the closing date the count is performed, the more difficult it is to show that inventory was missing *as of* the closing date.

Similar to the advice to sellers in the earlier discussion, if there is a dispute regarding the existence of inventory, the physical count procedures and supporting documentation matter. A haphazardly performed and sloppily documented inventory count is not nearly as persuasive as one performed in an organized manner with well-defined procedures and completed documentation. So, what does a well-performed inventory count look like? There should be documented procedures and controls governing the count, including:

- Documentation regarding when the physical count is started and completed
- Procedures that provide for the manner in which the count sheets (either paper or electronic) are to be completed, reviewed, and approved
- Procedures that provide for the appropriate identification and handling of damaged or junk inventory
- Procedures for consolidating the count sheets into an overall inventory count
- Procedures related to inventory pricing

Once the count is completed, the buyer can compare the results to the detailed accounting records of the acquired entity to identify any discrepancies. This is a simplistic explanation of what can be a very time consuming process, but it can nonetheless be worth the effort. For example, regardless of whether the physical inventory count results in the identification of any missing or damaged inventory, the results can be useful in confirming the opening inventory balance. If the physical count does result in the identification of missing or damaged inventory, the buyer is able to propose a purchase price adjustment to potentially recover the shortfall.

Assess the Valuation of Inventory Once the test for existence of the inventory is completed, the buyer can perform the valuation of the acquired inventory. This book is not a course on inventory valuation, so we will not be discussing the intricacies of every aspect of inventory valuation. Again, we will be focusing on the identification and valuation of excess and obsolete inventory.

A review for excess and obsolete inventory can be a very detailed process that is often performed at the individual product level. The buyer's assessment of inventory as excess or obsolete can involve an assessment of the historical sales and usage of inventory as well as the expected future sales and usage. As noted throughout this chapter, the expected future activity is subject to judgment and estimation, but the judgment and estimation exercised should be based on as much factual information as possible to be a useful determinant of value. In addition to sales and usage data, this information can include market factors, industry information, competitor products, and similar factors that have a real bearing on the salability and usability of the acquired products. For example, a conclusion by a buyer that there is excess inventory of a particular product can be supported by a combination of the recent history of sales/usage in combination with relevant market or industry factors impacting expected future sales and usage.

Buyers should be careful to not allow their own future plans for the acquired business or their own existing operations and accounting practices to create a bias in their review of the acquired inventory. For example, if the buyer has plans to cease production of a particular acquired product, those plans are by themselves often irrelevant to the determination of the utility of the acquired inventory as of the closing date. As discussed, purchase agreements commonly provide for the closing statement to be prepared as of a moment immediately prior to the closing and without giving effect to the transaction. In other words, the purchase agreement commonly prevents the seller from bearing the costs of buyer's post-closing plans for the acquired business.

Presenting the Buyer's Position to the Accounting Arbitrator Most purchase agreements require the buyer's proposed closing statement, including any proposed adjustments, to be based on the consistent application of the historical accounting practices and methodologies utilized by the company under seller's ownership, as long as such practices and methodologies are in compliance with GAAP. At a basic level, the buyer's argument for a purchase price adjustment related to inventory is commonly that the seller's accounting for inventory as of the closing date was not in accordance with GAAP and/or one or more relevant specific purchase agreement provisions. To be successful, the buyer's submissions to the arbitrator should present and support this claim as well as support that the buyer's position is in accordance with GAAP and any relevant purchase agreement provisions.

A buyer will have to be careful that the argument it sets forth regarding excess or obsolete inventory is not solely based on an assessment that it is more conservative, and therefore more compliant, with GAAP—i.e., better GAAP. Better GAAP typically does not trump GAAP-compliant past practices. A proposed reduction to inventory for excessive quantities or obsolescence should be founded in judgments and estimates that show the seller's accounting to be inaccurate or otherwise in violation of GAAP and/or the purchase agreement. For example, if the buyer can show that the company is overly optimistic in its future sales projections, and the buyer's arguments are based on historical sales/usage data and/or market factors, this could be very persuasive. In addition, while the company's documented historical practices may be GAAP compliant, the seller may not have actually applied them appropriately, thereby potentially rendering the seller's calculation demonstrably in violation of *past practices in accordance with GAAP*.

The information the buyer can provide the accounting arbitrator is very similar to the information the seller can provide. In essence, the information should be in sufficient detail to support the buyer's position. For example, an Excel file listing inventory and count totals could be provided with the buyer's initial submission as a consolidated inventory summary, but that file does not provide any evidence about the inventory count procedures or confirm that the inventory count procedures were followed. In other words, such a file could be insufficient if presented as the sole source of information regarding the count performed. In addition to the file, the buyer can explain how the count was performed and/or provide sufficient supporting documentation regarding the inventory count. Similarly, the buyer could provide inventory reduction calculations for excess and obsolete inventory with a discussion of how the buyer reached its conclusion.

An accounting arbitrator wants to arrive at the appropriate amount in accordance with the terms of the purchase agreement. To be successful, the buyer should provide sufficient information, discussion, and supporting documentation to help the arbitrator understand why the buyer's position should be adopted. As stated for the seller, the type of documentation discussed here, supported by discussions of the inventory and its characteristics, the relevant accounting guidance, and the relevant purchase agreement provisions, should provide a well-rounded argument to the arbitrator, resulting in the best opportunity for success.

RESOLVING INVENTORY-RELATED DISPUTED ITEMS

Inventory-related disputed items are often not resolved completely in favor of one party. Such disputed items frequently incorporate multiple arguments and moving parts, which can easily result in an answer that is somewhere between the two parties' positions, although not necessarily at the midpoint. As discussed in an earlier chapter, the parties have engaged the accounting arbitrator to render a determination on the disputed items. Inventory-related disputed items often require a significant amount of analysis in order to reach an appropriate and supported conclusion. In addition, the ultimate determination will often also require a certain amount of judgment on the part of the accounting arbitrator.

If the parties have supported their positions on an inventory disputed item, the accounting arbitrator will have likely received a significant quantity of detailed information regarding the inventory of the acquired company as well as other supporting documentation underlying each party's position related to the inventory valuation. If this level of information was not provided, the accounting arbitrator can request this information from both parties through the arbitrator interrogatories and document request process.

Analyzing the information provided by the parties related to inventory disputed items will likely require significant effort on the part of the accounting arbitrator and his or her team due to the volume of detailed information commonly provided. As noted above, inventory related disputed items are also frequently one of the most significant disputed items in terms of dollar amount. In addition, the determination of the appropriate inventory valuation involves exercising judgment based on the information provided by the parties, and the application and consideration of the provisions of the purchase agreement and the relevant accounting guidance. In other words, inventory disputed items are deserving of extensive review and consideration by the accounting arbitrator to arrive at an appropriate determination. Through analysis and review, the accounting arbitrator should be able to become familiar with all of the parties' arguments and the supporting documentation including those involving specific market factors and other unique considerations relevant to the inventory in dispute.

The arbitrator is engaged to render a determination in accordance with the terms of the purchase agreement. It governs how the dispute is to be resolved, including the relevant accounting guidance, consistency requirements, and any transaction-specific adjustments (e.g., non-GAAP measures such as exclusions or limitations of certain inventory items). Unless appropriate under the terms of the purchase agreement, the arbitrator should resist the temptation to rely on better or preferred GAAP instead of GAAP compliant past practices.

Reaching a final determination can be a difficult process because the accounting arbitrator is weighing the parties' arguments, which both necessarily involve judgment and estimation regarding the value of the inventory. The ultimate determination of the arbitrator will be documented in a written report delivered to the parties. The level of detail included in that report will generally have been agreed to during the engagement process and the greater the level of detail required (e.g., a fully reasoned award), the greater the level of specific information the accounting arbitrator will need to present in the award. Importantly, regardless of the chosen award format, the level of analysis performed by the accounting arbitrator should be thorough and complete. The award format is simply the communication vehicle, and should have no impact on substance of the work performed by the accounting arbitrator to arrive at the conclusion. In other words, the arbitrator should not shortcut the extent of his analysis and evaluation because he does not have to communicate it beyond his conclusion.

NOTES

1. *See* FASB ASC 330-10-20 Glossary at Inventory.
2. *See* FASB ASC 330-10-20 Glossary at Inventory.
3. *See* FASB ASC Master Glossary, at Current Assets.
4. *See* FASB ASC 210-10-45-3.
5. Regarding the valuation of inventory, there has been a recent revision to the GAAP guidance in ASC 330—Inventory, which

is effective for public companies for fiscal years beginning after December 15, 2016, including interim periods within those fiscal years, and is effective for all other entities for fiscal years beginning after December 15, 2016, and interim periods beginning after December 15, 2017. Historically, inventory has been valued (measured) and recorded at the lower of cost or market, with market being replacement cost, with the caveat that market must not exceed a ceiling of net realizable value or be below a floor of net realizable value less a normal profit margin. The revised guidance alters the measurement criteria to be the lower of cost or net realizable value. The exception to this new guidance is that companies that measure inventory using the last-in-first-out (LIFO) or retail inventory methods still apply the lower of cost or market. Given the time of the publication of this book, the new guidance may be relevant going forward, but is—dependent on the timing—not necessarily relevant for currently ongoing disputes. Throughout this chapter, we will reference a mix of current and pending GAAP content.

6. *See* FASB ASC 330-10-35-1. The cite is from current content, the language of which will be superseded by the pending content of FASB ASC 330-10-35-1A – 1C.
7. *See* FASB ASC Master Glossary, at Net Realizable Value.
8. *See* FASB ASC Master Glossary, at Market.
9. *See* FASB ASC 330-10-35-1B.
10. *See* FASB ASC 330-10-35-16.
11. *See* FASB ASC 330-10-35-1, 1B, 1C, and 2.
12. *See* FASB ASC 330-10-35-5.

CHAPTER 17

Accounts Receivable

Similar to inventories, a target company's accounts receivable, or more precisely, accounts receivable net of the allowance for doubtful accounts, are routinely subject to purchase price disputes. Buyers and sellers tend to disagree on the valuation of the accounts receivable or the associated allowance. Buyers often seek to write off or recognize a significant allowance for aged accounts receivable while sellers tend to believe in the ultimate collectability of the receivables and the sufficiency of the allowance. Accounts receivable write-offs and adjustments to the allowance are not the only accounts receivable issues that can lead to disputes. In some instances, the parties can have a dispute about the existence of certain receivables. Accounts receivable can also be the subject of specific provisions in agreements such as carve-outs and various non-GAAP treatments.

The types of receivables that are the topic of this chapter are commonly referred to as *trade receivables*. This chapter does not specifically discuss disputes-related non-trade receivables such as notes receivable, various loans, or other types of receivables, because they are far less common than disputes regarding trade receivables. Those other types of receivables can involve issues such as impairment of loans and effective interest rates, which are not directly addressed in this book. However, the advice and instruction offered herein is applicable to many forms of receivables that may be involved in an accounting arbitration.

As with any other financial statement item that involves estimates and judgment, there can be differences of opinion regarding the judgment exercised and the estimates utilized in determining the amount to be recorded. In a post-closing purchase price adjustment process, this can result in disputes regarding the appropriate net accounts receivable balance. Because purchase agreements often require GAAP compliance in the preparation of any relevant financial statements as well as all purchase price adjustment calculations, any estimates (and judgment) used to derive the closing date net accounts receivable balance must be in accordance with the relevant GAAP guidance. This chapter will discuss the relevant GAAP guidance, how to present arguments to an accounting arbitrator for accounts receivable disputed items, and how accounting arbitrators can resolve such disputed items.

GAAP GUIDANCE RELATED TO ACCOUNTS RECEIVABLE

For transactions involving U.S.-based companies, or any transaction utilizing GAAP as the basis for accounting, FASB ASC 310—Receivables and FASB ASC 450—Contingencies currently provide the most relevant accounting guidance.[1] The allowance for doubtful accounts, which is most often the source of disagreement, is a loss contingency, which are generally covered by the guidance in FASB ASC 450. Notably, FASB ASC 450 refers the reader back to FASB ASC 310 for specific guidance regarding trade receivables. We will focus on the guidance in FASB ASC 310 because it provides the necessary guidance for our purposes. Following is a brief discussion of accounts receivable, the allowance for doubtful accounts, and the relevant GAAP accounting guidance.

Accounts Receivable and the Allowance for Doubtful Accounts

A trade receivable, for purposes of our discussion, results from a credit sale to a customer with expected payment terms of less than one year (i.e., a current asset). The allowance for doubtful accounts is an estimate of the potentially uncollectable portion (a contingent loss) of the outstanding accounts receivable at the measurement date. The balance of accounts receivable is adjusted (reduced) by the allowance for doubtful accounts, resulting in the net accounts receivable expected to be collected. In practice, it is often not quite as simple as it may appear because the accounts receivable balance is adjusted throughout the period for credit sales, collections, and write-offs and the allowance balance is adjusted for write-offs and other activity impacting receivables and the allowance. Nonetheless, the basic principle remains that the allowance reduces the receivables balance based on an estimate of the ultimate collectability.

Example: Accounting for Accounts Receivable

- A company sells goods on credit. The company continuously adds to the allowance. For each sale on credit, the company adds a predetermined percentage of the sale to the allowance. That percentage can be set based on the company's own historical information, available industry information, and/or general economic indicators.
- In the regular course of business, when an outstanding account receivable is deemed to be uncollectable, the amount gets written off. That write-off gets charged against the allowance. The decision to write off accounts receivable can be largely formulaic based on account aging, size, and other predetermined factors. There is, however, commonly at least a human element to concluding the account should be written off or further pursued, if not for all accounts that potentially qualify for being written off, then at least for the larger amounts.
- The allowance gets evaluated as of the balance sheet date and adjusted as necessary. The company's analysis in order to finalize the allowance is typically a combination of analytics and management judgment. The analysis can include a stratification of the accounts receivable in aging buckets and a comparison of aging versus collection statistics against the company's own experience. Management can, for example,

consider the aging of the accounts and its view on market circumstances. While some of the analytics are typically mechanical in nature, the interpretation of those analytics by management and the translation into an allowance often incorporates substantial judgment.

At the time of a credit sale, the initial measurement of the trade receivable is the amount of the credit extended (the receivable). Generally, the new receivable does not specifically need an allowance at that time; if the seller did not expect the customer to ultimately pay the receivable, the seller would most likely not have extended credit to the customer. Notwithstanding, the company may as part of its process book an allowance as a percentage of each credit sale or total credit sales during a period as it recognizes based on, among other things, its overall historical collection experience that a loss has been incurred. Moreover, in specific situations, the company may, of course, extend credit to struggling customers for a variety of reasons, such as hoping the needed supplies will help the customer weather the storm or as part of an ongoing valuable or strategic relationship.

The subsequent measurement of accounts receivable is determined based on the total balance of the outstanding accounts receivable as well as the underlying specific factors resulting in a determination of the allowance for doubtful accounts.[2] The allowance can be determined in a variety of ways as will be discussed in the next section. The recorded balance as of any financial reporting date, or a transaction closing date, should reflect the best estimate of the collectable balance of accounts receivable. This is an estimate that involves judgment and as a result is subject to disagreement as evidenced by the frequent inclusion of accounts receivable disputed items in accounting arbitrations.

Determining the Allowance for Doubtful Accounts

As noted earlier, the primary driver of many disputes related to accounts receivable is the allowance for doubtful accounts.

The allowance for doubtful accounts is a contingent loss and is a subsequent measurement determination used in deriving the estimated net collectable accounts receivable balance as of any given date, such as the closing date. FASB ASC 310 states that the "conditions under which receivables exist usually involve some degree of uncertainty about their collectability, in which case a contingency exists."[3] A loss contingency is defined by GAAP as an "existing condition, situation, or set of circumstances involving uncertainty as to possible loss to an entity that will ultimately be resolved when one or more future events occur or fail to occur."[4] The common question for buyers and sellers is related to the magnitude of the contingent loss as of the closing date.

GAAP again provides some guidance in determining a contingent loss in both FASB ASC 450 and FASB ASC 310. In general, GAAP provides that a loss contingency should be accrued if (i) information available before the financial statements are issued or available to be issued indicates that the loss is probable and (ii) the amount of the loss (e.g., uncollectable receivables) can be reasonably estimated.[5] Both criteria must be met to qualify for accrual. We will discuss these criteria in more detail in a later chapter, but at a high level, "probable" means likely to occur,[6] which is a higher threshold than "more likely than not," and "reasonably estimable" commonly means that the amount can be reasonably estimated within a range of possible outcomes.[7]

This still does not answer the question regarding how the contingency is actually determined at any given time. Generally, it is an evaluation of the amount and probability of uncollectable accounts receivable. It involves judgment and estimation based on experience that are applied in a variety of ways by companies. Some companies only record an allowance for specific accounts receivable based on their knowledge of a specific issue. Other companies will evaluate the allowance based on a specific percentage of sales or accounts receivable based on a historical collection realization rate. Yet other companies base the allowance on the strict application of accounts receivable aging with an allowance percentage applied based on the age of the receivable. And still others utilize a combination of two or more of these allowance calculation methodologies. In practice, employing a combination of methodologies is very common.

BUYER'S AND SELLER'S DIFFERING VIEWS REGARDING COLLECTABILITY

In the context of a transaction, the typical requirement is the application of accounting practices and methodologies that are consistent with those employed historically by the company and in accordance with GAAP. In practice, sellers and buyers can disagree both on the implementation of past practices and/or whether those practices are in accordance with GAAP.

Even a well-documented and consistently applied set of procedures related to the determination of the allowance for doubtful accounts commonly includes mental processes and the application of judgment dependent on the facts and circumstances existing as of the balance sheet date. That can be problematic in the context of a post-closing purchase price adjustment. After all, the seller and the buyer may each arrive at a different allowance, each of which appears acceptable under the company's historical methodology.

Moreover, the company's historical methodology is not necessarily bulletproof. For example, the net accounts receivable balance could have been materially correct as of the last financial statement audit, but still be subject to an adjustment as of the closing date in a purchase price dispute arbitration. The company's historical practice of estimating the allowance for doubtful accounts using specific percentages based on aging could be utilized by the buyer but with different percentages for certain aging categories because the seller's percentages are in violation of GAAP based on the facts and circumstances existing as of the closing date.

Overall, the disagreement between buyers and sellers regarding accounts receivable can often be boiled down to differing views regarding the collectability of outstanding receivables and the means of estimating the level of collectability. These differing views can involve a different application of judgment to the same estimation methodology or they can involve different methodologies of calculating the allowance for doubtful accounts.

ACCOUNTS RECEIVABLE DISPUTED ITEMS

The most common types of accounts receivable disputed items fall into two categories: (i) those based on differing methodologies and (ii) those based on differing estimates of collectability. The basis of these two types of disputes is really the same—collectability—but the disputes are arrived at by different means.

Disputes Based on Differing Methodologies

GAAP does not provide a listing of "approved" methodologies for calculating the allowance for doubtful accounts. In general, GAAP "does not permit the establishment of allowances that are not supported by appropriate analyses" and prescribes that "[t]he approach for determination of the allowance shall be well documented and applied consistently from period to period."[8] It should be estimated using the guidance in FASB ASC 310 and 450, which requires that any loss contingency be both probable and estimable, which are both subject to judgment.

It is not uncommon for disputed items to involve a difference of opinion on the appropriate methodology to determine the probability of collection. By different methodologies we are referring to the various means to arrive at the allowance for doubtful accounts amount. Methods commonly include specific identification, percentage of sales/receivables, and aging of receivables. As noted earlier, many companies employ a combination of those methodologies. Of those three the most straightforward can appear to be the percentage of sales/receivables as it appears to consist of simple arithmetic, namely the determination of the percentage of sales/receivables expected to be uncollectable, multiplied by sales or receivables for the period. The percentage, however, can be subject to extensive debate. Moreover, under each calculation methodology the resulting allowance generally still has to be evaluated as of the balance sheet date using appropriate judgment. Less common, at least as a standalone allowance calculation methodology, is specific identification and measurement of individual receivables. It requires review of each receivable to assess its collectability. This method is most often used by companies with fewer customers.

In an accounting arbitration the parties will sometimes present different methodologies for determining the allowance and the resulting net accounts receivable balance. Sellers often argue that their methodology is consistent with past practices and GAAP compliant and therefore is the only acceptable methodology. Buyers often argue that the seller's amount is not in compliance with GAAP and therefore an alternative methodology is needed.

Sellers also commonly argue that they know their customer base best, including their collection history, and as such are best suited to determine the appropriate allowance. Buyers often counter this argument by stating that the seller is unrealistic in its assessment of collectability, that actual collections are much lower, and that the buyer's proposed method is a more conservative approach. Sellers may reply that the buyer is failing to properly pursue the collection of the receivables in the post-closing period and is thereby attempting to obtain a windfall by getting paid twice—once through the accounting arbitration and again when the customers ultimately pay.

A buyer's proposal of an alternative methodology without an analysis that shows that the seller's historical methodology would be in violation of GAAP as of the closing date typically fails under *past practices in accordance with GAAP*. Regarding accounts receivable, buyers at times tend to implicitly argue for better GAAP, which is commonly insufficient under the applicable purchase agreement. For example, a buyer may prefer an accounts receivable aging methodology as compared to a seller's historical percentage of sales methodology. The buyer should argue that its methodology complies with GAAP and that seller's methodology does not. Regardless, even if the buyer is correct in its claim that a seller's allowance is too low, the arbitrator may not use the buyer's proposed alternative methodology. Rather, the arbitrator may apply a revision to the seller's historical methodology (higher allowance as a percentage of sales) to bring it into compliance with GAAP as opposed to accepting a completely different methodology proposed by the buyer. In other words, in this example the seller's historical methodology is not the issue; it is the application thereof and the collectability estimate that is the issue.

Disputes Based on Differing Collectability Estimates

The potential loss a company will experience through the failure of customers to pay their receivables balance is a *contingency*. The determination of the contingency amount is not an exact science, nor is it, other than by happenstance, going to be 100 percent accurate. The estimate of the portion of receivables that is not collectible is an important management estimate that should generally be based on the historical experience of the company and other factors that can impact collectability, such as credit terms, the economy, and the specific industry, among others. Given the range of factors that can impact collectability, buyers and sellers can disagree regarding the allowance for doubtful accounts estimates.

Example: Collectability

- The company historically utilized a percentage of sales methodology to calculate its allowance for doubtful accounts. The company used 3 percent of sales for purposes of the reference financial statements.

- In the year leading up to the closing date, the seller relaxed its credit policies and payment terms for its customers in order to generate higher short-term sales.
- After the closing of the transaction, the buyer reviews the collection rates and the aging of the accounts receivable. It notices higher than anticipated rates of default and a growing population of older receivables as compared to the company's historical experience. Based on this analysis the buyer proposes an adjustment to the allowance reflecting an increase from 3 percent to 5 percent of sales as of the closing date.
- The seller disputes the adjustment, arguing that the 5 percent allowance percentage is not consistent with the seller's historical GAAP-compliant accounting policies.
- In the accounting arbitration, the seller relies on the consistency in accounting practices provision in the purchase agreement as support for its position. The buyer's proposed adjustment is based on the position that, while the buyer is proposing a different estimation percentage, it is consistent with the seller's historical methodology but utilizes an increased percentage that more accurately calculates the allowance based on the expected collectability.

In this example, the overall methodology remained consistent, but the allowance (estimate) percentage was changed by the buyer. The buyer could win this disputed item, especially if it shows that collectability has been reduced by the seller's more liberal credit policies. Such policies can, and often do, result in increased collectability issues, which would normally require an adjustment to the allowance calculation. If this is not done, the allowance could be insufficient and therefore not GAAP compliant based on the facts existing as of the closing date. This example highlights that consistency of the overall methodology can be maintained and still result in a dispute because of differing views on the appropriate implementation and the resulting loss contingency estimate.

Not all disputes regarding the percentage of allowance for doubtful accounts are as straightforward as the previous example. For example in the situation of stratifying accounts receivable by days outstanding, keeping the methodology consistent, the parties may still disagree regarding the collectability of specific receivables as well as the allowance percentages applied to the accounts receivable aging buckets. Companies that utilize accounting receivable aging as the basis of calculating the allowance for doubtful accounts may, for example, assign percentages to each aging bucket (0–30 days, 31–60 days, 61–90 days, etc.) based on experience and expected default rates for each bucket. What is the appropriate allowance percentage for each aging bucket? GAAP does not provide such specific guidance, because it is different for every company and can change over time. Each company must establish its own basis for the allowance percentages and it should be supported by the company's past experience and expected collection rates, including any relevant market factors and the composition of its customer base. For example, on an individual basis, a receivable from a small struggling company that is overdue by 90 days would be viewed as much more suspect than the same receivable from a reputable Fortune 500 company that has historically paid slow as a matter of course.

One of the more common disputes related to accounts receivable and the allowance involves a combination of write-offs of specifically identified receivables and an increase in the allowance based on aging. The write-offs aspect is driven by the buyer's assessment of receivables after the closing date and the identification of specific receivables that the buyer deems uncollectable. The allowance percentage based on aging disagreement is due to differing opinions on the percentage applicable to various aging buckets or categories of receivables. For example, the seller may utilize a 75% allowance for receivables in the 91–120-day bucket, while the buyer believes that a

90% allowance is more reflective of actual collectability. These types of issues are very common in accounting arbitrations, but common does not mean simple. Accounts receivable disputed items often require significant explanation and documentation to support and also require careful and detailed consideration by the accounting arbitrator to resolve appropriately.

PRESENTING AND RESOLVING NET ACCOUNTS RECEIVABLE DISPUTED ITEMS IN AN ACCOUNTING ARBITRATION

Due to the uncertainty associated with the collection of the accounts receivable, the closing date net accounts receivable balance is a financial statement item that involves judgment and estimation about future events (although it should relate to incurred losses as of the date of the financial statements). In an accounting arbitration each party should strive to fully support its respective calculation of accounts receivable, including the allowance for doubtful accounts.

The proposed purchase price adjustments from a buyer related to accounts receivable are of a wide range, including those impacting just a few specific receivables to those that challenge both the allowance methodology and amount. Despite the wide range, accounts receivable disputed items are rarely minor in nature. For example, even if a proposed adjustment is comprised of only a few specific receivables, those receivables are likely significant individually and in the aggregate. That, coupled with the frequency with which these disputed items occur, means that the presentation of each parties' position and the arbitrator's resolution are also very significant.

To present and support an accounting arbitration position on accounts receivable and the allowance for doubtful accounts often requires a fairly significant amount of explanation and supporting documentation in the parties' submissions to the accounting arbitrator. The explanation should discuss the rationale for the position presented, which is then supported by relevant and sufficient documentation. Simply stating that the calculation is consistent with past practices generally does not constitute an appropriate explanation or support. Similarly, a mere conclusory statement that the seller's methodology does not comply with GAAP is generally insufficient grounds to propose an alternative methodology. As previously discussed, it is generally not sufficient for an accounting arbitrator to simply select a midpoint to resolve disputed items. Resolving such disputed items involves the consideration of the arguments and supporting detail to arrive at the appropriate conclusion that is in accordance with the terms of the relevant purchase agreement.

Presenting Positions on Net Accounts Receivable Disputed Items

The basic concepts of presenting arguments to the arbitrator were discussed in some detail in Chapters 12 and 13. Here we will provide some specific advice to buyers and sellers related to accounts receivable disputed items. As previously discussed, determining net accounts receivable at any given date involves judgment and estimation regarding the ultimate collectability. The accounting arbitrator needs sufficient detailed information on which to base a conclusion on these disputed items and that information is best provided by the parties. As a result, the sufficiency and relevance of the information provided to the arbitrator is directly related to the success on any disputed item.

Advice Relevant to Both Buyers and Sellers Analogous to our discussion of presenting inventory disputed items, there are a few core components that commonly should be included in arguing the accounts receivable balance:

- A discussion of the general composition of the accounts receivable balance and any unique characteristics
- A discussion of the relevant accounting guidance and its application to the facts and circumstances of the company
- A discussion of the specific purchase agreement provisions

Accounts receivable may not seem to be an item that requires discussion regarding unique characteristics, but in many cases it does. For example, if in the normal course of business the acquired company typically has longer than normal collection times, this should be explained. Further, any significant market factors that positively or negatively impact the collection of receivables can be discussed as well. This may be information that in the view of the parties merely sets the stage, but it can nonetheless be crucial information to provide to the accounting arbitrator. As has been stated several times in this book, the accounting arbitrator has little if any detailed knowledge of the sold/acquired entity, its market, or its accounts receivable prior to receiving the parties' submissions. It is generally well worth the effort to discuss those factors.

Advice to Sellers In a purchase price dispute arbitration, the seller is often in the position of defending the company's historical accounting practices as they were applied as of the closing date in preparing the preliminary closing statement and/or the reference financial statements. Dependent on the documentation retained and the historical relationship with the company, the seller can be the party in the best position to judge the company's customers' ability to pay and the historical payment timing. This can be a clear advantage in an accounting arbitration. Notwithstanding this statement, this can also be a crutch for the seller as the company may have historically repeated the process without necessarily skeptically reviewing its implementation. Alternatively, a seller may so loosely apply the process that its proposed implementation actually deviates from the company's past practices. Thus, a seller is generally well-served by demonstrating (i) how the company has historically implemented the measurement of the accounts receivable (allowance), (ii) how it has applied that measurement as of the closing date, and (iii) how that measurement is in accordance with GAAP or otherwise in compliance with the purchase agreement. The arbitrator is seeking information as to why each party believes its position is correct. From a seller's perspective, presenting its positions to an accounting arbitrator related to accounts receivable disputed items can be supported by documentation such as:

- Documents reflecting the historical implementation of the estimation process, such as policies or company work papers
- Accounts receivable aging reports
- Historical collection history documentation
- Historical bad-debt documentation
- Other documents that support the seller's position, such as information regarding rights of offset

Post-closing, sellers can be at a disadvantage regarding certain of the supporting documentation listed here. If the seller was unable to retain the documentation after the closing or obtain it during the pre-dispute phase, the seller may potentially overcome the lack of documentation by informing the accounting arbitrator of the documentation that the seller believes supports its position. The accounting arbitrator may end up requesting that the buyer provides the necessary documentation, which is typically accomplished through the arbitrator's interrogatories and document requests.

The type of documentation discussed here, supported by discussions of the net accounts receivable, the allowance for doubtful accounts methodology, the relevant accounting guidance, and the relevant purchase agreement provisions, will assist in providing the arbitrator with a complete picture of the seller's position on the disputed item.

Advice to Buyers The buyer has an expectation, justifiably so, that the acquired receivables, less the allowance for doubtful accounts, will result in cash inflows to the acquired business. If the buyer's assessment of the outstanding net accounts receivable as of the closing date indicates that this is not accurate, the buyer can propose a purchase price adjustment to reflect the expected collectable amount as long as it comports with *past practices in accordance with GAAP*.

Proposed Adjustments Based on Methodology versus Estimates

In proposing purchase price adjustments related to accounts receivable, a buyer may be implementing the historical accounting practices of the company or an alternative methodology to comply with GAAP. In the context of an accounting arbitration, the buyer's assessment and resulting proposed adjustment should be based on a methodology that complies with the terms of the purchase agreement. A common argument proposed by buyers related to inventory disputed items also applies to accounts receivable related disputed items, namely that the buyer's methodology results in a more conservative (i.e., better GAAP) approach to determining the allowance for doubtful accounts. Regardless of any preference, "better GAAP" does not trump historical GAAP-compliant accounting practices as proposed by the seller under *past practices in accordance with GAAP*. Conversely, GAAP does trump the seller's proposed accounting practices, consistent or not, if such practices are not in compliance with GAAP as of the closing date. So, for proposed adjustments based on an alternative methodology, the buyer should endeavor to show that the application of the company's historical methodology does not comply with GAAP.

Beyond the methodology, the implementation, that is estimates that are a part of the company's historical practices, can be challenged and challenged successfully if such estimates can be shown to result in a misstatement of accounts receivable as of the closing date. Challenging underlying estimates may be very different than proposing an alternative methodology. The buyer's task in proposing and supporting adjustments in an accounting arbitration is to discuss and present the inadequacy of the seller's estimates under *past practices in accordance with GAAP*, as well as supporting the buyer's proposed revised estimates. In identifying a potential adjustment to accounts receivable, the buyer may perform a detailed analysis of the aging of accounts receivable balances, collection history, credit policies, payment terms, and any other relevant factors governing or impacting the acquired entity's accounts receivable balance.

Importantly, the buyer's estimation as of the closing date should generally assume that the company continues to pursue collection of outstanding receivables, including older and possibly problematic receivables, in the normal course of operating the business. Just because it may be more difficult to collect and may take longer than expected does not mean that a receivable is worthless and should be written off or significantly reduced through an allowance.

Presenting the Buyer's Position to the Accounting Arbitrator The buyer's purchase price adjustment related to accounts receivable should be premised on an argument that the seller's accounting for accounts receivable as of the closing date was not in accordance with GAAP, was not in accordance with the company's own past practices, and/or violated one or more relevant purchase agreement provisions. To provide the greatest opportunity for success, the buyer's submissions to the arbitrator should support this claim against the seller's accounting for accounts receivable and that the buyer's position is in accordance with *past practices in accordance with GAAP* and/or any other relevant purchase agreement provisions.

In presenting the buyer's position to the accounting arbitrator, the buyer can prepare an overall analysis of accounts receivable and how it supports its conclusion of the appropriate balance as of the closing date. The buyer's submissions can include much of the same information discussed for the seller. One item the buyer will have that the seller may not, at least for purposes of the initial submission, is the post-closing collection activity. Dependent on the purchase agreement, the post-closing period can be a key element of the buyer's analysis of the accounts receivable balance of the acquired entity. Whether that period is 30 days or 90 days, there will be payment activity, or lack thereof, that can provide insight into the expected realization of certain receivables.

Notwithstanding, just because a receivable was not collected during the subsequent event period does not mean it is automatically a bad debt. The post-closing period can, however, provide potentially valuable insight. For example, information can be presented to support the assertion that the company loosened its credit standards in the period prior to closing, which negatively impacted collection rates. The buyer's arbitration submissions can discuss this post-closing activity and can support conclusions drawn based on the activity. Notwithstanding, a demonstrated decline in collectability subsequent to the closing date is not necessarily informative of the appropriate allowance as of the closing date. By means of example, the decline in collections may be caused by a turn in the general industry or economy occurring after the closing.

Another argument that buyers commonly face is that the proposed adjustment includes write-offs of receivables that were not collected based on the buyer's failure to properly pursue collection. A way to overcome this argument can be maintaining records of collection efforts and the result of those efforts.

The buyer's submissions to the accounting arbitrator should include supporting documentation in sufficient detail necessary to provide the arbitrator a full understanding of the buyer's proposed adjustment and the basis thereof. This has been stated before, but it bears repeating that this type of documentation, supported by discussions of accounts receivable and the allowance for doubtful accounts, the relevant accounting guidance, and the relevant purchase agreement provisions, will provide a well-rounded argument to the arbitrator.

Resolving Disputed Items Related to Accounts Receivable

Accounts receivable disputes are often not resolved completely in favor of one party. The allowance for doubtful accounts is an estimated amount based on the judgment of the preparer.

Accounts receivable disputed items require a significant amount of detailed analysis to understand and assess in order to reach a determination. As stated throughout this book, the arbitrator should carefully consider all of the information provided as well as the relevant accounting guidance and the purchase agreement provisions in resolving the disputed item.

Accounts receivable is another disputed item that is often accompanied by a significant amount of information from the parties because of the detailed nature of the account and also because accounts receivable disputed items can be very significant in terms of the dollars at stake. The accounting arbitrator should generally receive a significant amount of detailed information, including accounts receivable listings, aging reports, collection reports, bad debts history, and other relevant information.

All of this information should be thoroughly reviewed and analyzed by the accounting arbitrator in order to reach an appropriate determination. The ultimate determination will be documented in a written report to the parties, which will present the arbitrator's findings in the agreed-upon level of detail (e.g., summary, summary reasoned award, or fully reasoned award). As noted in the inventory chapter, the format of the award should have no impact on the level of analysis performed by the arbitrator.

NOTES

1. In 2016 the FASB issued Accounting Standards Update 2016-13 Financial Instruments—Credit Losses (Topic 326), which will impact the recognition of credit losses related to various receivables.

   This revised guidance will impact the guidance in FASB ASC 310 related to the allowance for doubtful accounts. We have not addressed this change in guidance in this book because it will not be effective until 2020 for most entities. Early adoption is allowed for fiscal years beginning after December 15, 2018.

2. *See* FASB ASC 310-10-35-10.
3. *See* FASB ASC 310-10-35-7.
4. *See* FASB ASC Master Glossary, at Loss Contingency.
5. *See* FASB ASC 450-20-25-2.
6. *See* FASB ASC Master Glossary, at Probable.
7. *See* FASB ASC 450-20-25-5.
8. *See* FASB ASC 310-10-35-4-c

CHAPTER 18

Contingent Liabilities

Among the more common categories of disputed items are those involving a contingent liability or other form of loss or impairment. Earlier chapters covered some of these accounts, such as inventory and accounts receivable allowances. There are several other contingent liabilities that can impact net working capital as of the closing date and can result in proposed adjustments and disputes.

In this chapter we discuss various aspects of contingent liabilities, such as the applicable GAAP guidance and the importance of subsequent events. We also discuss three categories of contingent liabilities that frequently occur in practice. These include litigation accruals, warranty accruals, and taxes. Of course, post-closing disputes are not necessarily limited to those three categories (e.g., there can be a dispute about contingent environmental liabilities).

A loss contingency is defined in GAAP as:

> *An existing condition, situation, or set of circumstances involving uncertainty as to possible loss to an entity that will ultimately be resolved when one or more future events occur or fail to occur ...*[1]

In other words, a contingent liability generally incorporates an estimation of what might happen in the future. Just because an event might happen in the future, however, does not mean it should be recorded in a company's financial statements. To recognize (record) a contingent liability, GAAP (FASB ASC 450) provides two criteria, both of which must be met in order for a company to record the contingent liability:

> *A contingent loss shall be accrued by a charge to income [which results in recognition on the balance sheet as a result of double entry bookkeeping], if both of the following conditions are met:*
>
> *a. Information available before the financial statements are issued or are available to be issued ... indicates that it is probable that an asset had been impaired or a liability had been incurred at the date of the financial statements.... It is implicit in this condition that it must be probable that one or more future events will occur confirming the fact of the loss.*
> *b. The amount of the loss can be reasonably estimated.*[2]

Thus, in order to record a contingent loss, it must be probable (not 100%) and the amount must be able to be reasonably estimated. The usual suspects that are at the root of many disputed items related to contingencies are at play here—judgment and estimation. "Probable" is generally considered a high likelihood, which is a higher level of probability than "more likely than not." GAAP does not provide a percentage threshold to further define "probable."

The reasonable estimate can be a range of possible outcomes. In such cases, FASB ASC 450 provides the relevant guidance stating the following:

> *If some amount within a range of loss appears at the time to be a better estimate than any other amount within the range, that amount shall be accrued. When no amount within the range is a better estimate than any other amount, however, the minimum amount in the range shall be accrued.*[3]

In proposing, and objecting to, purchase price adjustments related to contingent liabilities, the disagreement is commonly rooted in the application of the GAAP guidance discussed earlier—the probability and estimation elements. Any number of factors come into play in these disputed items, several of which we have covered throughout this book. For some it is just a difference of opinion regarding what is probable, for others it is a disagreement on the estimable amount, and yet for others it is based on a preference for a more or less conservative approach in determining the probability or range of estimated loss. Given the fact that financial accounting involves, and in fact requires, the exercise of judgment about uncertain future events, coupled with the fact that buyers and sellers can disagree regarding the most likely outcome, it is not surprising that contingent liabilities are commonly disputed items. In addition, depending on the contingency, the dollars at stake can be significant.

Example: Probability Ranges and Estimates

- A company has introduced a new product. It recognizes a contingent liability for warranty obligations. Although it can estimate the obligation for its other products relatively precisely, it has very little experiential information for the new product on, for example, failure rates in practice.
- The seller estimates the range of the contingent liability at $1 million to $10 million and includes a $1 million accrual as of the closing date.
- The buyer agrees with the proposed range, but concludes that $8 million is the most likely outcome within the range. As a result, the buyer seeks a $7 million post-closing adjustment.

Finally, there can be an overlap between contingent liabilities and indemnification provisions. For example, the company may have tax accruals included in net working capital while the purchase agreement also contains an indemnification provision that allocates the financial responsibility for pre-closing related taxation to the seller. Further details related to indemnification provisions are provided in Chapter 21.

THE POTENTIAL IMPACT OF SUBSEQUENT EVENTS ON CONTINGENCIES

If a contingent loss is not recorded on the closing date, there can be events in the subsequent event period—insofar as such a period is used in the post-closing process—that may result in the need to record a contingency or update an existing contingent loss as of the closing date. For example, in preparing the preliminary closing statement a company may not have recorded a contingent loss related to an ongoing litigation matter. During the subsequent event period, the matter may settle or sufficient information may become available regarding the range of potential resolution of the matter. FASB ASC 450 provides, in pertinent part:

> *Accrual may be appropriate for litigation, claims, or assessments whose underlying cause is an event occurring on or before the date of an entity's financial statements even if the entity does not become aware of the existence or possibility of the lawsuit, claim, or assessment until after the date of the financial statements. If those financial statements have not been issued or are not yet available to be issued ..., accrual of a loss related to the litigation, claim, or assessment would be required if the probability of loss is such that the condition in paragraph 450–20–25–2(a) is met and the amount of loss can be reasonably estimated.*[4]

Chapter 9 discussed subsequent event considerations in more detail and the parties should be aware that such events can occur. If such events occur, it is not necessarily an indication that the preliminary closing statement was inaccurate, it may simply mean that additional information has come to light that provides additional clarity regarding existing contingencies or identifies previously unknown contingent losses. In this regard, subsequent events can be a component of the assessment of contingent liabilities in the context of the purchase price adjustment process.

LITIGATION ACCRUALS

The ultimate outcome of litigation is often very difficult to predict with any degree of certainty, which is why, from an accounting perspective, it is commonly a contingent liability. In some cases, the potential range of the outcome may be readily apparent; in other cases, the range may be zero to many millions of dollars. Complicating matters further is that buyers and sellers can disagree regarding the assessment of the range of potential outcomes of the litigation in question and on any best estimate of the outcome of the pending litigation within that range.

Accruals for pending litigation that involve some potential for damages or other costs to a company are a common contingent liability for companies and also a commonly disputed item in accounting arbitrations. Certain litigation matters can be more significant than others, both in terms of potential dollar impact as well as reputational impact. For example, a buyer reviewing a potential acquisition target may view threatened or pending litigation related to a workers' compensation claim for one employee much differently than a pending product liability lawsuit related to the target company's highest selling product. Unless the purchase agreement contains a specific provision to the contrary, the disclosure or recording of litigation matters should be assessed against the criteria of FASB ASC 450.

Regardless of the potential magnitude, the disclosure of pending or ongoing litigation is often included in a disclosure schedule to the purchase agreement. When considering post-closing purchase price adjustments, disclosure may have been a transaction agreement requirement, but whether some amount should actually be reflected in the financial statements is another question. Moreover, as discussed, the accounting classification, recognition, and measurement may be impacted by information obtained or subsequent events between the closing date and the date of the buyer's proposed closing statement.

In preparing the preliminary closing statement, sellers should critically assess their pending or threatened litigation and make appropriate accruals where necessary. Post-closing, buyers should perform the same critical assessment. Unfortunately, the parties often disagree regarding this assessment as to whether any amount should be recorded and the amount that should be recorded.

The theoretical accounting assessment of current, threatened, or pending litigation is not overly complex in many cases. For example, to provide the necessary practical information, letters from the company's attorney(s) regarding pending or ongoing litigation can be obtained. While the information provided in such letters can vary in in the level of detail, they will often at a minimum provide the current status of the litigation as well as any known range and possible timing of potential settlement (or other resolution). For example, an attorney letter may state that the litigation is pending, the company intends to defend its position vigorously, and no estimate of settlement can be made at this time. In other cases, the attorney letter may state that litigation has been ongoing for over a year and the current estimated range of potential resolution is between $1 million and $5 million. These relatively obvious examples can provide the information necessary to form the basis for a conclusion regarding the disclosure and/or recording of a contingent litigation accrual. After closing, the buyer may obtain updated legal letters that may provide additional information regarding any existing, pending, or new litigation as of the closing date that may inform the parties regarding the need for any related contingent accruals.

Disputed contingent litigation accruals often involve some additional complexity, such as accruing expected attorney's fees, potential insurance claim deductibles, or items not covered by any attorney letter. In these cases, the parties can discuss and describe the situation in the submissions to the accounting arbitrator, including the accounting guidance that supports the treatment proposed. For example, FASB ASC 450 includes a quote from an SEC Staff Announcement that discusses accrual of legal fees, observing both the inclusion of expected legal fees in litigation accruals as well as expensing such fees as incurred with the caveat that either policy should be the consistent policy utilized by the company.[5] So, if a seller has historically expensed attorney's fees as incurred and a buyer proposes an adjustment to add expected attorney's fees to the litigation accrual, the seller may prevail based on the buyer's departure from the company's past practices on that point, even though both methodologies may be acceptable under GAAP. As with all disputed items, it is up to the parties to educate the arbitrator regarding their respective positions and the basis therefor.

Resolving contingent litigation liabilities disputed items will require the review of the information provided by the parties that describes and discusses the specific matters in dispute. In cases where there is no independent assessment, such as an attorney letter, the arbitrator will have to reach an independent conclusion regarding the parties' rationale for their positions to resolve the dispute.

Many such disputed items may involve differing assessments of the contingent liability at issue between the seller and the buyer. Some of these differences can be significant such as a seller concluding that no accrual is warranted and a buyer claiming that a significant accrual is warranted. The accounting arbitrator will have to appropriately evaluate the accounting given the current status of the litigation matters that are part of the disputed items and the potential outcomes to establish a range of potential resolution on which to base the accrual.

WARRANTY ACCRUALS

Every product sold by a company that has an included or purchased warranty is subject to a claim under that warranty for product defects or other warrantied issues. In accordance with the guidance in FASB ASC 460—Guarantees, companies should assess the likelihood and amount of warranty claims expected to occur in future periods for goods that have been sold and, if necessary, record an accrual for that contingent liability.[6] As with most other commonly disputed post-closing adjustments, warranty accruals involve judgment and estimation.

The parties can disagree regarding the amount of any warranty accrual to be recorded as of the closing date. Disagreements commonly come into play with warranty accruals that involve new products or new product lines with little warranty history on which to base on estimate. In such instances, the parties can, for example, rely on comparison to similar products or similar product introductions, much the same way companies must estimate product returns.

More complex issues arise when special circumstances exist, such as a product recall or a significant product defect, resulting in a potentially high volume of expected warranty claims. In some instances, the product defect may not be identified until after the closing date. In situations where the product defect is known prior to the transaction, the parties may agree on a specific treatment, whether it is an agreed-upon accrual or an indemnification. Leaving such a potentially large volume of warranty claims open to competing assessments as of the closing date could result in a dispute.

Regardless of the complexity, in practice there are disputed items related to warranty accruals of all types. Accounting arbitrators should be well versed in the applicable guidance, but even more importantly they should be aware of any special provisions in the purchase agreement. Product warranties can be covered in special provisions to purchase agreements to either limit the level of warranties for which the buyer is responsible or vice versa. Such provisions can impact the determination amount. For example, based on the warranty claims, the determination of the accounting arbitrator solely under *past practices in accordance with GAAP* could be above the maximum amount allowed under the purchase agreement and should therefore be lowered in the award.

CONTINGENT TAX EXPOSURE

Taxes of all types are typically a consideration for transaction parties. Tax obligations are routinely subject to pre-closing due diligence. The parties also commonly include specific provisions related to taxation in the purchase agreement. For example, the purchase agreement can contain an indemnification provision based on which the seller is responsible for all taxes related to pre-closing periods. The interaction with indemnity claims is discussed in further detail in Chapter 21.

Taxes can also be at the genesis of various accruals as of the closing date. For example, the company may have prepaid its property taxes for the year. As of the closing date, the prepaid expenditure would be an asset that is part of net working capital. The company may also have accrued liabilities for known tax obligations.

In addition, a company can also have contingent tax liabilities. For example, the company may be subject to local sales tax audits that it expects to result in an additional tax obligation. While the amount may be unknown as of the closing date, the company may be able to estimate a range and include the estimate on the balance sheet as a contingent liability.[7]

Estimating tax contingencies may include the careful consideration of a variety of documentation as well as opinion letters from tax specialists.

POTENTIAL MITIGATION OF CERTAIN CONTINGENT LIABILITIES

Some contingent liabilities have the possibility of seriously impacting net working capital, especially in certain industries. By means of example, environmental liabilities can be very significant. The parties can attempt to prevent (or at least limit) specific contingent liabilities through explicitly excluding them from net working capital or otherwise defining special treatment. This can be especially attractive in the context of contingent liabilities that are also covered by indemnification provisions.

Example: Environmental Liability

- The target company operated a countrywide network of small retail and convenience stores. Some of the locations included fuel pumps and there may be environmental cleanup needed due to underground storage tanks.
- The purchase agreement has an indemnification for environmental liabilities.
- The seller disclosed the contingent liability in due diligence, but did not recognize it on the balance sheet because at that time the range of possible outcomes was from zero to $10 million.
- The buyer was informed of the obligation during due diligence. Subsequent to closing, the buyer commissioned a study as of the closing date, which found that the most likely required cleanup cost was $8 million and recommends cleanup within a year to prevent further contamination.
- The buyer proposed recording a contingent liability as a deduction to net working capital in an amount of $8 million, leading to a purchase price dispute.
- The accounting arbitrator ruled in favor of the buyer, determining that $8 million was an appropriate amount to recognize for the contingent liability as of the closing date.
- *Scenario 1:* The cleanup ultimately costs $9 million. The buyer receives an additional $1 million under the indemnification provision. The net effect is that the seller has paid for the cleanup (as the parties intended).
- *Scenario 2:* The cleanup ultimately costs $6 million. There is typically no mechanism or requirement for the buyer to pay back part of the net working capital deduction as the net working capital is based on the company's historical accounting practices in compliance with GAAP as of the closing date, not on the ultimate outcome. The net result

is a $2 million windfall for the buyer. The buyer received a $2 million discount on the purchase price for costs that were not ultimately incurred while the risk of the opposite situation was covered with an indemnity.

A possible approach to prevent this type of situation is to carve out the possibility of net working capital adjustments for contingent liabilities that are also covered by indemnification clauses. We discuss the interaction between indemnification provisions and net working capital in more detail in Chapter 21.

NOTES

1. *See* FASB ASC Master Glossary, at Loss Contingency.
2. *See* FASB ASC 450-20-25-2.
3. *See* FASB ASC 450-20-30-1.
4. *See* FASB ASC 450-20-55-11.
5. *See* FASB ASC 450-20-S99-2.
6. *See, e.g.*, FASB ASC 460-10-25-5 to 6.
7. Notably, FASB ASC 740 contains extensive guidance specifically related to income taxes, for which the accounting treatment is not necessarily the same as for other taxes.

CHAPTER 19

Revenue Recognition and Expense Accruals

As we discussed in the overview of disputed items, the recognition of revenue and accrual of expenses can be sources of adjustments and disputed items. Although the recognition of revenue and the accrual of expenses primarily relate to the income statement, the use of accrual accounting can result in an accompanying impact to the balance sheet, including net working capital.

In this chapter, we discuss revenue recognition in more detail and illustrate some of the disputes that can occur. We also discuss several expense accruals, including vacation and payroll accruals, bonus accruals, and tax accruals, that are frequently the subject of disputes between the parties. In general, those types of accruals center on the recognition of expenses—and an associated liability accrual—for amounts that have not yet been paid. We conclude the chapter with a discussion of the opposite situation—prepaid expenses.

REVENUE RECOGNITION

Disputes related to the recognition of revenue can, in general, be divided into two categories: cutoff issues and multi-period recognition timing. First, the parties may disagree on the manner in which the company recognizes its revenue in relation to the financial statement cutoff. For example, in the regular course of business the company may aggressively interpret accounting guidance to recognize revenue that is on the edge of whether it belongs in the current financial statement period or in the next one. In the context of the preliminary closing statement, early recognition of revenue can lead to the recognition of increased net working capital. Dependent on the circumstances, the buyer may argue that the company crossed the line and recognized revenue too early and thus failed to comply with GAAP.

GAAP includes specific criteria that determine when revenue should be recognized. The parties and the accounting arbitrator can apply those criteria to the dispute at hand. As the recognition of revenue depends on the facts and circumstances of the company, it is generally important for the parties to incorporate the applicable circumstances in their submissions as opposed to engaging in a GAAP debate set in a factual vacuum. Again, the parties will generally be well aware of the circumstances and understand the business practices of the company, while the arbitrator is new to the company when he or she is retained.

Disputes can also occur related to the manner in which the to-be-recognized revenue for a longer term project is to be deferred and recognized over the project or contract period. Dependent on the project, the appropriate revenue recognition can be ratable or non-ratable based on project milestones and the nature of the services performed.

Example: Ratable versus Non-Ratable Recognition of Revenue

- A company installs and services software. It typically offers its services in the form of long-term contracts.
- *Scenario 1:* The effort expended by the company servicing the software occurs smoothly throughout the contract period. The upfront installation effort is *de minimis*.
- *Scenario 2:* The company regards the contract as a multiple-element arrangement containing three distinct elements, namely the (i) initial sale of the license, (ii) installation and implementation of the software, and (iii) ongoing software maintenance.

- In the first scenario, the revenue will generally be recognized ratably over the life of the contract. In the second scenario, the revenue recognition may be non-ratably recognized, assuming the company can muster evidence for its breakout of the elements and can otherwise meet the criteria for non-ratable revenue recognition.

The GAAP guidance for non-ratable revenue recognition is complex and detailed. Its implementation depends on the individual facts and circumstances of the company, may require the company to muster evidence related to the breakout of the elements of its customer arrangements, and may differ from customer to customer if the contracts are customized.

Notwithstanding, even ratable recognition of revenue may lead to disputes between the parties.

Example: Ratable Revenue Recognition Dispute

- A company sells one-year service contracts on high-tech manufacturing equipment. The customer pays for the contract upfront.
- The company recognizes the contract revenue ratably over the course of a year with the first month of revenue recognized in the month the contract is executed.
- After the closing, the buyer takes the position that the company has recognized part of its revenue too early, which understates the deferred revenue liability.
  - The buyer argues that by recognizing revenue for a full month in the month the contract is signed, the company improperly recognizes revenue for part of the month for which the contract is not in effect.
  - As of the closing date the company has 500 service contracts in effect, for an average contract fee of $100,000, and an average of 6 months remaining on the contract.
  - The buyer's proposed closing statement recalculates the deferred revenue based on the effective dates of the service contracts. The buyer proposes an adjustment of $2.4 million.

- The seller takes the position that its revenue recognition methodology is an acceptable simplification under GAAP and that GAAP does not require day-by-day recognition. Moreover, the seller argues that even if its revenue recognition methodology is not in accordance with GAAP, a mid-month implementation would be appropriate. The seller concludes that no adjustment is necessary and that even if an adjustment is required, it should be $2.1 million (calculated on a midmonth basis).

Overall, companies that perform their services on a project basis or subject to period-based contracts can easily encounter one or more issues related to revenue recognition. Those issues can be of significant monetary value even if in situations where they are unexpected, such as in the previous example.

VACATION AND OTHER PAYROLL ACCRUALS

Vacation and payroll accruals can be relevant to any company that has employees and provides paid vacation to its employees. Buyer-proposed adjustments commonly relate to updating the vacation or payroll accrual as of the closing date. For example, the transaction closed on October 31, but the preliminary closing statement did not include the vacation accrued in October and instead included the amount as of September 30. Similarly, the preliminary closing statement may not include the accrual for the earned but unpaid payroll as of the closing date. These types of proposed adjustments are most frequently resolved without the need for arbitration because the need for a true-up is commonly obvious and easily corrected.

Notwithstanding, buyer-proposed increases to the vacation accrual can result in disputed items for other issues for which the seller claims that the buyer's adjustments fail to comply with the required consistency with historical policies. The proposed adjustment may include increases to the vacation accrual based on claimed inaccuracies in the seller's accrual calculation due to poor accounting records or regional variances in vacation polices. Vacation accruals can get granular. For example, another state in which the company operates may allow the carryover of more vacation than its home base. In the case of a small operation, the company may not sufficiently track such differences. The buyer may recalculate the vacation accrual and argue that the closing date accrual was insufficient due to the company not appropriately tracking unused vacation or other errors in the company's accounting records.

Payroll accruals also involve benefits and other items included in employees' pay checks. This can add some complexity to any proposed adjustments related to payroll accruals, but as with vacation accruals, such disputed items are typically relatively straightforward to resolve. The complexity that occurs in practice often involves bonus payments related to the transaction or annual performance bonuses for employees, which we discuss separately in what follows.

Overall, even when vacation and payroll adjustments become disputed items, such disputes are typically resolved fairly easily in an accounting arbitration because there is not much in the way of potential complexity, judgment, or estimation. As discussed in an earlier chapter, relevant errors may be identified by performing sell-side due diligence, which may avoid an unpleasant post-closing surprise adjustment. In presenting and resolving vacation and payroll accrual disputed items, documentation of accounting policies is key as are the terms of the purchase agreement.

BONUS ACCRUALS

The vacation and payroll accrual issues discussed earlier are primarily either cutoff issues that are sometimes not captured in preparing the preliminary closing statement, or mathematical or tracking errors. Bonus accruals are different in that they could just be missed or there could be a real question as to whether an accrual is required to comply with GAAP and the purchase agreement. There are three primary types of bonus accruals we will discuss: (i) transaction-related bonuses, (ii) annual or quarterly performance bonuses, and (iii) discretionary bonuses.

Transaction-related bonuses are frequently not an issue because they are often excluded from net working capital, or at least excluded from consideration in any purchase price adjustment, by a provision in the purchase agreement. This is done because the only way these bonuses are paid is if the transaction actually closes. Further, such bonuses are generally not related to the ongoing operations of the business. The same can be said for other transaction-related expenses (e.g., advisors, investment bankers, etc.), which are often also excluded from any purchase price adjustment metric.

The most common bonus accrual issues are related to quarterly and annual performance bonuses based on employee and/or company performance and discretionary bonuses. The timing of recording the accrual is what typically gives rise to proposed adjustments and disputed items. The question regarding the performance bonus is: When are they earned by the employees (in the case of employee/company performance bonuses) and when should they be accrued? Discretionary bonuses add another layer of complexity because there is typically no defined metric to meet to trigger the bonus payment. Such bonuses are paid exclusively at the discretion of management. The complicating factor, as with many such items, is that the transaction closing is rarely at a quarter- or year-end when such accruals are typically assessed and recorded.

Example: Bonus Payout Based on a Net Income Target

- A company has an annual performance bonus plan that is based on the financial performance of the company. Specifically, the bonus plan has three potential payment levels as a percentage of an employee's salary—5, 10, and 15 percent, depending on the company's success in hitting its target of 10 percent net income growth for the year. If the company hits 7 percent growth, the bonus payout is 5 percent, if the company hits 10 percent growth, the bonus payout is 10 percent, and if the company exceeds 12.5 percent growth, the bonus payout is 15 percent.

- The transaction closing date is October 15. Through that date the company's net income has grown 8 percent as compared to the prior year.
- The forecast for the last two-and-a-half months of the year is a bit murky because one of the company's premier products is facing stiff competition from two new competitors in the market. Sales for the product have declined 25 percent in the last 60 days.
- The company is launching an updated product with features exceeding those of the two new competitors, but it will not be available for sale until after Thanksgiving. Management's expectations of the new product sales are very high.

Based on the previous example, what level of bonus payout, if any, should the company record as of the October 15 closing date? Obviously, there is not enough information in the example to make an exact determination, but this example does highlight real issues that can have an impact on the judgment and estimation used to determine the timing of any bonus accrual. What if the company in the example was forecasting tremendous sales of the updated product, resulting in total net income growth for the year of 12 percent? What amount and related to what percentage should be considered incurred as of October 15? These and other considerations come into play regarding bonus accruals, which can be quite significant in dollar amount if such bonuses would be paid out to all or many of the company's employees.

In the case of discretionary bonuses, there is often no clear line to mark when a specific metric is met that would trigger the bonus payment. If the bonuses are truly discretionary, can they, or should they, be accrued before or only after management has made a firm decision to pay such bonuses and determined the amount to be paid? What if the company has a 10-year history of paying discretionary bonuses of at least 7 percent? What if the company's discretionary bonus payment history can really be tied to company performance? For example, the company does not pay a bonus every year, but it does pay a bonus in every year when sales increase over the prior year. It should be clear how such accruals can become an issue in a transaction setting. The parties can easily disagree regarding whether discretionary bonuses should be accrued as of the closing date, depending on many of the factors discussed in this section.

A possible way to minimize or avoid disputed items related to bonus accruals is to specify the amount of bonuses to be paid to employees, if any, in the purchase agreement. In the absence of such an agreement on the bonus accrual, the seller should fully disclose the bonus plan and the historical accrual methodology (monthly, annually, etc.) based upon how the bonus is earned. Of course, the accrual methodology must be in accordance with GAAP to be applicable.

TAX ACCRUALS

Taxes and tax accruals are commonly a consideration for the buyer. Without provisions to the contrary, the buyer—upon acquisition—becomes economically interested in the tax obligations of the company. Many purchase agreements contain protections for the buyer (and the seller) in the form of tax indemnities. For example, the purchase agreement may provide that the seller is responsible for taxes that become owed in relation to pre-closing periods and that have not been otherwise provided for as of the closing date (e.g., in the form of a net working capital accrual). Whether an indemnification is provided or not, the parties typically have a vested interest in the accuracy of the tax accruals as of the closing date. Tax accruals can include (i) "billed" liabilities, (ii) accrued liabilities for obligations that have been incurred, but for which a tax bill has not yet been received (or a return filed), and (iii) contingent tax liabilities (e.g., related to ongoing tax audits). In addition, taxes can also be pre-paid, which can result in an asset that needs to be recorded.

Upon the closing of the transaction, buyers commonly perform a detailed review of the tax accruals to gauge the sufficiency of such accruals based on the buyer's expectations. This review can result in proposed adjustments, some of which are resolved easily while others may become disputed items, on occasion very significant disputed items. These disputes often occur in transactions where the entity being acquired has locations across a variety of tax jurisdictions. Those types of companies require a significant effort to appropriately accrue, file, and pay a variety of taxes, including property, sales, and income taxes, to multiple local, state, national, and potentially international taxing authorities.

Such disputed items can be very document intensive to support and analyze for resolution. The disagreement rarely centers on different interpretations of tax law. Disputes are most often due to a different determination or estimation of taxes to be paid after the closing date. On occasion, the buyer may include proposed adjustments to reserve a contingent amount for potential taxes owed beyond the recorded tax accrual and without a direct basis in the known tax obligations of the company. This is generally a difficult position to support without a bill from a taxing authority or other evidence that the amount paid by the seller was insufficient, such as a sales reconciliation or tax audit results indicating additional amounts are due.

Taxes may sometimes seem to be a fairly straightforward issue on the surface. For example, a company sells items, collects sales taxes, and remits those sales taxes to the appropriate taxing authority. Errors in recording such accruals, however, are commonly caught as the books are closed for the period. Although this may result in a true-up, run-of-the mill accrual issues do not typically result in accounting arbitrations. Tax accrual disputes can relate to areas where judgment and estimation are involved. For example, the recognition of a contingent liability for the pending outcome of ongoing tax audits or proposed adjustments related to differences of opinion regarding the sufficiency of taxes paid in prior years can become subject to dispute.

Again, there can be overlap between the net working capital purchase price adjustment mechanism and the tax indemnification provisions of the purchase agreement. We discuss the interaction between indemnification provisions and net working capital in Chapter 21.

PREPAID EXPENSES

Prepaid expenses are a product of accrual accounting. These asset accounts include amounts for expenses that have been paid, but for which the period to which they relate has not yet (fully) expired. Prepaid expenses can include items such as insurance, interest, rents, and taxes.

The most common types of disputes related to prepaid expenses are those related to booking expenses on a cash basis and those due to the company failing to recognize a portion of the expense as of the closing date. Such treatment can become problematic for purposes of a net working capital adjustment dispute while not resulting in a problem in the preparation of the annual financial statements due to, for example, materiality considerations.

Disputed items related to the failure to recognize the current expense amount are often not very large in terms of dollar amount. For example, the property insurance premium may have been paid in full at the beginning of the policy period. The company should be recognizing 1/12 of that prepaid asset as an expense each month. If the company failed to do so in the month of closing, the proposed adjustment will only be 1/12 of the premium or less.

Cash-basis recognition of expenses can be a bit more problematic in terms of the magnitude of the dollar amount and the unexpected post-closing impact. By *cash basis* we are referring to a prepayment or a payment for a full year of service at the beginning of the relevant period, but rather than recognizing the prepaid asset the company expenses the full amount in the period in which it was paid. This is not accrual accounting and further does not recognize the expense in the proper period.

For example, a company that pays for a 12-month service contract for software may need to recognize 1/12 of the amount paid as an expense in each month of the contract term. On an annual expense basis, there is really no difference between recognizing the expense monthly or at the time of payment. In a transaction setting the impact can be significant depending on the closing date and the timing of the prepaid item.

Example: Prepaid Expenses

- The target company owns and operates high-tech logistics warehouses. It pays annual *ad valorem* real estate taxes in an amount of $12 million. The payment is made in January of each year. The company books the tax payment as an expense for the current period. The company's fiscal year is the calendar year.
- The company's financial statements do not show a prepaid expense on the balance sheet as of December 31 (the balance sheet date) nor should they as no payment has yet been made for the upcoming year. Its income statement for each year shows 12 months of real estate tax expenses. The company's financial statements accurately reflect the company's financial position and results on an accrual basis.
- The target company is sold and the transaction closes on January 31. The seller includes an $11 million prepaid expense for real estate taxes for the months February through December.

The previous example includes the seller appropriately recording the prepaid expense as of the closing date, which would be in accordance with GAAP. The buyer may be very unpleasantly surprised by the $11 million prepaid asset that appears in the preliminary closing statement. Moreover, the prepaid asset may not have been included in the target net working capital, resulting in a perceived sense of injustice. Such changes from historical practices, even to comply with GAAP, can create significant surprises for either party.

PART Five

Other Topics

CHAPTER 20

Governing Agreements and Contractual Choices

The purchase agreement is of great importance to the post-closing process and the accounting arbitration. Throughout this book, we have discussed a variety of items for which the implementation depends on the purchase agreement. We have also discussed some possible avenues for mitigation of potential complexities and ambiguities. In this chapter, we provide an overview of some of the choices that are available to the parties and their counsel regarding the post-closing adjustment process as they negotiate and draft the purchase agreement. We summarize some near-universal clauses and offer some more uncommon options for consideration.

We recognize that the post-closing adjustment process is only part of the entire negotiation and drafting process. The negotiation of that process is typically not the primary area of concern in the context of the transaction as a whole. Moreover, a desire to customize and optimize the post-closing process may result in taking scarce time and resources away from other parts of the agreement. Tightly regulating the process can even come at the cost of souring the relationship without much real benefit. In other words, the selected contractual considerations offered in this chapter are intended to be informative, but may be skipped over altogether if the facts and circumstances of the transaction do not appear to require the allocation of extensive time to this topic. We recognize that some uncertainty may simply be an appropriate price to pay for a smooth transaction negotiation and closing.

Dependent on the nature of the deal and the company that is being transacted, the net working capital component of the transaction can be of lesser or greater importance relative to the purchase price. The post-closing adjustment is commonly relatively small compared to the total purchase price, albeit perhaps a significant amount in absolute terms. However, that is not always the case. There are transactions for which the proposed adjustment can almost wipe out the entire purchase price. It is important to recognize relatively large exposures early, which may very well require a more than typical familiarity with the company, its accounting, and the post-closing process.

PAST PRACTICES IN ACCORDANCE WITH GAAP

The formula of *past practices in accordance with GAAP*, albeit more extensively described, is commonly used as the contractual framework for determining the net working capital at closing. We have discussed some of the advantages of this formula relative to other approaches. We have also discussed situations in which solely relying on this formula can turn out to be problematic.

Defining Historical Practices

The parties commonly define the company's past practices by reference to the company's audited financial statements. There are two issues that can occur when relying on historical financial statements. A specific accounting choice may not be covered in those financial statements or there may be inconsistencies in the historical financial statements.

There are several contractual choices available to mitigate those issues.

1. To mitigate the chance of encountering an accounting choice that has not been made, the parties can incorporate more than one set of reference financial statements, including potentially both annual and (unaudited) quarterly reference financial statements.

2. To mitigate the impact of inconsistencies between financial statements, the parties can adopt a hierarchy. For example, the reference financial statements can be the most recent three annual financial statements with the more recent one prevailing in the event of inconsistencies.
3. For remaining unaddressed accounting choices or inconsistencies, the parties can rely on a catchall provision as discussed in Chapter 5.

Past Practices in Violation of GAAP

A potential issue with solely relying on the formula of *past practices in accordance with GAAP* is that the application of past practices may not be in accordance with the applicable GAAP as of the closing date. Historical accounting practices could have been in accordance with GAAP as of the date of the reference financial statements, but may not be as of the closing date due to changes to GAAP. One way to try and avoid such issues is to perform research to identify if any such inconsistences are present.

A more efficient approach to mitigate this issue can be to evaluate GAAP compliance of past practices using historical GAAP. In other words, the parties would be using *past practices in accordance with [GAAP as it existed as of the reference financial statement date]*. Although this issue can occur in the context of a net working capital adjustment mechanism, it is more likely—and typically more impactful—in the context of an earn-out, which may extend a few years after the closing date.

Even in the context of contemporaneous GAAP, the company's historical accounting practices can be found in violation of GAAP. In the absence of applicable past practices, implementation of GAAP may lead to a broad range of possible outcomes. To narrow this down, the parties can preemptively agree to a fallback such as best/better GAAP, the nearest GAAP compliant methodology, the nearest GAAP compliant amount, or the midpoint of the parties' positions. We discuss some of the choices available as well as some related pros and cons in Chapter 5.

Multiple Potentially Compliant Outcomes

The above opportunities for mitigation notwithstanding, there can be instances in which the seller and the buyer take different positions, neither of which can be demonstrated to violate the requirement of *past practices in accordance with GAAP*. This could occur for a variety of reasons, including those due to the nature of GAAP and accounting estimates as well as limitations on the available documentation. There are several avenues available to the parties to preemptively cover such situations in the purchase agreement.

Among other things, the parties can elect to incorporate the selection of a baseline statement and/or allocate the burden of proof. For example, the parties can provide that the buyer's proposed closing statement stands unless the seller demonstrates that it does not comply with *past practices in accordance with GAAP*. The primary benefit of such a provision is that it eliminates the problem of multiple acceptable outcomes. That elimination, however, comes at a cost because it opens the door to the gaming of the inherent range of possible outcomes to maximize the position of the party that is benefited by such a provision. Moreover, attempting to provide for such a provision may well end up being a contentious element of the negotiation of the purchase agreement. We discuss the contractual selection of a baseline statement and the allocation of the burden of proof in more detail in Chapter 5.

An alternative is some sort of tie-breaker provision that incorporates a fallback in the event of multiple possible outcomes. The fallback can be, for example, the "nearest GAAP compliant amount" or the "midpoint of the parties' positions." Importantly, the tie-breaker provision should be broadly applicable. For example, a tie-breaker to "best GAAP" is not necessarily sufficient as "best GAAP" may not be identifiable as such. We discuss some of the choices available as well as some related pros and cons in Chapter 5.

If significantly divergent positions are expected, the parties can also mitigate some of the issues by including specific provisions (e.g., special treatments or carve-outs) to handle the related accounts. We have provided examples of such transaction-specific treatment herein and in Chapter 7.

Finally, the possibility of multiple appropriate outcomes does not necessarily become a problem in many cases. The parties may simply decide to accept some uncertainty to avoid the complications and expense of negotiating any deviations from the standard formula.

Effect of the Transaction: Timing and Transaction Costs

The implementation of appropriate GAAP encompasses the consideration of management intent and the overall strategy of the company. Differences in plans for the business can easily occur between those while it is under the seller's control versus under the buyer's control. By means of example, the buyer may want to shutter part of the business, rendering a large part of the inventory obsolete or excess, which may conflict with the seller's plans for the business had it not been sold.

To attempt to mitigate the difference in plans for the company, the parties routinely provide for the closing statement to be prepared (i) as of a time immediately prior to closing and (ii) without giving effect to the closing (i.e., without incorporating the impact of business choices new management will implement after the closing).

Purchase agreements also commonly provide for the allocation of responsibility for any incurred transaction costs, which are often excluded for the net working capital determination.

Parallel Application: Subsequent Events and Materiality

As discussed, GAAP provides guidance related to the consideration of subsequent events occurring between the balance sheet date and the date the financial statements are available to be issued. Therefore, to unambiguously apply this guidance to the post-closing process, the parties and the arbitrator would benefit from the setting of an end date for the consideration of subsequent events. For example, the purchase agreement can provide for the subsequent event guidance of GAAP to apply analogously as if the closing statement is a financial statement where the date that the financial statements are available to be issued is the date of buyer's proposed closing statement. Of course, the parties can also select another date or bar parallel implementation of subsequent event guidance altogether.

During the dispute process, it is not uncommon for parties to take the position that an adjustment is not necessary as it would not have been material in the context of the financial statements taken as a whole. Accounting arbitrators do not generally apply the concept of materiality in an accounting arbitration as it is applied by the auditor for purposes of an audit of financial statements. Thus, if the parties want to make sure a materiality threshold is applied, whether per item or overall, it would serve them well to explicitly address it in the purchase agreement. A practical alternative to the analogous application of GAAS may be the implementation of a hurdle, either overall or per item/account. We discuss hurdles in more detail ahead.

TRANSACTION-SPECIFIC TREATMENT

The parties may want to provide for a defined special treatment for one or more components of net working capital. For example, the parties may be aware that a certain (large) item was not accounted for in accordance with GAAP or is subject to significant outcome uncertainty.

We discuss some potential special treatments in the following. If the parties agree on any special treatment, they should also consider parallel implementation for purposes of determining the target net working capital. Without a parallel application of the special treatment, the post-closing process can lead to a purchase price adjustment without an underlying real difference as the final purchase price is often ultimately determined by comparing the final closing net working capital and the target net working capital.

Defined Accounting Treatment

The parties may question whether the historical accounting for a particular item will ultimately be found to comply with GAAP. In such instances the parties can choose to avoid uncertainty in the outcome of such an item—and a potential large swing in net working capital—by preemptively providing for the existing accounting to be treated as if it is in accordance with GAAP for purposes of the implementation of *past practices in accordance with GAAP*.

Alternatively, the parties can agree to a specific accounting treatment for certain items. Such an arrangement can be useful for both potentially non-GAAP-compliant items as well as items for which there is a potentially broad range of outcomes. For example, instead of relying on past management estimation processes related to the allowance for doubtful accounts, the parties can preemptively agree on a fixed percentage of the accounts receivable or fixed allowance amount as the applicable accounting treatment.

Accounting and Actual Carve-Outs

The parties can also carve out an item from net working capital altogether if the underlying accounting is perceived as either inappropriate from a business perspective or too uncertain. Of course, such a carve-out eliminates some of the benefits of *past practices in accordance with GAAP*, including the true-up of net working capital of the company to reflect the position as of the closing date.

If the parties know that they fundamentally disagree on the value of an asset or liability, they could—dependent on the structure of the deal—also agree to simply not transfer the asset or liability. Although it can lead to its own complications, a carve-out can be very effective to deal with some known problematic or potentially contentious items.

Back-End Sharing

Applying *past practices in accordance with GAAP* means quantifying each of the components of net working capital as of the closing date. Items that are subject to significant estimation as of the closing date can ultimately come out much higher or lower than expected. One of the benefits of *past practices in accordance with GAAP* is that it provides an objective framework, prevents a potentially lengthy ongoing relationship to determine the ultimate outcome of uncertain events, and can prevent disputes about whose fault it is that expectations have not been met.

In certain situations, however, the parties may find estimation in combination with the potential unpredictability of an accounting arbitration undesirable. The parties may also not be able to agree to an alternative formula as of the closing date as they simply have a very different view on the value of the underlying asset.

In such situations, the parties can agree to carve out the asset (or liability) from the estimation process and agree to share the actual benefits or losses realized at a later date.

Example: Back-End Sharing

- The company has significant accounts receivable as of the closing date. The company believes its lenient terms and collection policies will accelerate growth at the reseller level.
- The buyer views the receivables as over-aged and uncollectable. It does not want to pay for what it considers worthless paper. It finds an accounting arbitration on this topic an unattractive prospect as the amount at issue is too high and the outcome too unpredictable given the company's past practices and the necessary application of judgment.
- The seller believes that the receivables, while delayed, are substantially collectable and thus valuable. The seller also

finds an accounting arbitration unattractive as it recognizes the substantial risk that its past practices are not in accordance with GAAP. It recognizes that a substantial allowance or write-off may result in a situation where the buyer essentially gets part of the accounts receivable for free or for pennies on the dollar.

- Given the ongoing relationships as well as tax and legal complications, leaving the accounts receivable with the seller is not practicable.
- The parties decide to carve out the accounts receivable in question and share the back-end realization. As of the closing date, an allowance of 80 percent is recognized on those receivables. Any collection beyond 20 percent is split by the seller and the buyer 60/40.

Utilizing a back-end sharing formula has a clear downside. It tends to be laborious, introduces complexity, extends the relationship, and could possibly end up in a separate dispute. In addition, in the example the seller is effectively dependent on the buyer's collection efforts post-closing, which it may deem suboptimal.

Hurdles

The introduction of a hurdle in the purchase agreement can help prevent post-closing disputes by setting a threshold amount that must be reached before an adjustment can be proposed and implemented. The allowed adjustment can be the entire difference or only the amount exceeding the hurdle. In special situations, the parties can also agree to set hurdle amounts for individual accounts or groups of accounts. Mostly, that would be overly laborious and not practical given the continuous changes in the composition of net working capital as the business continues to operate leading up to the closing date.

Utilizing a hurdle recognizes that the setting of the target net working capital and the post-closing purchase price adjustment process are not necessarily an exact science. Moreover, it limits small disputes that may be worth pursuing given the relative efficiency of an accounting arbitration, but on an *ex ante* basis could be considered a waste of the party's resources.

Limits

Limits set a maximum on the potential post-closing purchase price adjustment either in total or for specific items. An overall cap on the post-closing net working capital adjustment can, for example, be set at a fixed amount or a percentage of the purchase price.

Setting an overall adjustment limit, especially at a relatively high amount (e.g., 10% of the purchase price), can seem silly, especially because the purchase price adjustment is commonly perceived to simply deal with day-to-day regular-course-of-business fluctuations in the net working capital. Intuitively, when the parties enter into the purchase agreement they often do not view the net working capital adjustment as a major component of the purchase price. And that is in many instances an accurate assumption. Sometimes, however, the net working capital adjustment can wipe out a much larger than expected portion of the purchase price, in extreme cases even the entire amount.

There are various factors that can contribute to such an event. A company can have net working capital that is of significant size relative to the transaction value, for example, a distressed service-oriented business that has significant accounts receivable and/or inventory. The existence or potential existence of (current) contingent liabilities such as potential tax exposure going back multiple years, litigation exposure, and environmental obligations can also contribute to such situations if they have not been carved out or otherwise separately addressed in the purchase agreement.

PROCEDURAL CHOICES

The purchase agreement can to a greater or lesser extent detail the procedures of the post-closing purchase price dispute resolution before an accounting arbitrator. Many purchase agreements include a general requirement for submissions to the accounting arbitrator and can also explicitly mention rebuttal submissions. Rebuttal submissions are often defined as limited in scope to rebuttal of initial submissions and should not otherwise include new information. In addition, purchase agreements can provide for a timeline for all or some of those items and various other procedural choices.

More detailed procedural choices are often made once the potential for a dispute becomes a reality. As described in Chapter 11, in regard to the dispute resolution procedures, the arbitrator's retention agreement is often more detailed in that regard than the purchase agreement. By means of example, the parties may decide prior to the retention of the arbitrator that they want to have a hearing to present their positions, which is then incorporated into the agreed upon process. As the arbitration proceeds, the parties may jointly decide that there should be further changes to the proceedings, such as changes to the schedule.

In the end, the arbitration is based on an agreement. So, if both parties decide—and they commonly do—on a specific implementation, they can typically effect it. If they do not agree, the arbitrator will make the decision based on the purchase agreement, the retention agreement, and other considerations (such as whether additional information is needed to render an appropriate opinion).

The Selection of the Accounting Arbitrator

In Chapter 11, we discuss the selection and retention of the accounting arbitrator. The purchase agreement can set forth the procedure for selecting the accounting arbitrator, which can range from a very narrowly defined process to a very broad process.

On one hand, the parties can preemptively identify potential individual arbitrators and include their names in the purchase agreement. The primary advantages are that the parties can typically relatively easily agree on arbitrators while a dispute is not yet on the horizon. Such a designation in the purchase agreement can streamline the post-closing appointment of the accounting arbitrator. On the other hand, in some cases it may take substantial effort between the parties to come up with a list of arbitrators while the transaction may not end up in a post-closing dispute. A named arbitrator or a list of potential arbitrators is often combined with a fallback position in case of conflicts of interest.

The parties can also simply agree that an accounting arbitrator will be needed and a competent arbitrator will be appointed jointly. The primary downside is that at the time an accounting arbitrator is needed, the relationship between the parties can be outright hostile. Moreover, one or more of the parties may believe it is in its own best interest to delay the process (e.g., if it is likely that it will end up paying some amount or if it believes relevant ex-post information may become available in the meantime). The result is that the selection of the accounting arbitrator may be significantly delayed. It is typically advisable to at least include a fallback option if the parties cannot reach an agreement on the selection of the arbitrator.

Limitations on the Proceedings

The procedures before an accounting arbitrator are typically relatively informal. By means of example, the accounting arbitrator does not typically apply legal rules of evidence. Further, hearings are mostly in the form of presentations without the presence of a court reporter or other courtroom formalities.

If the parties want a more formal proceeding, to have more opportunities for discovery, and/or to have formal rules of evidence applied, they can include such requirements in the purchase agreement and/or the retention agreement. Notably, without including such considerations in the purchase agreement they may end up not being implemented as the parties may no longer agree on the procedures to be followed when it comes time to retain the accounting arbitrator.

The parties may also take a wholly different approach and agree to have the procedure be more limited in scope than usual to limit costs. For example, the parties can agree that there will only be initial submissions. In the end, the procedures and related limitations are generally up to the parties.

Form of the Award

As we discussed in Chapter 14, the form of the accounting arbitrator's award can range from a single schedule to a fully reasoned award that incorporates the arbitrator's considerations on each disputed item. From the perspective of the independent accountant, the form of the award is typically at the discretion of the parties. From the perspective of the parties there may a variety of legal and other considerations. Often, the parties want a summary reasoned award as, among other things, having a reasoned award tends to render any clerical errors identifiable so they can be addressed, and having the arbitrator disclose his reasoning contributes to ensuring that the arbitrator has applied the mental discipline necessary to appropriately consider all relevant factors. Notwithstanding, parties at times simply want an answer at the lowest possible cost and thus choose an award consisting of a schedule only.

The form of the award is typically decided jointly by the parties. If left to the arbitrator, the arbitrator will often—but not necessarily always—issue a (summary) reasoned award. If one or both parties feel strongly about receiving the award in a certain form, they can provide for it in the purchase agreement to preempt disagreements down the road.

Setting Limits on the Arbitrator and the Parties' Positions

The parties may want to formally restrict the accounting arbitrator's determination to one that is inside the bookends as set by the parties' positions on the disputed items. This can be done to prevent the accountant from going off the proverbial reservation. Although such a situation would be highly uncommon in the context of professionally advised parties and a competent arbitrator, it may be wise to err on the side of caution and contractually mandate bracketed arbitration. Finding out about the unexpected technical bias or pet issues of an accounting arbitrator in the form of an out-of-bounds award is generally very undesirable.

If so desired, although relatively uncommon, the parties can also agree to other forms of arbitration that have their own benefits and drawbacks. An example is to structure the arbitration as a baseball arbitration in which the arbitrator must choose between the parties' positions (and cannot split the difference or select an alternative position). An important benefit of such a proceeding is that it incentivizes pre-arbitration elimination of negotiable issues. It also assists in preventing the parties from taking extreme positions in an attempt to profit from anchoring bias or a perceived tendency of arbitrators to split the baby.

Handling the Arbitrator's Fees

The parties commonly provide in the purchase agreement for the allocation of the fees and expenses of the arbitrator. Purchase agreements often provide for either 50/50 allocation or an inverse proportion allocation. To avoid confusion in the event of a party abandoning a position during the arbitration, the purchase agreement can provide for the fee allocation to be based on the award and the positions of the parties as reflected in their initial submissions, in the accountant's engagement letter, as presented in rebuttal submissions, or another benchmark.

Either way, the fees of the accounting arbitrator are typically periodically (i.e., monthly) billed to, and paid by, the parties over the course of the arbitration in a 50/50 ratio. The financial impact of the award of the arbitrator's fees and expenses on an inverse proportion basis is typically allocated in the award in accordance with the purchase agreement.

Pre-Award Interest

The post-closing dispute process is typically relatively swift. Notwithstanding, there are disputes that end up being protracted processes that end up taking multiple months or even years before full resolution. To deal with such instances, the parties could find it appropriate to include pre-award interest in the purchase agreement. If the agreement contains such a provision, the responsibility for calculating the interest is often assigned to the accounting arbitrator and is included in the award.

Handling of Clerical Errors by the Accounting Arbitrator

Although it should not occur, the arbitrator's award may contain typographical or arithmetical errors. Dependent on the form of the award, those clerical errors may or may not be obvious. In the case of obvious errors, for example, the summary schedule contains a typo and the amount does not match the award amount discussed for a specific disputed item later in the award, the parties typically ask the arbitrator for clarification or correction.

To mitigate some of the issues that can occur if the parties end up in procedural fights over such clerical errors, the purchase agreement can explicitly provide for the option to bring possible clerical errors to the attention of the arbitrator (e.g., within ten business days of receiving the award) and for the arbitrator to correct such errors.

CHAPTER 21

Interaction with Indemnification Provisions

Purchase agreements commonly incorporate indemnification, representation, and warranty provisions to protect the parties and to allocate some of the economic risks and benefits associated with the ownership between the buyer and the seller. The resolution of disputes related to indemnification provisions, representations, and warranties is not typically handled by accounting arbitrators. These types of issues generally take the form of contractual disputes, and they are therefore handled by civil courts or attorney-arbitrators. Notwithstanding, those provisions can sometimes overlap and otherwise interact with net working capital provisions, and as such can represent important considerations for the parties.

INDEMNIFICATION PROVISIONS

Indemnification provisions allocate the economic burden of selected risks and obligations of the company between the seller and the buyer after the closing. An indemnification provision arranges for the indemnifying party to hold the other party harmless in whole or in part for certain known or unknown obligations.

Example: Usage of Indemnification Provisions

- The seller indemnifies the buyer for any tax payment required by the company related to periods prior to the closing date. In other words, insofar as there is any after-the-fact tax audit that results in a post-closing payment by the company for tax obligations related to periods prior to closing, the seller is responsible for payment or reimbursement.

- The seller and the buyer have agreed that the buyer will (indirectly) assume all of the company's environmental obligations with the transfer of the business. The buyer indemnifies the seller for any payments made by the seller (e.g., due to group liability toward third parties) for environmental cleanup obligations of the company.

Indemnification provisions are typically accompanied by certain related arrangements to, among other things, provide the indemnifying party an opportunity to limit its exposure. In the previous tax audit example, the seller may have contractual rights to be timely informed and to decide whether the company should appeal the post-audit tax assessment.

REPRESENTATIONS AND WARRANTIES

Representation and warranty provisions are exactly that—provisions that include one party representing or warranting certain things to the benefit of the counterparty.

Examples

- The seller represents and warrants that the company holds legal title to all of its assets and has no debts or liens that are not explicitly disclosed.
- The seller represents and warrants that all previously sold toys in the United States meet the requirements of ASTM International's Standard Consumer Safety Specification for Toy Safety (F963).

The following section will discuss the interaction of the net working capital adjustment process with indemnification provisions. The interaction is generally more relevant and more common in the context of those provisions because indemnification provisions are more likely to lead to payments. Indeed, the primary purpose of an indemnification provision is to address the expectation that there could be a payment and it should be preemptively allocated between the parties. On the other hand, representations and warranties are generally not anticipated to lead to payments. Notwithstanding, the discussion regarding possible overlap can be, at least in part, applicable to representations and warranties as well.

THE NET WORKING CAPITAL ADJUSTMENT PROCESS CAN OVERLAP WITH INDEMNIFICATION PROVISIONS

Indemnification payments can relate to items that are also included in the calculation of net working capital. In such situations, without a provision to the contrary, an indemnification could result in a party making a (partial) payment for an item that has already been accounted for in the determination of the adjusted purchase price.

Example: Overlap between Net Working Capital and Indemnification

- The purchase agreement provides for the seller to indemnify the buyer for any tax payments related to periods prior to the closing date.
- As of the closing date, there is a tax audit underway. The seller's preliminary closing statement does not include a related tax liability.
- The buyer's proposed closing statement incorporates a related $1 million expected tax obligation as a contingent liability. The accounting arbitrator rules that this contingent liability, which effectively reduces the purchase price, is required under GAAP.
- Without a provision to the contrary, the buyer could potentially be reimbursed for this obligation twice: first, in the form of a discount to the purchase price for a $1 million

contingent liability in net working capital and second, upon the indemnification payment of the taxation the buyer could seek reimbursement for under the indemnification provision.

To preempt this issue, purchase agreements often limit indemnification payments to amounts that have not already been included in the (final) net working capital. Although that seems straightforward enough, there are several complications that can be associated with implementing such a provision.

Accounting and Post-Closing Complications

The parties may recognize that the net working capital as of the closing date may include contingent liability accruals that could potentially overlap with the indemnification provisions, such as the tax audit accrual in the previous example. To preclude an overlap of these issues, the parties may include a provision that limits indemnification payments to amounts that have not already been included in the (final) net working capital. In doing so, as the purchase agreement is signed, the parties may believe that they have fully addressed the potential overlap in relation to the contingent tax liability. Through including such a provision, the parties have, however, implicitly relied on the company's historical accounting and the therein encompassed classification of that contingent tax liability. Changes as a result of the post-closing adjustment process may result in that reliance being ultimately insufficient.

Example: Reclassification

- The purchase agreement includes an indemnification for tax obligations related to pre-closing periods. The purchase agreement also excludes any amounts already included with net working capital to be excluded from the indemnity payments.
- Included with the preliminary closing statement is a contingent liability for expected payments related to tax audits as

part of net working capital. The buyer takes the position that the contingent liability is non-current and should be reclassified out of net working capital. The accounting arbitrator agrees. As the purchase agreement calls for a net of debt calculation of the purchase price, the reclassification of the contingent liability does not impact the purchase price. The reclassification increases net working capital (higher price) and debt (lower price) in equal amounts.
- When the tax statement comes in, however, the buyer seeks indemnification without imputing the related contingent liability as it is not included with the (final) net working capital.

The result in the previous example is that the post-closing purchase price adjustment mechanism ended up impacting the indemnification payment. That impact was effected through a GAAP-required accounting reclassification that did not even impact the total purchase price. In other words, sometimes the interaction and effects can be unexpected.

Consideration of the Level at which the Deduction Takes Place

Purchase agreements that provide for the deduction of related amounts in net working capital from indemnification payments do not necessarily provide for the level at which this deduction should take place. That can result in a perceived ambiguity.

Example: Level of Deduction

- The seller indemnifies the buyer for post-closing tax payments that relate to pre-closing periods. The purchase agreement provides that any indemnifiable amounts that are already included with the net working capital as of the closing date shall be deducted from any indemnity payments.
- The target company has multiple levels at which this deduction could potentially be applied.

- It could be implemented at the overall indemnity level (i.e., "tax"). Under that approach, an indemnity payment is only due insofar as the total tax payments exceed total tax liabilities (a discussion on netting out tax assets and refunds is excluded for simplicity purposes).
- It could also be implemented at the level of the financial statements (i.e., the account in which the indemnifiable obligation would have been included in the financial statements). By means of example, if the financial statements distinguish between income tax and sales tax, that distinction would apply.
- Another possible choice is tying the deduction to the general ledger (i.e., using the general ledger account in which the indemnifiable obligation would have been booked).
- Or the parties can take a fully granular approach and tie the deduction to the individual item. In other words, the deduction would have to relate to that specific tax bill. Of course, the books are not necessarily kept at this level of granularity (especially as it relates to contingencies).

A perceived upside of an interpretation at a higher level is that it will be tied to a level that the parties agreed on or that an accounting arbitrator has ruled on. Although ultimately the amount of the high-level balance sheet accounts will be set, that is not necessarily so for the underlying composition of those amounts. A broader interpretation also is more likely to prevent the risk of perceived double-dipping. An easily underestimated downside is that a broader interpretation means a broader accounting of all relevant payments and receipts to arrive at the amounts that should be paid under the purchase agreement's indemnity provision. The process can be laborious and can significantly delay the process and any payments.

Timing Issues

A practical issue in the implementation of a net working capital deduction can be timing. The calculation of the indemnification claims can require the deduction of any related amounts in the final net working capital (i.e., after the resolution of any disputes between the parties). An indemnification claim, however, may very well materialize before the net working capital is final. This can result in the indemnification payment being put on hold until the net working capital dispute is resolved or, for example, the deduction being preliminarily based on the position least favorable to the indemnified party.

THE COMBINATION OF NET WORKING CAPITAL AND INDEMNIFICATION PROVISIONS CAN LEAD TO A WINDFALL

Even without duplication of payments through the net working capital adjustment and the indemnification provisions, the combination of net working capital and indemnification provisions can lead to a windfall (including on an *ex ante* expectation basis).

We demonstrate this through an example that is broken up into multiple scenarios. All scenarios are based on the same situation, namely the sale and purchase of a company that has known environmental exposure. In the first scenario, we assume that the purchase agreement provides for a net working capital adjustment, but not for an indemnity provision related to that exposure. In the second scenario, we assume that the purchase agreement does not have a net working capital adjustment provision, or it does not apply, but does provide for an indemnification of the environmental exposure. In the third scenario, we assume that the purchase agreement includes both a net working capital adjustment mechanism and an environmental indemnification. For each of the three scenarios, we analyze the expected benefit or loss for the buyer dependent on the actual amount of the environmental expenditure. Of course that amount will likely deviate, whether higher or lower, from the estimated amount as of the closing date.

Example: Environmental Exposure – Scenario I: NWC Adjustment Mechanism by Itself

- A company has a known environmental exposure. The range of probable cleanup expenses is \$10 million–\$20 million. The most likely outcome is \$15 million. The company includes a \$15 million contingent liability in net working capital.
- If the cleanup ends up costing \$15 million, there is no *ex post* benefit to either party. If the cleanup ends up costing \$10 million, the buyer ends up benefiting in the amount of \$5 million. If the cleanup ends up costing \$20 million, the buyer loses \$5 million.
- On an *ex ante* basis, there is no expected benefit or loss for the buyer as it can go both ways.[1]

In the first scenario, there can be an after-the-fact benefit or loss to buyer. That is the result of the net working capital being based on an estimate before the actual expenditure. The ultimate amount spent can of course turn out to be higher or lower than the estimated amount.

In the second scenario, the purchase agreement only contains an indemnification provision. The indemnification payment is solely based on the actual expenditure as determined after the fact.

Example: Environmental Exposure – Scenario II: Indemnification Provision by Itself

- Assume the same company was purchased and sold without a net working capital adjustment mechanism, but with an environmental indemnification provision.
- Whether the ultimate outcome is \$10 million, \$15 million, or \$20 million, the indemnification payments would be equal to the expenditure. There is no net benefit or loss for buyer after-the-fact. Nor is there an expected benefit on an *ex ante* basis. (*Note:* This, of course, ignores, among other things, credit risk.)

On a combined basis, however, the indemnification and the net working capital provisions can interact in a manner that results in a benefit to the buyer on an *ex ante* expected probability-weighted average basis. Effectively, the indemnification payment eliminates the risk of underestimation in the net working capital while not doing the same for the possible benefit associated with overestimation.

Example: Environmental Exposure – Scenario III: Both NWC and Indemnity Provisions

- Assume the same company was purchased and sold with both a net working capital adjustment mechanism and an indemnification provision included in the purchase agreement.
- If the environmental cleanup ultimately costs $15 million, there would be neither a net benefit nor a net loss to the buyer. The ultimate expense matches the amount included in net working capital and has thus been deducted from the purchase price.
- If the environmental costs end up being $20 million, there would also be neither a net benefit nor a net loss to buyer. Buyer would receive $15 million as an effective purchase price reduction through the net working capital and a supplemental payment of $5 million pursuant to the indemnity provision.
- If the environmental costs end up being $10 million, however, the buyer would end up with a net benefit of $5 million. After all, it received a $15 million purchase price discount through the net working capital provision, but did not actually incur $15 million in expenses. The indemnification provision does not subsequently reduce this amount.
- On an overall basis, the buyer can either break even on the combined provision or receive a net benefit. The combination of both provisions, however, does not lead to a net loss whether the actual expenditure is lower or higher than expected.

The result is that the net working capital adjustment for indemnifiable items is an opportunity for a windfall for buyer.

To exacerbate matters, accounts that overlap with negotiated indemnification or guarantee provisions, such as contingent liabilities, can require significant judgment. A relatively low environmental accrual may become a much larger contingent obligation in the accounting arbitration in order for it to be in accordance with GAAP.

An interesting side-effect of this can also occur during the post-closing negotiation of the proposed net working capital adjustments. Horse-trading one account for the other can have an unintended ultimate outcome if the parties are not careful.

Example: Impact on Negotiation

- The buyer and the seller disagree on two items: the inventory allowance (buyer's position: $2 million / seller's position: $1 million) and the contingent tax liability (buyer's position: $2 million / seller's position: $1 million).
- The buyer proposes to drop the tax liability if the seller agrees to accept the inventory allowance. If the purchase agreement contains a tax indemnification provision, the two are not the same. Rather, assuming both positions are equally meritorious, the buyer's proposal works greatly to its advantage.

The above analysis and examples are simplified. Among other things, the interaction can be further complicated by, for example, basket and/or cap clauses related to the indemnification provision. Such clauses can limit the seller's indemnification exposure as the basket establishes a threshold and the cap a ceiling regarding the indemnification.

EXCLUDING INDEMNIFIABLE ITEMS FROM THE NET WORKING CAPITAL CALCULATION

Given the potential economic effects and the swings that can be associated with including indemnified obligations in net working capital adjustments to be resolved in an accounting arbitration, the parties may seek to carve out the indemnified obligation from net working capital or the purchase price adjustment process. Such carve-outs are not free of downside. They introduce collection risk for the amount that would have otherwise been included in net working capital and can add a variety of complexities. Among other things, carving out indemnifiable items from net working capital may require carving out parts of a variety of accounts, which can become very complex and may require intimate knowledge of the company's accounting to perform unambiguously.

Moreover, if the indemnification provisions and the accompanying carve-outs from net working capital are broad in nature, the effect can be a laborious post-closing process that may drive an accounting arbitration as well as lead to civil litigation. For example, a company can easily be exposed to many tax liabilities for multiple types of taxes (such as income tax, real property tax, personal property tax, and sales tax), owed to many taxing authorities at different levels of government (from municipalities to federal taxes), and for multiple periods (for example, from current-year tax estimates to audits for a period five years ago). A multitude of legal entities and international operations can further increase the complexity of tax obligations. Many of these obligations are routinely tracked and booked into the accounting system. Eliminating the resulting balance from net working capital at closing means that each payment will be subject to the indemnification process.

In other words, taking the essentially opposite approach (i.e., carving out from net working capital as opposed to deducting from the indemnity) is not necessarily the mitigation of complexity and effort that it can seem to be at first glance.

NOTE

1. This statement assumes the probability distribution is symmetrical. If not, there may be a difference between the measurement of the contingent liability on a GAAP-compliant best-estimate basis versus the probability-weighted expected value of the liability.

CHAPTER 22

Other Mechanisms, Earn-Outs, and Locked Boxes

Net working capital adjustment mechanisms are not the only source of post-closing purchase price adjustments and disputes. M&A disputes can also relate to, for example:

- Adjustment mechanisms based on the company's pre-closing EBIT, EBITDA, or another income measure. The parties can disagree on the measurement of that financial performance.
- Earn-out disputes, which are related to the company's post-closing financial performance. The parties can disagree on the measurement of the financial performance.
- Other adjustment mechanisms based on the financial position of the company as of the closing date, such as debt or cash adjustment mechanisms.
- The parties can disagree on the allocation of the purchase price. Although this does not impact the total amount of the purchase price itself, the allocation of the purchase price can have real consequences.
- The indemnification provisions included with the agreement. Indemnification payments can be accounted for as purchase price adjustments.
- The purchase agreement may include a provision that restricts the seller from certain capital expenditures or requires a minimum in pre-closing capital expenditures, which can lead to a dispute.
- Allegations of transaction fraud, which can lead to significant disputes.

Many of the items included in the preceding list can end up before an accounting arbitrator. We discuss the first two categories of disputes in more detail in the following sections. Although there are large commonalities between those disputes and net working capital disputes, there are also several distinct differences. We also briefly discuss CAPEX mechanisms and the impact of transaction fraud. Notably, the latter is not typically brought before an accounting arbitrator.

In addition, we also discuss locked-box transactions. Contractual locked-box provisions are an alternative to net working capital adjustment mechanisms. The intent is to prevent the need for post-closing adjustment mechanisms and, thus, any related disputes. In practice, the locked box itself introduces certain unique aspects, such as permitted and non-permitted leakage, which as we will discuss, can lead to significant disputes.

PRE-CLOSING EBIT/EBITDA ADJUSTMENTS AND DISPUTES

Purchase price adjustment mechanisms based on pre-closing performance expressed in the form of EBIT (earnings before interest and taxes), EBITDA (earnings before interest, taxes, depreciation, and amortization), or other income stream measures can occur in practice. Similar to net working capital, the final EBITDA for the relevant pre-closing period (e.g., the trailing 12 months) is generally not available until the books are finalized. The parties may disagree regarding the appropriate amounts for the various components of the companies' income stream.

EBITDA is a measure of financial performance that is commonly used in valuations. However, it is not a GAAP-defined term (although its components generally are part of GAAP-based financial statements). Furthermore, for purposes of M&A purchase price adjustment clauses, EBITDA—or an alternative measure—is typically calculated based on a definition that is customized for the transaction (i.e., "Adjusted

EBITDA"). The parties will generally want to normalize or otherwise customize the historical income stream being measured to arrive at a measure to meet their needs. The result is the formulation of a customized version of a non-GAAP measure, which tends to be more susceptible to errors in implementation, ambiguity, and various complications. The effect can be exacerbated by the fact that the reference period for measurement is typically also the period immediately prior to the transaction closing and thus the period in which the company may very well be preparing for its separation.

Arriving at an agreed-upon, unambiguous definition is complex and can easily be underestimated. Many of the issues described in earlier chapters for net working capital—based purchase price adjustments apply analogously to purchase price adjustments based on pre-closing EBITDA or other measures of financial performance.

In general, the income stream measure for any potential purchase price adjustment will have a much broader basis than a net working capital–based adjustment. The net working capital based adjustment typically relates to only a portion of the balance sheet while an Adjusted EBITDA measure can incorporate almost the entire income statement. Thus, issues that do not normally affect net working capital, such as impairment of long-lived assets, may very well impact the income stream–based adjustment. Interestingly, impairment is separate from depreciation and amortization and can lead to potentially significant unexpected adjustments without a purchase agreement provision that specifically excludes it from the Adjusted EBITDA calculation.

An Adjusted EBITDA definition may include references to specific general ledger accounts and one or more examples of the calculation may be included with the purchase agreement. Defining the income stream measure used to value the company can be complex as it may have to rely on granular adjustments based on the company's general ledger or chart of accounts.

Similarly, providing for the definition and exclusion of one-time items from the income stream can be complex. The parties may have to rely on the company's trial balance/general ledger, as opposed to the income statements as included with the financial statements, in order for the information to be granular enough to be useful. We have previously discussed some of the issues that can arise in the context of relying on the accounting below the company's financial statement level. Those issues analogously apply here.

Also, as discussed, the balance sheet and the income statement are communicating vessels. The balance sheet reflects the financial position of a company at a given moment in time while the income statement reflects the financial performance over a period of time. Thus, in a sense the income statement explains the transition from one balance sheet to the next (excluding possible capital contributions, withdrawals, or other bookings that flow directly to equity). Not surprisingly, similar issues related to, among other things, management judgment as discussed in relation to the net working capital can impact the income statement.

Example: Balance Sheet and Income Statement Effects

- The conclusion that inventory in an amount of $1,000 is obsolete can be booked as follows:
  - Debit: Inventory obsolescence expense $1,000
  - Credit: Inventory obsolescence allowance $1,000
- The credit part of the entry ends up on the balance sheet, where it results in lower net working capital. The debit part of the entry ends up on the income statement, where it lowers net income.

Another complication is that the EBITDA purchase price adjustment mechanism may be implemented on a multiplier basis. For example, the final purchase price may be calculated as (i) $50 million minus (ii) the lesser of (a) $10 million and (b) the greater of six times Target EBITDA minus Adjusted EBITDA and zero. In such situations, any change to the company's income can have an impact that is higher than the dollar-for-dollar impact of a net working capital—based adjustment. In such instances the seller can be, among other things, incentivized to underreport costs. For example, due to the multiplier effect, the seller would potentially benefit from absorbing costs at the group level that should arguably be accounted for at the company level.

EARN-OUT ADJUSTMENTS AND DISPUTES

An earn-out is an agreed-upon provision included in certain purchase agreements whereby the seller has the opportunity to receive additional future payments (i.e., additional purchase price) depending upon the future performance of the sold business. In multiple-year earn-outs, the business performance is normally measured annually and can include annual earn-out payments and/or a cumulative earn-out payment based on the business performance over the entire earn-out period. Many transaction agreements with earn-out provisions also include a closing date–based purchase price adjustment process. Therefore, such transactions have two potential dispute phases—one as of the closing date to adjust the closing date purchase price and another related to the calculation of the metric underlying the earn-out calculation.

Earn-outs can provide a compromise solution for buyers and sellers that are not able to agree on the purchase price, primarily due to differing views on the expected performance of the business and its impact on the current valuation of the business. Earn-outs are often utilized in situations where a seller is optimistic about the future financial performance of the firm (and its growth) while a buyer is cautious and wants to avoid paying for future increases in performance that may never materialize. If the buyer and the seller would have to agree on a fixed purchase price, the negotiations may break down over the divergence in expected outcomes and risk. The implementation of an earn-out allows for the accommodation of both views as the earn-out will be paid based on the future realized performance of the company.

This all sounds like a good compromise with a straightforward measurement method; however, it is often not so straightforward. Unlike a closing date net working capital purchase price adjustment, an earn-out is based on the measurement of future performance, which includes many unknown variables. Earn-out calculations are notorious for ending up in disputes for a variety of reasons that impact the metric underlying the earn-out calculation, including integration of the acquired company, changes in management decisions, changes in the business direction, changes in the economy, changes in applicable GAAP, changes in GAAP methodology, loss of a major customer or contract, and other reasons. In many cases the calculation of the actual earn-out owed, or lack thereof, becomes a sticking point.

Accounting Issues

Earn-out out provisions can be based on a variety of financial performance measures (e.g., the earn-out may be based on EBITDA, EBIT, sales, or net income). The different metrics can have various pros and cons dependent on the facts and circumstances surrounding the business and the transaction. For example, a perceived benefit of a sales-based earn-out may be that, under the right circumstances, the accounting may be very straightforward and unlikely to lead to any significant disputes. On the other hand, if the seller keeps managing the company post-closing, which is not uncommon in earn-outs, the seller-manager may be incentivized to grow the company's top line at the expense of its profitability. In practice, earn-out calculations may also include multiple metrics. For example, there may be a primary earn-out payment based on EBITDA and a secondary payment based on the company achieving a sales growth target post-closing. The remainder of this section uses Adjusted EBITDA as the assumed metric for the earn-out. The usage of such a metric is common in practice.

Analogous to net working capital adjustments mechanisms, purchase agreements may require the determination of Adjusted EBITDA to be based on the company's historical accounting practices and in accordance with GAAP. Notably, although EBITDA itself is not a GAAP metric, its components generally are. The consistency and GAAP compliance requirements may be implemented, for example, by providing for the Adjusted EBITDA to be calculated based on the company's financial statements, which are to be prepared using *past practices in accordance with GAAP*.

In addition, and similar to our earlier discussion related to customizing EBITDA, the parties will typically want to agree on an Adjusted EBITDA measure for the earn-out that eliminates certain nonrecurring items and otherwise normalizes the EBITDA to meet the needs of the parties. Not surprising, defining Adjusted EBITDA for purposes of calculating earn-out payments generally runs into some of the same complexities as can be encountered when customizing a net working capital metric.

In addition, there can be multiple additional complexities that can come into play. The Adjusted EBITDA commonly has to be applied multiple years into the future. In other words, it requires a robust consistency framework to withstand changes in facts and circumstances without resulting in ambiguity.

Moreover, as the earn-out period progresses, GAAP may change. Those changes in GAAP can have a real impact on the calculation of EBITDA and the earn-out unless otherwise provided for in the purchase agreement. It is nearly impossible to anticipate and account for all changes in GAAP that may impact an earn-out calculation, especially for longer earn-out periods. The primary means of mitigating such issues is to restrict the applicable GAAP to GAAP as it was in effect as of, for example, the date of the last pre-closing audited financial statements or the closing date.

To complicate the accounting further, the Adjusted EBITDA has to be calculated for the company, which, after the closing may be part of a new group with various new group relationships. Purchase agreements often provide for maintaining separate accounting for the acquired company. However, the walls between the accounting of the company and its new parent often break down over time as the company is naturally integrated, even if somewhat unintentionally.

Even if the accounting remains separated, the simple closing of the transaction may introduce new intra-group business relationships that can impact the operations of the acquired business as well as the acquiring business. For example, the group may use the intellectual property of its newly acquired subsidiary to its advantage. Purchase agreements may provide for the accounting for transactions between the group and the acquired company to be accounted for at arm's length. Regardless of any such provisions, identifying those transactions and accounting for them can be complicated and lead to disputes.

Example: Intra-Group Transfer Usage of Intellectual Property

- The company has an impressive intellectual property portfolio, including proprietary formularies and production processes as well as various other trade secrets.
- The company had $100 million in sales prior to its acquisition by the buyer, but had been rapidly growing as it managed to monetize the competitive advantage of its intellectual property.
- The buyer is much larger and had $10 billion in sales prior to the acquisition of the company. After the closing, the buyer leverages the intellectual property of the acquired company to increase its sales to $15 billion by the end of the earn-out period.
- The acquired company's sales and growth, however, stagnate as its former competitor—the buyer—is now on a level playing field.
- The buyer does not account for the use of the acquired intellectual property within the group. Under its accounting, the buyer determines that no earn-out is due to the seller.

The seller believes the intellectual property usage by the group should result in substantial EBITDA for the company under the contractually required at arm's length basis for intercompany transactions. It demands the full earn-out payment.

Business Issues

In certain earn-out situations, the sellers are the owner-operators of the business while the buyers are a larger company or private equity fund. It is not uncommon for the parties to agree that the target company will not only be accounted for on a segregated basis, but will also be allowed to operate on a semi-standalone basis. The former owner-operator(s) may be retained to serve as executive(s) with great autonomy in running the business. From the perspective of the sellers, this can provide an opportunity to, or at least appear to, safeguard their earn-out against actions by the buyer that may be in the buyer group's best interest, but are at the expense of the acquired business. For example, the buyer may want to introduce a new product that cannibalizes some of the acquired company's market share and may, without a provision to the contrary, decide to shutter part of the acquired company.

Such a provision, whether in the situation of an owner-operator that continues to be involved or not, can be much more complicated than it appears. Over time, acquired companies tend to become more integrated with the group they now belong to. Indeed, in many situations the company can benefit from group resources. Moreover, as time progresses, the market circumstances may change, requiring adaptation by the company.

Consistency of Company Management Upon the closing of the transaction, the buyer assumes control of the business. In some transactions, the purchase agreement will specify that certain members of the sold company's owner-operator management team will continue on in a similar role or other role (e.g., advisor) for a defined period of time, often a six-month or one-year transition period. In other cases, none of the existing management team stays with the company after the closing. If members of the company's management team stay on for the transition period, especially if the purchase agreement requires the company to continue to be run in a similar manner and the continuing management includes members that have a stake in the earn-out, this can help in avoiding earn-out disputes. This is even more likely if these management members are onsite and involved in running the business as it had been run historically. This does not always avoid earn-out disputes, but it can help avoid or minimize many disputes.

If the management team does not stay with the company, the buyer assumes the daily operations of the acquired company without any input or guidance from the seller. This can result in differences in the daily operations of the acquired business, including decisions that are made regarding the course of the acquired business. If the acquired business does great and meets the metrics to achieve an earn-out, everybody should reap the rewards as planned. If not, the seller may have questions as to how and why this occurred. The reason that the acquired company, from an operations perspective, failed to achieve the performance sufficient to result in an earn-out can be varied and could include, for example:

- The seller was overly optimistic about the company's future.
- The company lost a significant contract or customer.
- Significant receivables were not collectable.
- An economic downturn occurred that negatively impacted the business.
- Manufacturing or product issues occurred.

The *how* of the failure to meet the earn-out criteria can be easy to identify. The *why* can be much more challenging. All of the above issues impacting the earn-out calculation could have occurred naturally and could just be bad luck and timing.

Regardless, the resulting lack of an earn-out, or a greatly reduced one, may be challenged by the seller on the basis that the buyer did not run the business in a manner consistent with the historical operations of the company. In some cases, there may be some truth to this claim; in other cases, it may just be an unfortunate reality for the seller.

For example, post-closing the company could have lost a major customer because, in the ordinary course of business, that customer chose a different supplier. Alternatively, the buyer could have not renewed a contract with the customer because it was seeking more favorable terms that the customer was not willing to accept. As another example, the company could have experienced higher-than-usual accounts receivable write-offs during the earn-out period. The cause for this could have been an adverse change in the economy or financial difficulties of a significant customer. Or it could have been due to liberal credit policies instituted by the seller in the pre-closing period to boost sales. It could also have been due to a failure on the part of the buyer to actively pursue collections. It can attempt to make up the loss by not having to pay the earn-out.

Notably, even if the management of the company stays the same, its authority may be limited in practice or it may not receive the resources it needs, and believes it should get, in the normal course of business from the new group. The specifics of such situations may be difficult to anticipate, and therefore to provide for, in the purchase agreement.

Standalone Operation of the Purchased Business Another significant issue that occurs related to earn-out disputes is that it is often nearly impossible and undesirable to operate the acquired company on a completely standalone basis post-closing. Even if operated as a separate company, the acquired company is often integrated at some level such as the sales team, the accounting team, the preparation of financial statements, management, and so forth. This integration creates a level of complexity in attempting to assess the performance of the acquired business on a standalone basis, resulting in a greater potential for disputes.

Even when the purchase agreement prescribes separated accounting and such accounting is implemented with separate books, there can still be many issues as a result of even limited integration with the new parent company. Such integration can include the allocation of costs from the group to the new subsidiary, the usage of the company's intellectual property by the group, and many others. Both the recognition and measurement of those issues can lead to complications and significant disputes. Notably, complete segregation for the period of the earn-out will typically defeat the purpose of the transaction and hinder the buyer from obtaining the synergistic effects that provide value and which often are shared with the seller through the earn-out.

Another business issue can be the provision of capital by the new parent and the distribution of earnings. For example, if the company gets to retain its earnings during the earn-out period, those earnings can be used to increase the capital base of the company and its earnings. On the other hand, if the earnings are extracted by the new parent as part of its group cash management system, while only sparsely providing additional capital to the acquired company, it can stunt the acquired company's growth. Although this may seem counterintuitive as the buyer also benefits from the company's success, the group will look at its overall capital needs and potential returns in allocating capital. The acquired company can "lose" its anticipated capital allocation, because an unrelated subsidiary has additional capital needs and promises even greater returns.

To facilitate the earn-out there is nonetheless a common requirement of separate accounting. If that is truly the intent, there needs to be some sense of how the balance will be struck between the need to operate the business to allow for a separate measurement of the financial performance of the acquired entity and the need to allow for the desired level of integration to make the separate operation and/or accounting not unnecessarily burdensome or even detrimental. For example, how will items such as transfer pricing, shared liabilities, and cash management be handled in the context of the separation of operations and assets? Of course, maintaining completely separate operations with no crossover of functions, sharing of intellectual property, and so on may defeat the point of the acquisition or at least delay it until after the earn-out period.

Unanticipated Events Impacting the Earn-Out Even the best-laid plans are susceptible to unexpected events. In an earn-out, the measure of the financial performance of the acquired entity may have been expertly provided for in the agreement, leaving little room for judgment or manipulation. This does not, however, protect the seller or the buyer from potential world, economic, or market factors that can have a direct or indirect impact on the performance of the acquired entity. These are realities that cannot necessarily be provided for in a purchase agreement, but can occur to the detriment of the buyer, the seller, or both.

Caps on Earn-Outs

Commonly, the total dollar amount of an earn-out that a seller can receive is capped in the purchase agreement. For example, the earn-out could be determined based on a multiple of EBITDA, but capped at a specific dollar amount regardless of the actual calculation. The earlier example regarding the 50 percent increase in sales of the buyer's preexisting business is an example of where earn-out caps come into play. Caps limit the upside for the seller and the exposure for the buyer. This is often a heavily negotiated provision. The seller will want to maximize any upside while the buyer will desire to manage the ultimate potential payout.

The buyer may also desire to protect against any potential short-term unsustainable performance of the acquired entity that drives a huge earn-out payment while not resulting in continued long-term success of the company. The seller generally does not want to be limited or miss out on any short-term upside that it felt was already present in the business at the time of acquisition. The negotiated cap on the earn-out is typically the result of a compromise between the seller and the buyer.

Business-related disputes that can impact the earn-out can be more difficult for the accounting arbitrator to resolve because they may be wholly separated from accounting matters. Various breach-of-contract allegations that are part of an earn-out dispute are commonly resolved in civil court or before a panel of attorney-arbitrators. Many disputes related to the accounting for and quantification of the earn-out payments, however, are resolved by an accounting arbitrator.

ADJUSTMENT MECHANISMS RELATED TO CAPITAL EXPENDITURES

Dependent on the nature of the business, the target company may require continuous capital expenditures. In practice, the seller and the buyer may agree upon a capital expenditure provision to account for capital expenditures in the period leading up to the closing of the sale of the business. Several considerations go into drafting the relevant clause.

Prior to closing, the buyer, as the future owner of the company, has an interest in the level of capital expenditures, because such expenditures directly relate to assets that are for the long-term benefit of the company. Dependent on the buyer's future plans for the acquired company, the buyer may want to prevent underinvestment in the pre-closing period because it plans to accelerate the company's growth and wants to prevent having to play catchup on the assets. On the other hand, the buyer may seek to institute some strategic changes upon acquisition of the company and may want to prevent the company from expending resources on CAPEX that do not fit with its future plans. The buyer may also want to prevent overinvestment in capital assets. The target company may be part of a larger group that supplies part of the target company's capital asset base. The buyer may want to reduce the occurrence of what may ultimately be excess purchases from the buyer's perspective.

To manage the capital expenditure level in the pre-closing period, the parties may agree to any number of specific purchase agreement provisions such as thresholds and ceilings. Importantly, any contractual provision related to capital expenditure levels may also more generally interact with other potential adjustments to the purchase price, which, unless appropriately considered in the purchase agreement, may lead to unwanted side effects.

Example: CAPEX and Net Working Capital

- The purchase agreement contains a net working capital purchase price adjustment clause.
- The purchase agreement also contains a clause that allows the buyer to propose capital expenditures in the three months leading up to closing.
- At the buyer's direction, the target company replaces some of its manufacturing equipment. The company spends $1 million. At the time of purchase the company books reflect the following:
  - Debit: Equipment $1 million
  - Credit: Accounts Payable $1 million
- The first entry recognizes the new fixed asset, which is not part of net working capital. The second part of the booking recognizes the company's obligation to pay for the equipment. That current liability is part of net working capital and could, without an arrangement to the contrary, result in a downward purchase price adjustment.

Commonly, capital expenditure adjustments are sufficiently straightforward to prevent them from ending up before an accounting arbitrator. Some capital expenditure provisions, however, can be more complicated in their design.

THE LOCKED BOX: AN ALTERNATIVE TO POST-CLOSING ADJUSTMENTS?

Throughout this book, we have primarily focused on net working capital—based post-closing purchase price adjustment mechanisms. Such post-closing mechanisms are needed because on the closing date the composition and amount of the net working capital necessarily includes some estimated items, or potential errors or omissions, that could prove to require adjustment. As a result, the final purchase price is only determined after the post-closing purchase adjustment process is completed. An alternative to post-closing adjustments is to arrange for a situation that effectively locks up the business pre-closing and sets the final purchase price retroactively so that a post-closing adjustment is, at least in theory, not necessary. This chapter does not attempt to cover every aspect of locked-box-based transactions. Rather, it provides an overview of what they are and a comparison to the more familiar closing accounts.

In a purchase agreement with a net working capital–based purchase price adjustment provision, the transaction follows a pattern, including:

1. The parties enter into a purchase agreement that contains a purchase price subject to post-closing adjustments based on the components of net working capital.
2. The parties close the transaction (a few to many months) subsequent to entering into the purchase agreement based on a preliminary closing statement. The legal ownership of the business is formally transferred to the buyer as of the closing date and the buyer starts enjoying its economic benefits.
3. The parties finalize any adjustments to the amount of net working capital as of the closing date among themselves or with the assistance of the accounting arbitrator and the final purchase price is set based on the adjustments.

By contrast, the locked-box mechanism takes a retroactive approach to setting the purchase price. A locked box provides for the price to be set based on (historical) reference financial statements, often the most recent audited financial statements or a balance sheet prepared for that purpose. A fixed purchase price is set as of the date of the reference financial statements, referred to as the locked-box date, that is not subject to adjustment except for any leakage that occurs between the locked-box date and the actual closing date. Leakage typically includes any value extracted from the business by the seller between the locked-box date and the closing date that is not provided for in the negotiated purchase agreement. Such leakage can include undisclosed items such as dividends, transfers of assets, and transaction-related bonuses. In other words, locked-box provisions commonly distinguish between permitted and non-permitted leakage.

In setting the fixed purchase price and agreeing to a locked-box process, the seller is assured of receiving the fixed purchase price at closing (barring any leakage not already agreed to by the parties). A key element of the locked box is that the buyer effectively assumes the risks and rewards of ownership of the company as of the locked-box date, even though no payment to the seller occurs until the closing date. To assist in preventing inappropriate activity in the interim period, locked-box purchase agreements typically contain significant protections against leakage between the locked-box date and the closing date. In other words, the company is effectively walled off or placed in a locked box. In return for continuing to run the company in the interim period between the locked-box date and the closing date, and as compensation for the lost opportunity cost, the seller can receive some form of agreed-upon interest payment based on the value of company.

From the buyer's perspective, because the price is fixed as of the locked-box date and not subject to adjustment post-closing, the buyer will need to perform sufficient due diligence on the reference financial statements to get comfortable with the accounting and ultimately the purchase price. While this may sound like a straightforward process to avoid potential post-closing purchase price adjustments, it is often not without issues.

1. In setting the price, the buyer will necessarily have to rely on the information provided by the seller, augmented by the buyer's own due diligence, which is by its nature limited. In other words, the post-closing information and adjustment process between the parties is effectively replaced by the accounting as disclosed by the seller and reviewed by the buyer. Dependent on the situation, that may be wholly acceptable or completely undesirable.
2. Dependent on the relationship between the seller and the target company, the implementation of the locked box may be relatively straightforward (if the seller is a conglomerate of distant investors) or a theoretical *fata morgana* (if the seller and the target company are part of a tightly integrated group). If it has not already been done preemptively, it takes time and effort to unwind corporate relationships, if it can and should be done at all. The alternative is extensive permitted leakage, which can easily defeat the purpose.
3. The seller will have to implement and abide by the locked-box process, including running the company for the greatest benefit of the buyer in the interim period. As opposed to a situation in which a post-closing net working capital adjustment is defined, in a locked-box transaction the seller does not get paid for great performance and typically is not punished for poor performance (and certainly not for performance at the low end of mediocre).
4. A common response to some of the issues is to create the proverbial windows in the locked box. Indeed, the separation as described earlier often cannot be achieved. Instead, the seller engages in a hybrid form between a locked box (it will not pay dividends) and an integrated company. Of course, that can also easily defeat the point.

In summary, a locked-box transaction can be a means of avoiding post-closing purchase price adjustments and related disputes for some companies. In a way, however, it just shifts the dispute potential from one primarily focused on net working capital adjustments to one based on leakage, indemnities, and representations and warranties. Those disputes are often much more costly to resolve. Moreover, the post-closing net working capital adjustment process is in many situations collaborative. Unpermitted leakage, however, is more readily associated with misbehavior, resulting in parties starting off at odds instead of in collaboration.

Moreover, the locked box imposes a level of due diligence on the buyer that is often not practicable and can be overly expensive. Similarly, the distinction between permitted and non-permitted leakage can easily result in extensive negotiations that are otherwise unnecessary, only to find out that the specifically negotiated and permitted leakage is overly broad or too narrow for the circumstances. Combined with the potential misalignment of economic incentives, a locked-box approach can easily create more problems than it solves. Those problems are, then, often also more expensive and time-consuming to resolve.

Companies and transactions can vary in the extent to which a locked-box approach can be appropriate. For example, in certain situations the retroactive transfer of economic interest can be attractive independent of the impact on potential post-closing disputes. Even in the case of more suitable transactions, however, the door to post-closing disputes often remains wide open. As a result, given the remaining potential for an expensive and heavily contested post-closing dispute, it can in many instances be much more efficient to proceed with the traditional post-closing adjustment process. Indeed, the situation in which the implementation of a locked box is least likely to lead to disputes is also often the situation in which a post-closing adjustment mechanism would have been implemented smoothly and without dispute.

TRANSACTION FRAUD

Transaction fraud can be a real threat to deal value. As a result, many purchase agreements contain a provision related to any fraudulent behavior on the part of either transaction party. We briefly discuss transaction fraud because it can result in significant disputes that can result in adjustments to the purchase price or even the complete unwinding of the entire transaction.

In the case of alleged transaction fraud, one of the parties is typically accused of wrongfully and intentionally misrepresenting or omitting pertinent facts in order to obtain a higher transaction price. For example, the seller may falsify revenue through the creation of fake purchase orders and the recording of false and uncollectable accounts receivable.

Again, provisions against such nefarious activity are typically included in the representations and warranties or indemnity provisions. As indicated earlier, fraud is at its core an intentional deception to the detriment of the other party. Not surprisingly, many purchase agreements remove any limitation of liability for damages due to fraudulent activity.

Transaction fraud can take multiple forms, which often go hand-in-hand with a material misstatement of the financial statements. An example could be a seller intentionally failing to record, or intentionally reducing, certain liabilities. Or a seller could intentionally inflate earnings through techniques such as channel stuffing or other misrepresentations of sales.

Transaction fraud is a very serious matter that can erode or even eliminate all deal value. Transactions can end up completely unwound due to the severity and/or pervasiveness of the fraud detected. Although accountants generally do not handle transaction fraud matters as an arbitrator, the unwinding of the fraud and its impact often involves forensic accountants.

CHAPTER 23

International Considerations

Due to the high volume of cross-border transactions, and the general globalization of commerce, this book would not be complete without addressing some of the unique considerations related to transactions between parties from different countries. Net working capital adjustments mechanisms, commonly included with the terms completion accounts or closing accounts outside the United States, and other adjustment mechanisms such as earn-outs are also implemented internationally. Since we are focused on accounting-related post-closing adjustments and disputes, we will address some of the common differences in the applicable accounting guidance and the consideration of such differences in purchase agreements. Our discussion is not meant to be all inclusive regarding potential issues related to cross-border transactions. Rather, it is meant to illustrate the fact that such differences can have a real impact on the purchase price adjustment process if not sufficiently addressed in the purchase agreement.

Beyond the accounting differences, other aspects of cross-border transactions that may not always be considered or may be considered less important can also have an impact, such as language barriers and differences in terminology. This chapter will also call attention, at a high level, to some of the differences in the legal systems that may have an impact on the post-closing process and the ultimate resolution of any post-closing purchase price dispute.

U.S. GAAP, IFRS, AND LOCAL GAAP

The International Accounting Standards Board (IASB) is the independent standard-setting body of the IFRS Foundation that is responsible for the development and publication of International Financial Reporting Standards (IFRS). While IFRS is not the authoritative accounting guidance in the United States, IFRS is the required basis for financial statements in many major financial markets in the world. There has also been continued convergence between local country GAAP guidance and IFRS guidance in much of the world. Even in countries that have not adopted IFRS or have only adopted them for the reporting of public companies, local GAAP can be increasingly similar to IFRS in many respects. Notwithstanding such convergence and conversion, there can be important differences between local GAAP and IFRS that can impact transaction agreement provisions and post-closing purchase price adjustments. Further, as a result of the prevalent use of IFRS globally, many cross-border transactions involving U.S. and non-U.S. entities may encounter U.S. GAAP vs. IFRS differences.

Even though differences still exist, there are also signs of continued convergence between U.S. GAAP and IFRS. For example, through 2016, under U.S. GAAP inventory was measured as the lower of cost or market. For financial reporting periods beginning after December 15, 2016, U.S. GAAP will require inventory to be measured using lower of cost or net realizable value under certain circumstances, which brings it more in line with IFRS guidance. In addition, the IASB has added more detailed guidance and rules in a variety of areas, which is more similar to the more detailed U.S. GAAP guidance. Even with convergence, differences remain and the differences highlight the fact that the transaction parties should consider the potential impact on the purchase agreement provisions, including the applicable accounting standards and any post-closing purchase price adjustment process.

Transactions between companies utilizing the same GAAP guidance means they are at least speaking the same language, at least from an accounting perspective. When there are differences between the applicable accounting guidance for the transaction parties, accounting complications can really take them by surprise. For example, IFRS prohibits the use of the LIFO inventory costing methodology while it is allowed under U.S. GAAP. Other examples include differences in the impairment of long-lived assets (e.g., impairment reversal may be prohibited under U.S. GAAP while allowed under IFRS) and the recognition of contingent liabilities (e.g., differences include that "probable" under IFRS is generally considered more likely than not, which is a lower threshold than what is commonly used in practice in the United States). Such differences can have a potentially disproportionate impact on the calculation of net working capital and should therefore be identified and considered by the parties.

Rules-Based U.S. GAAP versus Principles-Based IFRS

Colloquially, U.S. GAAP is often referred to as rules based while IFRS is considered principles based. In reality, both U.S. GAAP and IFRS are based on principles. The differences between the two sets of standards (other than content differences in guidance) are in the level of detailed guidance (i.e., "rules") to assist in applying and following the principles. The extent of specific rules in U.S. GAAP is generally perceived to be greater than in IFRS. U.S. GAAP is also perceived as being more narrowly prescriptive in many situations while IFRS is perceived as providing more freedom for the company to tailor the accounting to the specific facts and circumstances.

Notwithstanding, both sets of accounting standards contain extensive rules. Dependent on the topic, U.S. GAAP rules may provide the company with more or less freedom than under IFRS. Overall, the two sets of standards are generally more alike than different for most commonly encountered accounting issues. Both standards relate to accounting, and the underlying principles, although at times different in implementation, are largely the same. Ultimately, this leads to similar accounting in many circumstances.

Notwithstanding, it may serve the parties well to be cautious. Small differences in the provisions of the accounting guidance and its implementation can result in large monetary swings in outcome for purposes of post-closing adjustment mechanisms.

Differences Between U.S. GAAP and IFRS

As discussed earlier, U.S. GAAP is in general perceived to include more detailed application guidance than IFRS. Ahead we discuss some examples of differences in the detailed "rules" between the two standards. We have not attempted to include all or even most of the differences between U.S. GAAP and IFRS. Our goal in discussing this small sample of differences is to highlight the necessity of considering the potential impact of the applicable accounting guidance in cross-border transactions. Following are summaries of several differences between these two accountant standards.

Inventory The LIFO inventory costing methodology is acceptable under U.S. GAAP, but is not allowed under IFRS. For transactions involving U.S.-based companies that utilize LIFO, this could be a significant consideration. The LIFO method typically results in a lower valuation of inventory, because the older (typically less expensive) inventory items are maintained while the newer (typically more expensive) inventory items are recognized as if they were sold first. Depending on the level of inventory held by a target company, a large increase in inventory valuation could occur for a U.S.-based company using LIFO that is required to convert to FIFO or other costing methodology.

Under U.S. GAAP, the write-down (impairment) of inventory establishes a new cost basis for the inventory that cannot generally be reversed. Contrarily, IFRS does allow for the reversal of such an impairment if and when the reasons for impairment no longer exist.

Long-Lived Assets Similar to inventory, U.S. GAAP generally does not allow the reversal of the impairment of long-lived assets while IFRS does allow the reversal of impairment for assets other than goodwill. This could, dependent on the metric used, potentially have an impact on transactions involving an earn-out.

In general, U.S. GAAP utilizes historical cost as the carrying basis for most long-lived assets and does not allow revaluation except for certain financial instruments and other assets. IFRS utilizes historical cost initially, but can more broadly allow, dependent on the circumstances, a revaluation model based on fair value for certain assets such as some intangibles and property, plant, and equipment.

Contingent Liabilities U.S. GAAP requires the accrual of a loss contingency if it is probable that the liability has been incurred and if the amount of the loss can be reasonably estimated. Under IFRS, a contingent liability without an actual obligation is not recognized. A provision is recorded under IFRS if three criteria are met: (i) a present obligation related to past events exists, (ii) an outflow of resources to settle the obligation is probable, and (iii) a reliable estimate of the amount can be made.

The phrase used in IFRS of "present obligation" may result in the delayed recognition of liabilities as compared to U.S. GAAP because under U.S. GAAP the probability of the existence of the liability can still result in recording the liability, whereas IFRS requires the obligation to exist before recognition becomes possible (although disclosure may be required).

Moreover, the term "probable" under U.S. GAAP is intended to represent that the event is likely to occur, which is not specifically numerically quantified. GAAP merely provides that this is a higher probability than "more likely than not." In practice, "probable" is considered a high likelihood of occurrence, such as 75 percent or more (in which the referenced percentage of 75 percent is for illustrative purposes only and does not attempt to quantify the actual demarcation line).

Under IFRS, "probable" refers to an outcome that is more likely than not, which generally denotes anything greater than 50 percent.

Thus, U.S. GAAP may require the recognition of a contingent liability that remains off the balance sheet under IFRS and vice versa. Moreover, the measurement can also be different under U.S. GAAP and IFRS. U.S. GAAP requires accrual of the best estimate and, in the event of a range with equally likely outcomes, the low end of the range is accrued. IFRS requires the provision to be measured as the best estimate of the expenditure required to settle the present obligation at the end of the reporting period. That may be the most likely amount, a probability-weighted expected amount, or another amount dependent on the circumstances.

Balance Sheet Classification Under certain circumstances, the refinancing of debt can change the classification of the debt in question under U.S. GAAP, but not under IFRS. For example, if a note has been called by the lender and the lender has requested payment within 90 days, the entire outstanding balance of the debt is a current liability under both sets of standards. The company may also be negotiating an extension of that debt. If that negotiation is successful and completed after the balance sheet date, but prior to the issuance of the financial statements, U.S. GAAP would allow the company to move the long-term portion back out of current assets. IFRS would not allow this reclassification if the refinancing was completed after the balance sheet date.

Such specific circumstances may be rare and may in practice be irrelevant under a contractual framework that covers both net working capital and debt. Under certain circumstances, however, it could impact net working capital by a significant amount.

Revenue Recognition The U.S. GAAP revenue recognition guidance is extensive and varied. It contains many detailed rules underlying the basic tenets of recognizing revenue when it is either realized or realizable and earned. IFRS contains various conditions for the recognition of revenue for sale of goods and rendering of services. Those conditions consider, for example, whether the economic benefits of the transaction will flow to the entity, and whether the revenue and the relevant costs can be measured reliably. As a result, there can be differences in the timing of the revenue recognition and ratable versus non-ratable recognition.

By means of another example, there are also significant differences between U.S. GAAP and IFRS related to construction contracts. Among other things, U.S. GAAP allows the use of the completed-contract method while IFRS prohibits this method.

Notwithstanding some of the differences described above, revenue recognition is on a path to convergence between IFRS and U.S. GAAP. The FASB and the IASB have issued a jointly created revenue recognition standard—FASB ASC 606 and IFRS 15—Revenue from Contracts with Customers. At the time of publication of this book, the standard is scheduled to become effective for U.S. companies with financial statement periods beginning after December 15, 2017. For IFRS financial statements, the new standard is scheduled to be effective as of January 1, 2018.[1] This new standard will represent some significant changes for certain companies as it becomes effective.

The previous summaries of a variety of differences between U.S. GAAP and IFRS are only a few of the many differences that still exist between the two sets of standards.

In addition, there are differences between other local GAAP and other sets of standards that we have not addressed here. As a result, the party that is having to apply or consider accounting standards different than their own local GAAP should pay careful attention to the differences and the potential impact on the transaction calculations. Moreover, caution can also serve the parties well if financial statements under a different set of standards than the company's day-to-day accounting have been (or will be) prepared for purposes of the transaction. The differences between local GAAP and the applicable accounting guidance for the transaction can have a real impact on the calculation of net working capital or other post-closing metrics.

DIFFERENCES IN LEGAL SYSTEMS

There can be significant differences in the legal systems between countries. Those differences may or may not be directly relevant to the contract and the transactions. Provisions that may be impacted can include those related to the accounting arbitration. By means of example, differences in enforceability in an international context may be a contributing factor in choosing between accounting arbitration and expert determination.

The differences in the general legal frameworks can also drive differences in expectations between the non-lawyers involved in the transaction and/or the post-closing process. By means of example, in many countries the discovery process is much less extensive than it is in the United States. The U.S. discovery process—even the limited discovery process as part of an accounting arbitration—can be perceived as intrusive in some legal cultures.

In addition, participants from different countries can have different views regarding the use of party-retained independent experts in civil litigation. In many countries one independent expert may be appointed by the court to advise on his or her area of expertise as opposed to the common U.S. practice of each party retaining its own experts.

OTHER CONSIDERATIONS

In addition to differences in accounting guidance and legal systems there are other issues that can impact the transaction and the post-closing process, including language differences, various cultural differences, and logistics. Those differences are generally not decisive in pursuing a transaction or the ultimate outcome of the accounting arbitration, but could still be a consideration for the parties. Examples include:

- International travel is often time consuming and may be a burden. For many transactions, senior-level executives are involved as well as accounting and legal professionals in the local area of the respective parties. As a result, in a dispute setting, an opposing party may have no desire to travel and/or pay the expenses of an entire team to travel, to attend a negotiation meeting, or for a hearing in an arbitration.

- Time differences can impact the ability to have team conferences on short notice. Moreover, work and vacation schedules can vary across cultures.
- Language barriers, while not as much of a concern for English-speaking countries, are still very real. For example, while non-native speakers in European countries may have a good grasp of "business English," local language nuances may be lost. This can create unexpected misunderstandings.
- The certifications and titles held by a variety of professionals such as accountants and lawyers can vary across the world. While it can be a distinction without a difference, the professional and educational background of people holding apparently similar titles can vary significantly.
- There are also differences in terminology for the same items. For example, in the United States we commonly refer to the proposed closing statement or closing balance sheet. In many foreign countries, the terms *closing accounts* or *completion accounts* are used for those items.

NOTE

1. We note that the effective dates of the new revenue recognition standards have been repeatedly pushed back and may be again.

Index